Living With Grief After Sudden Loss

Suicide

Homicide

Accident

Heart Attack

Stroke

Typography

The cover, the title pages and the chapter heads of this book have been set in a typeface called *Mistral*.

The body text is *Christiana*.

The dictionary describes *mistral* as a "violent cold dry northerly wind of the Mediterranean provinces of France." The root of *Christiana* reminds us, of course, of rebirth.

—G.S.

Living With Grief After Sudden Loss

Suicide
Homicide
Accident
Heart Attack
Stroke

EDITED BY KENNETH J. DOKA, PH.D.

HOSPICE FOUNDATION OF AMERICA

Taylor & Francis
Publishers since 1798

Ordering information:

Bookstores and individuals order additional copies from:

> Taylor & Francis
> 1900 Frost Road, Suite 101
> Bristol, PA 19007

To order by phone, call toll free 1-800-821-8312
or send orders on a 24-hour telefax, 215-785-5515
Orders can be placed via Internet at bkorders@tandfpa.com

For bulk quantity orders, call Hospice Foundation of America, 1-800-854-3402
or write:

> Hospice Foundation of America
> Suite 300
> 2001 S Street, NW
> Washington, DC 20009

Book and cover design and typesetting by Ginny Sherman.

Hospice Foundation of America staff assistance from Lisa McGahey, Treena Greene, Norman Sherman.

Library of Congress Cataloging-in-Print data available upon request.

ISBN: 1-56032-578-X

Contents

CONTENTS

Foreword

JACK D. GORDON
PRESIDENT, HOSPICE FOUNDATION OF AMERICA

Hospices have an obligation, which they accept gracefully, to serve families of their patients—counseling a family even ahead of a death, listening to the anguish of a depressed survivor of a recent loss, arranging a bereavement visit from a hospice social worker or clergyperson. They do all of that and more, naturally and routinely. But they don't stop there.

Close to 90 percent of hospices in the United States reach beyond their own patients and families to become, in a variety of ways, a community resource on grief and bereavement. They often sponsor regular support groups for people who are dealing with complicated mourning that may have begun long before and outside of hospice. It certainly requires providing counseling or guidance at the time of a community crisis. It may involve offering a speaker for schools, service clubs or church groups. Simply it means being there whenever they are needed for as long as they are needed. That is the hospice mission and that is an important service that the Hospice Foundation of America encourages and tries to support.

It was out of that spirit that our first teleconference on living with grief was arranged in 1994. We began with a limited vision of what we might do, hoping for at least 50 sites (or downlinks) and possibly 2,500 people. We exceeded that in a week and ended with an ad hoc network of over 900 sites. The next year we rose to 1,170 sites and about 55,000–60,000 participants. This year we expect to reach 2,000 sites. If we do, we will have an audience of at least 100,000 people who in turn may touch the lives of millions of people each year of their professional careers. That is an exciting success story.

What is equally exciting is that we, like the hospices themselves, are reaching out beyond our limits. We are pleased that we now involve a far wider group of site sponsors than ever before, including hospitals, community colleges, university departments of social work, mortuary science and nursing, military bases, government agencies, including police and EMS personnel, state departments of aging and funeral homes.

This book is the outgrowth of our 1996 teleconference, *Living With Grief: After Sudden Loss.* We were joined again by the Association for Death Education and Counseling (ADEC) and welcomed Mothers Against Drunk Driving (MADD) as cosponsor. Major funding came to us from the Open Society Institute's Project on Death in America and from Service Corporation International, Inc. and its associated funeral homes. The American Medical Association (AMA) and the American Nurses Association (ANA) have been new and particularly helpful allies. Cokie Roberts, volunteer moderator of each of our teleconferences, contributes in ways beyond simple description or measure.

Because we are a small foundation, our ability to produce and distribute the teleconference and to fund our many activities depends on support from other organizations and individuals. We thank all of those who have been of such precious help, partners truly.

While the teleconference is our most visible activity each year, we also publish a monthly bereavement newsletter, *Journeys,* edited by Ken Doka. In February 1996, just a year after we started, we distributed 28,300 copies to subscribers through 204 hospices to surviving families and through public libraries to senior citizen groups. We hope to double our distribution this year.

Our foundation makes a special effort to reach out to the military services with their unique problems and needs and to both clergy and physician education programs on end-of-life issues. This year we have increased our support of AIDS education and prevention projects, particularly involving church-connected pastoral care programs in some areas.

Finally, I wish to thank the authors of the chapters contained in this book. Some of their contributions have appeared in other places and sometimes in other forms, but all are joined here in a particularly moving and instructive document. Once again, Ken Doka has attracted the authors, gathered the material as editor, and led us sensitively and firmly to a satisfying result. He deserves, and we offer, our deepest gratitude for his guidance and counsel.

Dedication

To all my colleagues in the Association for Death Education and Counseling and in The International Work Group for Dying, Death and Bereavement for all the stimulation and all the nurturing and support.

Acknowledgments

To produce a book for a teleconference, but which can stand on its own, requires exceptional cooperation from many people. I have called on old friends and new ones, and they have all come through wonderfully. Every author has my gratitude for a contribution made in good spirits and within a very tight time frame. We shared the goal of offering useful and informative material to a broad audience with widely different interests, training and professions.

I have benefited from the assistance of the staff of the Hospice Foundation of America, and particularly from the vision and commitment of its president, Jack D. Gordon, not only in this project, but in others. In addition, my support staff at the College of New Rochelle, and especially my secretary, Rosemary Stroebal, has been invaluable and always helpful.

Finally, I want to acknowledge the support and nurturing of my own family and friends. My son, Michael, Kathy and all those who are part of the fabric of my life provide the strength, love and support that allow me to live life fully even in the shadow of loss.

Kenneth J. Doka
Poughkeepsie, New York

1. Journey of a Young Widow: The Bombing of Pan Am 103

VICTORIA CUMMOCK

On December 21, 1988, when John Cummock was murdered, with 269 other people, on Pan Am 103, I lost not only my husband, but my best friend and the father of my three children, Christopher, 6, Matthew, 4, and Ashley, 3. It was on that day that my world was totally shattered. Not only had I lost John, but everything about my life from that point on changed forever. I lost a little bit of my country on that day because, I realized, the terrorists were going after the American flag on the tail of the plane and not anyone specifically on that flight—a fact unacknowledged for months by my country—the State Department and the U.S. Congress.

I lost the economic security provided by a two-income household, a wonderful marriage, the possibility of raising our small children with John and of growing old together. The journey of healing in the past seven years has been, for each member of my family, an individual and ongoing complex journey.

MY REACTION

The process of waiting for official information after a disaster is complicated by a range of emotions including disbelief, growing anguish and deep grief itself. No one is ever prepared to deal with news that someone they love has been brutally murdered, but, in the case of the Pan Am 103 families, we never even received any official information or notification. Like the rest of the world, the only information we gleaned was from television! This compounded our disbelief. When malice is involved, the process of connecting the horror of such an unthinkable act to the loved one is kept at bay for various reasons.

First and most important are the issues of hope and loyalty. It is natural to hope against all hope that somehow a loved one has been spared the cruel fate of a violent murder. It is not uncommon for families to hold out hope for their loved one's survival for days or even weeks as the effects of shock alter the perception of time to that of endless minutes, rather than hours or days. Holding out hope is driven by a deep sense of loyalty to the victim. To give up this hope is to abandon one's family during the time of its greatest need. Thus, a strong sense of denial is maintained at all cost and remains in effect until official notification of death is received and/or a body is recovered. It is at this juncture that families can and must let go of life as they have known it and accept the reality of death with the horror and anguish that it brings. It was with the return of John's body, *two weeks* after the explosion, that I accepted his death and began to let go of hope, thus beginning my grieving process.

Searing anguish typified every day, compounded by total mental fragmentation. I thought I had gone insane. I had no idea whether it was day or night. If I looked at my watch and it said three o'clock, I'd have to go look out a window to see if it was daytime or nighttime. I didn't feel hunger until somewhere in May of the year after. Initially, coping meant trying to get through minute by minute, then expanding it to hour by hour, and after a time I could manage a morning or a day.

For my part, when people did not acknowledge what truly happened, but minimized the atrocity of John's death by calling it an accident, I felt as though my feelings of anguish didn't correspond to such a passive event as an "accident." I kept wondering how much John and his fellow passengers had known and had suffered as the plane exploded at 31,000 feet. By not calling a spade a spade, I was pushed further into despair and isolation because I wasn't given permission to feel my feelings or ask my questions.

The events that exacerbated my anger, my grief and my loss were unanticipated. Because Americans feel that we are an invincible young country, terrorism is not something that our society often has to think about or live with. Hence, people always try to make nice of everything, including murder. It's our way of coping.

Nobody wants to dwell on something that's morbid. When people said "I'm sorry your husband passed away," I found no consolation. Instead, my anger was piqued. I would respond by saying, "I guess he passed away like the Jews passed away under Hitler." It seemed that most people chose not to recognize John's murder nor the enormity of the bombing of Pan Am 103.

My isolation and that of other Pan Am family widows was increased with remarks such as "You're young. You'll find another husband." I didn't want to hear that. I had just lost my husband, and I wanted him back. Such words of hope often pushed me further into my grief and a greater sense of loss. I felt no one understood my feelings, and I became more stuck in my anger and confusion.

Another coping tool that people tried to impose on me, in order to avoid being confronted by my active grief and anguish, was to offer me jobs in order to keep me busy. But, immediately after such profound trauma, it is not the time to forget. It is the time to grieve, to find consolation and comfort.

I found consolation and comfort from the advice of my therapist who encouraged me to feel my feelings, to accept that grieving is hard work and, lastly, to realize that there is no timetable for the healing process. I had to accept that each of us in my family and in the Pan Am 103 family would cope in different ways and at different rates. I had to decide either to be a victim or a survivor, and decide what effect this tragic event would have on my life and that of my three children. I didn't have a choice about what happened to John, but I did have a choice about how it would impact me and his legacy. The terrorists were not going to be victorious by ruining four more lives from the Cummock family.

THE CHILDREN'S REACTION

For my children, coping was a very different process. Because of their ages (ranging from 3 to 6 years), they thought death was a temporary state like going to work or traveling. For example, Ashley would ask me, "Mommy, when Daddy finishes dying, is he going to come home and tuck me in?" The permanence of death was a very difficult concept for me. I had to explain to them that dying is a time when your energy or your soul goes to God. I explained, "You know when Christopher's battery-oper-ated car stops because there's no more energy in the battery? That's what's happened with your dad. His energy, or his soul, has gone out of his body; he is no longer with us. He's with God."

When John's body came home and they saw him, they wanted to bring him home. They remembered the movie *E.T.* and that *E.T.* had hidden in the closet with the stuffed animals. Perhaps daddy could stay in the closet too, even if he wasn't very energetic. Then they could visit him whenever they wanted to.

The children expressed missing their father in many surprising ways. For example, one day we were walking out of a parking lot and one of the boys darted out in front of a car. I said, "Honey, you can't do that. A car could not see you and you could be killed." My son answered, "Well, that's all right because I could be with Dad." Recognizing their altered value system, I said, "I'm glad you don't have a fear of dying, but we need you here. Even worse, you could be crippled for the rest of your life." Over the years, depending on their ages and ability to cope with the enormity of death, each of them at different times "searched" for their dad. And, often, their bafflement with death and their dad's absence gave way to anxiety in varying degrees. As they entered different stages of awareness developmentally, their loss or anxiety would peak, requiring therapy. At age three, Ashley would cheerfully and as a matter of fact tell you, " My daddy was murdered." At age six she found out what murder was and was devastated. All three children, particularly Ashley, suffered from nightmares and other post-traumatic stress disorder (PTSD) symptoms for a very long time, requiring therapy for years, as issues developed.

Pan Am 103 Families

Being involved in the formation and leadership of the Pan Am 103 Families group, I have seen how 270 families have journeyed through the grieving process. Some chose to utilize different resources to help and support themselves. When faced with a highly complex emotional event such as murder, those who didn't get professional mental health counseling have had a very long and tough struggle dealing with their issues of grief and, especially, anger. Seven years later, many are still stuck in the different stages of the process and, regrettably, have not been able to move on in their lives.

THE ROLE OF THE MENTAL HEALTH PROVIDERS

Most mental health professionals are aware of the different stages of the grieving process: the initial shock, denial, sadness, anger, guilt, loneliness and despair and gradual acceptance. But when the loss of a loved one is complicated by a sudden, violent and intentional act, such as murder, the reactions of survivors are also sudden and violent in their own way—intense, severe and extremely profound. Recovery becomes a multifaceted process. Although there are common variables affecting survivors' bereavement reactions to any loss or trauma (i.e., previous traumas and history of preexisting mental illness, coping skills for stress and/or conflict resolution, level of support), there are marked differences that can compound the recovery process for homicide survivors. This includes the length of time awaiting official notification and the return of remains, the degree of intrusive outside influences (e.g., media/public involvement). The role of the mental health provider can result in a markedly different or compounded post-traumatic environment.

Unlike most losses in which there is a time to mentally prepare and say good-bye to one's loved one, the sudden and violent nature of murder leaves the surviving families with an immense burden, a burden further weighted by the survivors' "unfinished business" with the victim. Unresolved issues related to earlier resentments or conflicts, to hopes and dreams and to unfulfilled promises require attention. Survivors and those who support them particularly benefit from learning that the depth and duration of the healing process is prolonged, and that *the state of acute grief may last longer than a year*. Learning that each person grieves separately, differently and at his or her own pace can be of great comfort to the bereaved. In short, educating the bereaved to the many stages of the grieving process helps to normalize and validate the range of intense and often contradictory emotions. The mental health provider serves to give the bereaved the confidence to continue through the grieving process and avoid getting "stuck" in any one reaction.

Helping the bereaved to understand their own state of mind, as well as to interpret the range of emotions of others around them, is an important tool in preventing isolation and fragmentation.

Remaining close relationships can become unraveled when others choose a variety of coping mechanisms, which are unexpected by the bereaved, such as minimization or various degrees of denial.

The recovery process is further complicated as families of homicide victims contend with the criminal justice system. The enormous challenge of learning how this system works and its untimely demands amplify the already distressing states of disorientation and disorganization. Mental health providers can normalize the emotional highs and lows that the next-of-kin frequently experience as they seek to find closure through the attainment of justice. For many, justice will never be served, and it is vital to help the bereaved avoid the demoralizing effects of alienation. Referrals to long-term therapy or participation in support and/or advocacy groups is recommended as a means to give the bereaved ongoing support, a sense of belonging, a sense of purpose and encouragement.

Other intrusive influences such as mass media or expansive public involvement, at the outset of a murder, can greatly complicate the grieving process. Families are on an emotional overload leaving them disoriented, vulnerable and defenseless. In trying to identify and connect with the range and intensity of their feelings, it is important to provide a supportive environment that allows private time to be introspective and minimizes additional unnecessary external variables.

Repeated media images of the carnage, devastation and destruction further intensify the shock, keeping survivors confused and isolated. The families' need for truth and official information must be protected and held as a priority. Based on their acute emotional state, it is imperative that families be given firsthand official information about their loved ones, thus allowing them a private time to cope with the facts *prior* to public consumption. Again it becomes an issue of loyalty to the deceased in that the families want to respect, honor and protect them. Once the deceased becomes a public persona entering the public domain, families have lost yet another part of that person during a time that they have not learned how to cope with their initial loss.

Since the nature of news is what is "new," the pace in which the press intrudes in the victims' families is uncaring and often quite relentless. The media often tries to sensationalize tragedy when the truth and facts alone are hard enough for the families to cope with. It is important to honor the needs of the families to privacy and minimize unnecessary outside influences to avoid compounding and adding yet another dimension to their loss. The addition of the media, attorneys and the judicial system into the lives of homicide survivors is so overwhelming and confusing that it prevents families from regaining a sense of balance and control in their lives. Often it prevents or postpones their grief work as it relates to the loss of the victim, but also around the loss of their own life as they have known it.

OKLAHOMA CITY—OBSERVATIONS OF THE VICTIMS' FAMILIES

The personal hell I went through after the bombing of Pan Am 103 echoed across thousands of miles to me when I heard of the Oklahoma City bombing. I immediately sent a letter expressing our sympathy, love and prayers to the victims' families with a floral wreath in the shape of an American Flag. I needed to make sure that this country expressed solidarity and support at all levels for these families. I then sent a fax to senior White House aide Bruce Lindsey stressing the extreme necessity for the President to acknowledge their tragic loss and offer them words of hope and a promise to pursue justice. The President quoted from my letter in his speech at the Oklahoma City memorial service. This communication led to my involvement and consoling efforts for eight days in Oklahoma City. Under the sponsorship of the American Red Cross, I spent 12 to 14 hours daily working with many of the 168 victims' families still waiting to hear about their loved ones trapped in the Murrah Federal Building. For weeks they gathered at the First Christian Church, (a center set up by the Red Cross exclusively for next-of-kin), to await official information or death notification. Much of what I have observed over the last seven years about traumatic loss and the grieving process of survivors of homicide was confirmed.

For the families of the 116 victims left trapped in the Federal Building ten days after the bombing, the parallel process of holding vigil and awaiting notification was striking. Initially, the conversations were of hope for survival. Many spoke of the physical strength, stamina and endurance of their loved one and his or her ability to overcome extreme adversity. As the days progressed into weeks, the conversations evolved from hope of survival to hope of recovering a body. Slowly, the degree of denial changed as they gave themselves permission to let go just a little bit of hope and let a bit of reality take its place. The rate in which this process took place varied dramatically from one person to another, depending on their ability to deal with the degree of horror, anguish and pain that came with the acceptance of reality.

There was a critical juncture in the two weeks of waiting for notification. It came on May 1 when reports—false, as it turned out—claimed rescuers were ending the search for bodies because the remaining structure of the building was too near collapse. Governor Keating and Fire Chief Marrs went to the center at First Christian Church to reassure the families who were still missing kin that rescue work was, in fact, continuing. The governor and the chief were uncertain how they should describe the severe realities of the search. Chief Marrs brought a plan of the Murrah Building indicating where they thought the remaining bodies were located.

Before the two men faced the families, they sought advice from the volunteers and counselors. I was adamant in my opinion: they must disregard the rumors, and focus on the truth. The families were so fragmented that it was a waste of time to deny rumors of which they probably were not even aware. I stressed to the authorities to be straightforward and truthful with the families. Tell them the facts and then be prepared for the next two questions from the families: "What are the conditions of the bodies?" and "Would everybody be accounted for?"

Following the counselors' session, the governor and the chief went down the hall to the gathered family members. Brothers, sisters, fathers, mothers, husbands and wives, people of every economic status, every generation, every background waited for them. Almost immediately, the governor was asked if there was any chance of anyone now being found alive. Responding as honestly as he felt able, he said "The chance is very, very remote." The pain in the room was palpable. Acutely aware of the emotions of the families, Chief Marrs carefully and precisely explained that the hardest bodies to reach were those located where several floors had fallen and been compressed into the "pancake." He produced the rescuers' plan which several groups pored over when his talk ended. A family member, clearly distressed, hugged the chief and thanked him, on behalf of everyone, for his honesty and his help. The families thanked the fire rescue staff for risking their lives to recover the dead. Everyone in the room held hands and tearfully prayed.

The healing would take a long while, but the journey had begun for all of them.

CONCLUSION

The role of mental health providers for victims of mass murder is paramount in the recovery of the survivors. It is important to realize that denial serves as a primary tool utilized by the victims' families at the outset of a murder. Denial is an adaptive reaction that protects survivors of homicide from the full force of the tragedy. This coping mechanism is a gradual and graceful way to deal with the murder of a loved one, allowing families the time that they need to make the transition from shock and denial into the grieving process.

Educating the survivors as to the grieving process and the importance of honoring their feelings is essential work. Survivors must also learn the stages of recovery, the reality of variables for themselves and for others, and the unpredictability of the length of time required for the healing process. Finding personal resolution after such a violent act will be a lifelong journey for the victims' families. As each bereaved family member enters a different stage in his or her own life, a multitude of issues will develop. It is the mental health provider who must be trained to support, educate and give the bereaved the confidence to continue their lives and their loved ones' legacy.

Sudden Loss: The Experiences of Bereavement

COMMENTARY BY KENNETH J. DOKA, PH.D.

There can be few more powerful introductions to the topic of sudden loss than Victoria Cummock's very personal account of the loss of her husband when Pan Am 103 was bombed. Her story is echoed daily by survivors of those who are killed in other terrorist actions, the Oklahoma City bombing of the Murrah Federal Building, for example, as well as the survivors of countless victims of inner city violence, crime, drunken driving and other causes of sudden death. Cummock's chapter is a poignant reminder that death totals are more than just statistics; they are events seared indelibly into the lives of all who survive them.

Sudden loss, death without forewarning, understandably creates special problems for survivors. Three of the most common include intensified grief, the shattering of a person's normal world and the existence of a series of concurrent crises and secondary losses.

Grief is often intensified since there is little or no opportunity to prepare for the loss, say good-bye or finish unfinished business. In addition, the nature of the loss can bring on grief reactions such as anger, guilt and hopelessness, among others. There can also be a lingering sense of disorganization and consuming obsession with the person who died.

Survivors of this kind of loss often experience a heightened sense of vulnerability and anxiety. Nothing appears safe anymore. Activities previously casually undertaken, such as driving a car, now can seem fraught with danger. Survivors may have to deal with pressures of media interest and intrusion, and of police or legal entanglements. They may experience secondary losses, too, like lost income or even their homes, and the inevitable search for the meaning of the loss can challenge spiritual resources.

The grieving process is, simply, very complicated, intensified, and demands possibly even more than normally that a survivor struggle to cope both with the loss and its aftermath.

There are a number of factors—I list six—that further affect the nature of any particular sudden loss. They exist on a kind of continuum, and where a given loss falls on this continuum can affect how survivors experience the loss.

1. NATURAL—HUMAN MADE

Some losses like a heart attack or a hurricane are natural while others such as a homicide or a bombing are the result of individual hostile actions. In natural losses the anger may be directed toward the deceased person ("Why didn't you watch your health better?") or even toward God (How could you allow a hurricane to kill?). In human-made events the anger is likely to be directed at persons held responsible.

2. THE DEGREE OF INTENTIONALITY

Some losses are the result of highly intentional acts such as homicide. Others such as vehicular homicide due to reckless or drunken driving have a degree of intentionality. Here, the individual responsible made choices that resulted in another's death, but there was no premeditation. In other cases such as an accident there is no clear intentionality. In intentional deaths anger and blame can be highly directed.

3. THE DEGREE OF PREVENTABILITY

Some losses like a sudden heart attack may not be perceived as highly preventable. Others such as a homicide may be highly preventable. When deaths are perceived as preventable, there may be a strong obsession with the losses, a constant replaying of the "What ifs?" ("What if we came home later?", "What if he did not go out?"). Preventable deaths are also likely to increase a sense of guilt (if one holds oneself responsible for the loss) or anger (if one holds others at fault).

4. SUFFERING

In some losses, the death is instantaneous. But in other situations there may be the question whether the deceased suffered anxiety or physical pain. While the perception of suffering may complicate reactions to loss, instantaneous death may also leave feelings that the person who died had no time to prepare for death.

5. SCOPE

The number of people affected by the loss may also affect the intensity of grief. When large numbers of people are involved, the ability of others to offer support may be limited. But conversely, large-scope losses may also provide for support from the larger community and allow opportunities for survivors to bond together.

6. THE DEGREE OF EXPECTEDNESS

Some sudden loss may still have a degree of expectedness. For example, the heart attack of someone at risk or the sudden loss of someone struggling with a life-threatening illness, even supposedly in recovery, may not be a total surprise. Other losses, though, may have no forewarning at all.

All of these factors remind us that sudden losses, like all losses, are highly individual and are likely to affect survivors in very different ways. Each loss may have factors that complicate or facilitate grief of survivors. That becomes a critical recognition. One cannot compare loss. Each loss, whether sudden or not, creates its own issues. Losses are not more or less difficult. They are different. One, after all, cannot measure pain.

The articles in the succeeding section carry that theme. They remind us of the nuances of each particular type of loss. Stephen Hersh's chapter begins by exploring the issue of sudden loss through natural causes such as stroke or heart attack. Such losses illustrate many of the issues previously discussed. For example, survivors may experience shock. There may be unfinished business that leaves a void. Survivors may constantly review the death, wondering if they misread early signs or could have taken more effective action. In addition, since many causes of death are influenced by prior behaviors, survivors may feel deep anger or guilt. This should remind caregivers to explore whether survivors had prior fears about the death.

Janice Lord, director of Victim Services for Mothers Against Drunk Driving (MADD) has a sensitivity to the variety of difficulties that drinking and driving deaths leave for survivors. She explores both the pain of survivors and the role of advocacy in providing an outlet for grief. In similar fashion, Judith Stillion explores the impact of suicide on survivors. Stillion notes that anger at the person who committed suicide and guilt are common reactions to this form of sudden loss.

Stillion also notes a key complicating factor in suicide. Survivors often fear rejection from others who believe that suicide brings a stigma to the survivors. In my own work, I have discussed disenfranchised grief that occurs when a loss cannot be openly acknowledged, publicly mourned or socially supported. Grief can be disenfranchised for a number of reasons. The relationship is not acknowledged (a friend or lover), or the griever is not perceived as capable of grief (a person with developmental disabilities or a growing child). But there are also disenfranchising deaths, such as suicide or victim-precipitated homicide, where the very circumstances of the loss can complicate the survivor's ability or willingness to attract support. In certain losses, such as suicide, survivors may be ashamed to share their loss with others.

Stillion, like Lord, provides very practical guidelines for organizations to deal with the aftermath of a suicide. One might also add that groups such as schools can also do much by building self-esteem and problem solving skills, thereby helping to prevent adolescent suicide.

Lula Redmond's chapter powerfully describes the ways that homicide complicates grief. Again Redmond explores the intense anger survivors experience as well as guilt and vulnerability. Redmond also notes that many homicide, like suicide, survivors experience stigmatization and disenfranchisement. And, as with suicide, there are negative effects resulting from the intrusion of law-enforcement agencies, the criminal justice system and the media. Redmond's chapter has particular relevance to understanding the destructive effects of the violence that plagues inner cities. Here the anger, cycles of revenge and distrust of law enforcement, criminal justice and the media fuel a heightened sense of vulnerability and hopelessness.

Bonnie Carroll notes that military deaths are different. They are often unexpected and traumatic. Survivors are ripped suddenly from the protective environment that military life can allow and stripped of their identities, thrust into a civilian world that they may not have experienced recently and left to grieve alone. Bonnie Carroll, Lisa Hudson and Dianne Ruby offer not only their touching and compelling stories, but clear lessons on sensitivity to the special needs that both the military and clinicians need to hear.

Carroll's chapter also evokes Dan Leviton's 1991 work on horrendous death, which reminds us that we need not simply pick up the pieces after the sudden loss, but, in some instances, can prevent it. Leviton's work also reminds us that horrendous death or massive, large scale, sudden and often intentional death found in a bombing like Beirut deeply affects not only survivors, but society as a whole.

Sudden loss creates distinct issues for survivors even as it shares many reactions common to the grief process. In highlighting certain sudden loss, there is no attempt to minimize other types of sudden loss. Each type of sudden loss, whether a heart or a terrorist attack, leaves survivors bereaved, dazed and vulnerable.

2   After Heart Attack and Stroke

Stephen P. Hersh, M.D., F.A.P.A

Each year 1.25 million Americans suffer a heart attack, and about 500,000 people die from some form of cardiac-related death. 250,000 people die within an hour of an attack and about 20 percent of them die before they ever reach an emergency room. These sudden, if not instantaneous, deaths occur frequently without family at hand, among strangers or alone.

And then there is the companion killer, stroke, which is the third most common cause of death in developed countries. In the United States 550,000 occur annually and result in about 150,000 deaths. Not all of those deaths are sudden and unexpected, but many are. In any case, heart attacks and strokes are major causes of death in our country, thus creating a vast number of bereaved people needing help with their mourning.

What is important for the family member, clinician, therapist and clergy to remember is that the survivors of a death of a loved one from heart attack and stroke live with many of the same after effects as survivors of suicide, homicide and automobile and airplane accidents. The consequences of those deaths are well documented in this book by those who have survived the horrific loss of someone close as well as by those who have studied the survivors and those who are involved in providing professional assistance.

Survivors of traumatic deaths suffer a uniquely wrenching loss that starts with shock and may end in familial and personal dysfunction. Along the way there are emotional challenges that cannot be avoided: disruption of family functioning; redefining responsibilities and roles of individual family members; challenges to faith; indifference or short-lived support from institutions previously depended on; financial change and burdens; possible intrusions by media (private anguish too often becomes a kaleidoscope for public voyeurism) and words and actions by friends and family that, often inadvertently, hurt.

There is loneliness and sadness that lingers following traumatic death. There are feelings of guilt arising from self-accusations about things one should have said or done that will not disappear or good memories that cannot gain equal time. The bereavement road at the beginning seems to the survivor a hilly one with many ups and downs: the route marked by moments of high-functioning and then moments of confusion, disbelief and despair. Sudden death is a dreadful burden dropped heavily on the existential shoulders of survivors without the advantages of anticipation or the marshalling of personal resources.

It is easy to lose sight of the fact that sudden loss of a loved one from heart attack or stroke can be as unexpected and devastating to the family and friends of the deceased as suicide, homicide and accident. These "natural" deaths do not carry with them exactly the same dimension of horror or stigma, and they do not have the terrorist or criminal who caused the death to focus on as a target of wrath. But, in fact, sudden natural death does result in many of the same symptoms of anger, guilt, fear and rage that the more dramatic deaths do.

PSYCHOSOCIAL ISSUES

The psychosocial reactions to sudden unexpected death generally involve the survivors, immediate family, observing members of the community and some medical staff. Family members and the family network and community react with shock and disbelief. They are denied the opportunities to generate some understanding of the death that is to come, to say good-bye, and in so doing receive from the deceased permission to go on with their own lives. Survivors are deprived of any possibilities of anticipatory grief and its associated social rituals, as well as development of support networks that greatly help all of us when we face death.

The age of the deceased does seem to make a difference in our reactions. Even though most strokes and heart attacks occur in adults, particularly older adults, they do occur in children and adolescents and young adults as well. When death involves a child or young adult, our cultural bias in the Western world is that a greater injustice is involved than when there is a death of an older person. That feeling correspondingly relates to greater feelings of sorrow, anger, regret and outrage. (Yet for the family involved, any death, regardless of age of the deceased, is a shock.)

Additional important issues influencing reactions to a sudden death are the deceased person's role in the family; his or her gender; whether family members knew of preexisting health problems. As in all situations of death, the reactions of survivors are also shaped by the structure and health of the family system, the prior personal experiences of survivors with death, as well as their beliefs about death and what happens in death.

THE EVENT

Death from stroke usually is not instantaneous. When it is immediate, stroke deaths to the observer may differ from heart attack only in being preceded by obvious, rapid dramatic changes in motor functioning or speech.

The usual observer's immediate reactions are panic and fear. Both accompany actions directed first toward checking the individual, then attempting to help them—from calling 911 to CPR interventions. Confronted with the unconscious person, the involved family and non-family members find themselves aroused to a high pitch of activity, often but not always purposeful activity.

Once it becomes clear that the person has died, the excitement and energy associated with crisis change to numbness, and even distant or dreamlike feelings. Actions then become quietly purposeful or they just stop, depending upon the situation and the roles of the survivors present with respect to the deceased.

Ideally, the closest family members or friends will be able to see and touch their loved one, verifying for themselves that life has departed. They may begin the process of saying good-bye.

Very quickly the responsible family members are forced by the hospital or community to focus on immediate demands as well as needs—organ donor decisions, a postmortem examination or not, disposition of the remains, funeral or memorial service plans, the associated financial issues. There is simply no time off.

We move directly from shock through a fog of emotions to irrevocable decisions. It is tough. At the same time, there is a blur of having to relate to extended family, friends, employers—giving out information on what happened, dealing with their responses, learning about possible commitments left by the now-deceased loved one. Then, if, as is usually the case, the deceased is an adult, issues of estate and wills may follow.

The chaos of the immediate is followed by lingering long-term difficulties. Moments, often at night and into morning, of being alone leave the surviving loved ones with their feelings of numbness combined with awareness of their own altered reality, more so than if one had had time to prepare for the death. It is a time when eating may have no appeal, sleep is less restful, absent-mindedness around small ordinary chores increases, the capacity to read, get involved with a television program or movies diminishes or totally disappears. Yet one functions, noting the behaviors of others but often not immediately relating to them.

If personal problems are immense, social relations match them. A death may alter relationships in the family and often even in the community. Siblings misunderstand each other's expressions of emotion. Spouses think their children are ignoring them at a time of need. One family member may think someone grieves too much or not enough. The wife of the minister or rabbi may suddenly have no continuing role in the church or synagogue. The wife of the truck driver may feel isolated from the couples' group they used to chum with. No matter who you are or what the deceased person did, there is change. All of this will lead to discomfort at best, anger and hard feelings at worst.

Close family members lose a part of their identity in a death. An inability to recognize and deal with this change is basic to understanding prolonged, pathological grief or grief that results in increased psychological, occupational or social dysfunction. When death is sudden, the bereaved person in his or her state of shock feels that life has been irreparably damaged, not just changed, by this unprepared-for death. If neglected, this feeling can inhibit survivors from establishing new roles for themselves. When the sudden death involves an adult, if that person was a major support such as a homemaker and/or breadwinner for the family, the family integrity and economics, location in the community and lifestyle are all affected.

Generally, during the three to six months after sudden death, survivors note mood changes in themselves, especially short tempers and other forms of irritability. They may have moments of fear about their own mortality and being suddenly "taken away." Questioning the meaningfulness of life may occur, with wondering (depending on religious and other beliefs) about where and how the deceased is at that moment. Sleep can be restless, absent of or full of disturbing dreams. Uncomfortable experiences can occur, such as a startle reaction to a familiar silhouette, or body stance, or hair color that reminds one of the deceased. There is shock and embarrassment for an individual who buys the usual two tickets for a movie when there is only one person to use them. Even physical health is altered with an increase over the normal number of colds or bouts with the flu or other infections; there may be problems in stabilizing one's diabetes or blood pressure. Loneliness may be dealt with by seeking the numbing effects of alcohol or too much medication. It is simply a time of endless misery and adjustments, looking back while trying to forge ahead.

During this time, school-age survivors experience problems in sleep, increased minor illness, poor school performance, increased oppositional and defiant behaviors. Teenagers may withdraw from the surviving parent and siblings in reaction to feeling overwhelmed by the loss. They may also alternate between extreme cynicism, combined with overuse of available substances such as alcohol, and oversolicitous involvement with the surviving parent. Children of all ages will seek and should be both permitted and encouraged to take selectively some of the possessions and clothing items of the deceased—a concrete reminder, reassurance and comfort.

Even more intensely than with other losses, as the months roll by, spouses in particular may find themselves reviewing in their memories the moments, hours, days and weeks prior to their loved one's death. "If only" questions to self are posed: If only I had made him/her go to the doctor. If only I had paid more attention; If only we hadn't had that argument, etc.

Generally friends and other acquaintances made aware of these thoughts attempt to be helpful. When they *just* listen, comforting the bereaved with that listening and their presence, *they are helpful.* Some, however, create anger and pain by their belief that they have to give specific reassurances and responses, in general missing the point, with homilies such as " It was the will of God." The result—from friends, acquaintances, clergy—just heightens feelings of "this all can't be real" as well as the sense of aloneness and anger.

Others may begin to note that in various ways survivors take on the identity of the deceased. This may be in the form of clothes, color, food or music preferences, or likes and dislikes of certain people and experiences. These behaviors represent unconscious ways to keep alive and further incorporate the deceased into life. There may be moments when this feels "spooky" or otherwise uncomfortable. A survivor needs just to ride with these feelings, accepting them as part of normal bereavement, especially in situations of sudden loss.

Long-term manifestations of positive adaptation to sudden loss allow for ritual, reviewing in one's mind and with friends and family the loss and time around the death, including an intellectual understanding of what brought about the death. Normal bereavement adaptation is marked by decrease in feelings of numbness and distance from things, an increase in capacity to be involved with people, ideas, experiences, community, work.

Long-term unsuccessful adjustment manifests itself through bitterness, chronic anger, poor self-care, poor health, alcohol or other substance abuse, sexual dysfunction, loss of pleasure in life, loss of hopefulness about life experiences, inability to maintain old relations combined with inability to initiate new ones. The bereaved family member feels distant from people and events, often continuing to feel dreamlike in day-to-day activities. These characteristics mark severe problems in adjusting to loss. Professional consultation always is called for when such situations are noted.

WHAT HUMAN SERVICE AND CLINICAL PROFESSIONALS CAN DO

Know that sudden death from heart attack and stroke requires more availability and practical support than the more gradual, prepared-for death. Know that sudden death from heart attack and stroke leaves lifelong feelings as well as memories with loved ones who often can be heavily burdened by both guilt and fear. Practical support in the immediate post-death period means observing that the primary family members are functioning adequately, offering them support in that functioning, but moving in aggressively to assist if requested, or without invitation if an important lack of practical functioning is noted. Whenever possible the exact cause of death should be determined through postmortem examinations. This provides the emotional anchor of having some kind of explanation for the death.

Do *not* offer tranquillizers or other sedating medicines. Offer practical help and your presence. There is nothing specific for you to fix! Do not argue back if you are told you don't understand. Listen, share your caring and interest in caring. Help the survivors with post-death decisions when requested or if they need help, but don't force yourself on anybody. Help set up appropriate rituals and services marking the death. Be sure to meet with the survivors at two weeks, two months and six months after the death of their loved one, if not more frequently. Do not suggest widow/widower or other bereaved persons' groups too soon. One month post-death is almost always too soon. Be available to intervene if long-term problems of acting out behaviors, especially with children, such as depression, alcohol abuse, inability to work or parent or study occur.

SELF-CARE FOR THE SURVIVORS

Survivors need to be patient with themselves. (I offer a general timetable, knowing that it may not describe any particular person. But it is what I have usually seen in my practice.) The rollercoaster of emotions will be dramatic for at least six months, and one won't descend from it for at least another nine or ten months. Survivors should anchor themselves in all the activities of daily living. Acquaintanceships and friendships should be maintained. Self-care should follow Ben Franklin's precept: Early to bed, early to rise. Human systems, both physical and emotional, rebalance themselves with regular rhythms.

Here is what I would tell survivors. Allow yourself to mourn at your own pace, but seek out a support group when you feel ready. Remain in one that works for you for at least 12 months. For surviving spouses, seek companionship, but don't let your loneliness and the interest of others confuse you into a new long-term commitment with someone before a minimum of 15 months from the time of death. The ongoing struggles with fear, guilty thoughts, angry, raging outbursts may indicate that you need professional attention, especially if these persist six months or more after the sudden death experience.

When the sudden death involves a parent of minor or young adolescent children, the surviving parent would benefit from three to five counselling and parenting-during-bereavement educational sessions with a knowledgeable trained professional within three or four weeks of the spouse's death. This should be followed by several family therapy sessions.

Symptomatic children—with sleep problems, toilet regression, school, social problems—should have individual counseling. Checkups on their dealings with the loss should be made at one year, 15 months, two years and three years after the loss.

For the unusual situations where the sudden death was that of a child or adolescent, both parents and surviving siblings should seek short-term help in two or three counseling sessions within the first six weeks after a death and again with the same counselor at six and 12 to 15 months after death.

Engaging in the above forms of self-care acknowledges the powerful impact of sudden death on survivors. Such acknowledgment and advocacy for self and family makes the difference between a future without significant fear and disability or one in which future quality of life is forever impaired.

Despite the emotional challenges of sudden loss, honest acceptance of feelings combined with patient mobilization of personal, family and community resources over time will always result in adaptation.

3. America's Number One Killer: Vehicular Crashes

JANICE HARRIS LORD, A.C.S.W., M.S.S.W.

Before the 1980s, vehicular crash-related death and injury were considered merely unfortunate. Victims were thought to have been in the wrong place at the wrong time, unable to avoid "accidents." With the advent of Mothers Against Drunk Driving (MADD) and other highway safety groups, crash victims are no longer considered simply an amorphous mass of statistics. They are considered legitimate victims of crime if the cause of the crash was drunk driving or another form of extreme negligence.

Due to emphasis on victim assistance, prevention programs and aggressive public policy issues, vehicular crashes are declining steadily, particularly drunk driving deaths, which are down 35.4% since 1980 (NHTSA, 1995). However, the problem remains very significant, as revealed by the following statistics:

- About 780 people are killed in vehicular crashes every week— an average of one every 15 minutes (NHTSA, 1995).

- Vehicular crashes are the number one killer of Americans between the ages of six and 29 (NHTSA, 1995).

- Traffic crashes are the major cause of death for children under the age of 15, with 21.4% of those killed having been a passenger with an intoxicated parent or other caretaker (NHTSA, 1995).

- Alcohol-related crashes cost society $44 billion in 1993, including $6 billion in medical costs. An additional $90 billion was lost in pain, suffering and lost quality of life in these cases (Miller & Blincoe, 1994).

While these numbers are quite compelling, they become even more significant when we acknowledge that for each person killed, a myriad of parents, siblings, spouses, colleagues and friends find their lives forever changed by what has happened.

Amick-McMullen, et al. (1989) found that 23% of family members of someone murdered or killed by a drunk driver developed post-traumatic stress disorder at some point after the death. Interestingly, very few differences were noted between the two victim populations, thus destroying the myth that crashes are mere "accidents" that should not result in as much trauma for family members as murders or other homicides.

This study (and others) also found that the minimal criminal justice sanctions that drunk drivers received, as compared to those who killed with a gun or knife, added to the difficulty of the families' grief and mourning recovery.

TREATMENT ISSUES

Many counselors, clergy and others who work with crash victims still base their grief counseling on early traditional studies in death and dying. The Elisabeth Kubler-Ross model is still proclaimed gospel by many who use it as both diagnostic and prescriptive for the unfortunate souls who cross their thresholds. This is so, regardless of the fact that Dr. Kubler-Ross never intended for her "stages" to be considered concrete, nor did she generalize her research beyond the terminally ill.

Although similarities can be drawn from traditional and pioneering works, a death that is sudden, violent and senseless, accompanied by confusing and frustrating interactions with the criminal justice system as well as significant financial expenses, is more different than similar. Understanding these critical differences can enable the helping professional to create an environment of support and healing for surviving family members.

LACK OF ANTICIPATION

Vehicular crashes are among the most unanticipated of deaths. The offender is not usually known to the victim, nor does s/he selectively choose the victim. A high percentage of murders are committed by someone known by the victim, so while few families anticipate murder as an end result, they may have been experiencing anxieties related to assault, stalking, etc. that serve as something of a psychological preparation for the death. Families of children who die of gang-related murder do not expect them to be killed, but they, too, may have had some degree of anticipatory stress because of their worries about their children. While many people experience fatal heart attacks or strokes with no warning, many others have had health concerns prior to the sudden death.

In most cases of vehicular crashes, family members say "good-bye" one very normal day, fully expecting their loved one to return at a designated time. Instead, several hours after his or her expected arrival, a police officer knocks on the door, bringing the family the worst news of their lifetime. Or even worse, the unexpected message comes by phone. None of this is to say that one kind of traumatic loss is worse than the other. Whatever happens to a given family is the worst for them. But having no psychological preparation is different from having some preparation.

Inappropriate death notification can leave lasting scars on family members and can become the subject matter of post-traumatic stress disorder symptoms, including nightmares, flashbacks and an exaggerated startle response to the sound of door bells or ringing phones. A death notification by phone to someone home alone frequently results in a traumatized person who needs emotional support and sometimes physical assistance. For example, not long ago in Fort Worth, Texas, a young man was burned to death in a vehicular crash. The law enforcement agency did not notify the family, and the man's father learned of his son's death when the medical examiner called him for dental records. The father was alone, and after hanging up the phone, he suffered a heart attack and died.

Counselors should routinely ask, "How did you find out about the death?" because survivors need to tell of the notification experience time and time again. These discussions usually lead to emotional reactions of deep regret about lack of opportunity for closure. Frequent laments include "I didn't get to say good-bye," "I love you," or "I'm sorry."

The suddenness component, coupled with lack of closure, often leads survivors to feel driven to go immediately to the body of their loved one, regardless of its condition. This can present a dilemma if law enforcement is still actively investigating at the scene because investigators must "secure or maintain the crime scene" for the sake of a successful prosecution, make measurements, take photographs and administer other investigative techniques before anyone touches or moves the body. Family members can usually understand this if it is clearly explained to them. The compassionate officer will not restrain family members (in some cases, family members have been handcuffed and placed in the patrol car) but will carefully explain what is being done and why it is being done. After the on-the-scene investigation is concluded and evidence has been preserved, they may allow the family member who wishes to, to sit beside, touch or hold their loved one. Law enforcement officers and chaplains are encouraged, however, to tell family members *exactly* what they will see before they approach the body. If they are told that they will see serious trauma, dismemberment, significant amounts of blood, etc., they may change their minds, though many won't. Officers are sometimes reluctant to tell the family about the condition of the body for fear of further traumatizing them. However, restraining without explanation, or allowing them to see their loved one without preparation, is far more traumatizing.

As one father said, "The worst thing that could happen to me already had. I knew her injuries were so severe that they killed her, and I was prepared for that. What I was not prepared for was the resistance. I knew what I could handle in asking to see her."

Because of their need to get to their loved one's body, many family members will want to go to the medical examiner's office or to the hospital morgue rather than to wait until the funeral home has prepared the body. We encourage medical examiners to allow this—after the body has been cleaned up as much as possible and after the family has been told exactly what they will see. They can, again, based on this description, make an informed choice.

Professionals who work with surviving families must understand that the unexpected nature of crashes can result in significant problems. For example, one study found that parents whose adult children were killed in vehicular crashes suffered more overall psychiatric distress, guilt and expression of health complaints than parents whose children died of cancer (Schanfield et al., 1987). It may be hypothesized that the reason is lack of opportunity to spend loving time with the victim before death. If there was no closure opportunity, getting to their loved one as soon as possible after the crash may feel like the final protective act they can do for their child. Yet, they often experience significant resistance from others in allowing them to do so. As one mother eloquently said:

> Permission was finally granted for me to see Timothy on the condition that I "didn't do anything silly." As they watched, I presumed that meant I was not to touch him or disturb anyone. But Timothy was my child; he had not ceased to be my child. (He had not suddenly become a corpse, a body or the deceased.) I desperately needed to hold him, to look at him, to see his wounds. These instincts don't die when your child dies. I needed to comfort and cuddle him, to examine and inspect him, to try to understand and most of all to hold him. Yet, I had been told "not to do anything silly." If I did, I feared my watchers would run in, constrain me and lead me away. So I betrayed my own instincts and my son by standing there and "not doing anything silly." Our society has lost touch with our most basic instincts— the instincts we share with other mammals. We marvel at a mother cat washing her kittens. We admire the protection an elephant gives her sick calf. We are tearful and sympathize when an animal refuses to leave its dead offspring, nuzzling him and willing him to live again. That is exactly what a mother's human instinct tells her to do. If a mother is not able to examine, hold and nuzzle her dead child, she is being denied motherhood in its extreme (Awooner-Renner, 1993).

VIOLENCE

We tend to think of intentional murders when we hear the words "violent death." However, the extremely severe trauma experienced in vehicular crashes—so severe that it caused death— becomes a crucial component of bereavement counseling. This is particularly true if loved ones were not given time with the body at the scene, at the medical examiner's office or at the funeral home. One's imagination can sometimes lead to the development of imagery more grotesque than reality. This phenomenon is common when family members are not told the truth about the body, and they, therefore, fill in the blanks between the bits and pieces they overhear from investigators, medical personnel, or the media. Rynearson & McCreery (1993) studied 18 young adults whose loved one had been killed a mean of 2.5 years ago. Seventeen of the 18 were still experiencing intense, terrifying intrusive images of the fantasies they had developed from the minimal facts they had obtained. Rynearson discovered, as have others who work with trauma survivors, that grief work cannot begin until the trauma is first dealt with. A significant component of grief work is remembering and developing the memories one wishes to retain, even as he or she is letting go of the physical person.

When the suggestion to "remember" is accompanied by traumatic imagery, the value of the remembrance is lost. Rynearson concludes that some short-term, anti-anxiety medication and classical conditioning techniques may be indicated to calm the survivors, help them sleep and reduce intrusive imagery and nightmares. The combination of grief (longing, pining, guilt, idealized attachment to the deceased) with intense traumatic imagery should alert practitioners that significant treatment is needed—preferably by a trauma specialist who understands that trauma work must precede grief work.

The sense of helplessness from knowing that a loved one suffered physically is insurmountable. People are intimately attached to the bodies of their loved ones, and no matter how strong their faith that their loved one's soul or spirit is in Heaven, they significantly mourn what happened to his or her body and, at some point, will need to talk about it.

Over time—and the time must be of their choosing—many will want to learn more about what really happened. They may seek out the officer or paramedic who was their final link to their dead loved one and ask for details. They may decide to ask the law enforcement agency, the medical examiner or the prosecutor to show them pictures.

These are not bizarre requests to be denied because of a professional's sense of overprotection. People do not ask for these things unless they are ready to know. Professionals should become assertive advocates for the survivors in these cases to assure that they get the information they need. Parents of Murdered Children has developed a protocol for viewing photographs that seems to work for most people.

1. The family member wishing to see photographs is asked to bring their strongest support person with them.

2. The agency places each photograph in a separate manila envelope or folder, arranging them so that the most offensive photo is on the bottom and the least offensive photo is on top.

3. The support person looks at the first photo and describes it in detail to the surviving family member. The survivor, thus, has two sources of preparatory information: (a) s/he has observed the personal reaction of the support person upon seeing the photo, and (b) s/he now has concrete information about the contents of the photograph.

4. The survivor has the opportunity to choose, again, whether s/he really does want to see the photos now.

Most survivors want to see only the top photo, because it serves the purpose of making the death and the victim's identity a reality. Some will choose to see the entire set of photos. Some will decide not to look now, but to have a set of the photos to take home so they can look at them when they *are* ready.

Obviously, photos may not be removed until the criminal case has been concluded because they may serve as evidence for the prosecution. However, prosecutors should be encouraged to allow family members to view photos that may be projected onto a screen during the trial if they will be in the courtroom when they are shown. After the trial is over, caregivers should support survivors in viewing and/or obtaining photos, if that is their desire.

Grief counselor Kelly Osmont (1993) describes the experiences of three women who decided they wanted to see photographs of their loved ones who had died tragic deaths within the last few years. None of the women had previously viewed their loved one's body. One was a bereaved parent, and the other two were widows. They chose to view the photos in their support group. After facing extreme resistance on the part of the keepers of the photos, Osmont was finally able to obtain them for the survivors. The widow whose husband had overdosed on drugs three years earlier said she had not had one positive memory of their life together since his death. All she could envision was the imagery she had developed about how he may have looked. Two days after viewing the photos, she began having positive memories of fun and loving times with her husband.

The other widow had been adamant in insisting that her husband's death two years earlier was a murder, not a suicide as his death certificate stated. The photos gave her the necessary evidence to begin to acknowledge that it was a suicide; and shortly thereafter she was able to acknowledge that he was, indeed, depressed enough to have committed suicide.

The mother seemed to speak for all three of the women when she said, "After the initial shock and pain (of looking at the photos), it was better. Before seeing the photos, my imagination had been painting horror pictures. I was relieved to see him, I think, to hold him in my mind, to know now that he really was gone, and to get on with my grief work." Osmont noted that, for the first time since coming to the group, this woman stopped wearing an artificial smile, and the group noted sadness in her eyes.

CAUSE OF DEATH

Most people are generally angry that with all of our scientific achievements, we have not found cures for AIDS, cancer, leuke-mia or the myriad of other terminal illnesses that plague us. However, a vehicular crash (as murders and other homicides) is *somebody's fault*. While the specific victim was not preselected and run down, the offender was usually negligent through intoxication, speed, lack of attentiveness, allowing exhaustion to set in, etc. Therefore, the crash could so easily have been pre-vented. Working through this component will likely take many therapeutic hours.

The "what ifs" and "if onlys" can burden a family for a long time. Out of this sense of powerlessness about what happened, many survivors conclude that active involvement in the criminal justice system may be their last protective act for their loved one. Many survivors join MADD and other activist groups that can educate them about laws, the criminal justice system and local criminal justice procedures. They become highly invested in the criminal case, possibly out of their drive to see some sense of justice, possibly because it is their only tangible outlet after staring at the empty chair each morning.

Counselors, clergy and other caregivers must not assume that this involvement in the criminal justice system is a defense to prevent them from facing the pain. It *can* be used for that, but our experience is that investment in the criminal case is an essential component of the grief process for many, not an adjunct or a barrier to it.

Therefore, the wise caregiver will also learn about the criminal justice system so it can be discussed intelligently. If possible, caregivers should attend the trial as a support to the survivors. They may assist the family in writing Victim Impact Statements to present to the court at the sentencing hearing. (For samples of Victim Impact Statements, call your local MADD chapter or the national MADD hotline, 1-800-GET-MADD.)

Language issues of survivors should be respected when working through this component of grieving. Because the act was "sense-less," many survivors feel the words "accident" and "dead" are too passive. "Accidents" are truly accidental. But since bad choices are usually the cause of vehicular crashes, many survivors prefer the words "crash," "collision," or "crime." These are stronger words, more descriptive of what actually happened. These victims did not simply "die." They were "killed." Most survivors prefer "killed" because it suggests that the life was taken, not simply lost—and it was a criminal act, in many cases.

According to Dr. Alan Wolfelt (1992), creating a context of meaning for the death is a significant component of recovery. This is challenging in the face of a "senseless" death. Some survivors find meaning in their personal faith journey; others find it through activism to prevent future crashes or through "victim advocacy" as they reach out to help others. Some make value and lifestyle changes such as staying home with the family more and saying "I love you" more often. Creating a context of meaning out of the senseless does not explain the killing or make it acceptable; but it does help the survivor identify outcomes that appropriately honor and memorialize their loved ones.

FINANCIAL NEEDS

Most victims of vehicular crashes face even more stress than
grief reactions and criminal justice frustrations. Caregivers and
advocates must be prepared to advise them against premature
insurance offers that are not policy limits before the full extent of
present and future financial costs are known. If the offending
driver was clearly negligent, policy limits frequently increase. It is
a relatively simple matter to obtain three estimates on damages
to the vehicle and settle on property damages. Personal damages
are more complex. It may take some time for all the bills to come
in on final medical care for the person(s) who died. If injured
victims survived, it can take months, even years to obtain a full
and complete diagnosis and prognosis. The family should not
settle on the medical component of liability until rehabilitation
experts, specifically trained to assess the lifetime cost of medical
care, lost wages, etc. for a victim who suffers permanent injuries,
evaluate the case. The more complex the recovery issues, the
more advisable that the family seek out a personal injury attorney with expertise in the particular type of injury the surviving
victim(s) suffers.

On the other hand, the family should be cautious about prematurely entering into a contingency agreement with an attorney if
the case is relatively simple and policy limits are clear. Giving an
attorney one-third of the settlement in these cases may not be
necessary. Seeking advice from an attorney who specializes in
wrongful death and personal injury cases on an hourly-fee basis
is advised before entering a contingency agreement.

All caregivers of people who have been involved in vehicular
crashes should be knowledgeable about their state's Crime
Victim Compensation program. These funds are available only
when alcohol was involved or following hit-and-run crashes, and
they are funds "of last resort." In other words, they are reserved
only for families in which expenses are not covered by insurance
or other financial resources. In most states, the fund pays funeral
expenses, medical expenses, counseling expenses, loss of wages
and child care (if a parent has been killed). Compensation maxi-
mums range from $10,000 to $25,000 and are available only if
the family is cooperative with law enforcement as they complete

their investigation. Compensation application forms are available in most prosecutors' offices and many law enforcement agencies.

Several of the "Recommended Reading" resources at the end of this book may be useful in seeking additional means of financial recovery for families in need.

FAITH/PHILOSOPHY OF LIFE

Just as there are unique physical, mental, emotional, social and financial components to every sudden, violent death, there are spiritual ramifications as well. Those who have never thought much about God before will do so after a loved one has died traumatically. Also, those faithful persons who feel they have given as much of themselves as they understand to as much of their God as they understand, and therefore assume that what happens to them is God's will, are forced to reshape their faith positions to incorporate the fact that bad things do happen to good people.

In a study of 184 family members of someone killed in a drunk-driving crash, Dr. Dorothy Mercer (1991) found that those reporting having had a lot or some faith before the sudden death of their loved one found their faith strengthened by the crisis they had endured. Those having little or no faith prior to the killing of their loved one found their faith staying the same or weakening. Overall, nearly three times as many claimed their faith was strengthened as was weakened as a result of the crash.

Among those whose faith became stronger, it was clear that the process of rebuilding their faith with integrity took a significant amount of time, and that it was primarily an internal process. Respondents were highly critical of the lack of support they received from their clergy and faith community following the death. Reasons for dissatisfaction included being told they shouldn't be angry and/or that they should forgive the drunk driver. They felt unsupported or unaccepted when they "fell apart" at church, often being told that this was a sign that they didn't trust enough in God.

As with other components of grief and mourning, simply reminding the survivor that it will take time to reestablish their relationship with God and that they need not say or do things that feel unauthentic to them (such as saying "I forgive you" when they don't) will help them feel understood and respected.

Even if spiritual issues are outside your expertise, acknowledging that the faith community can sometimes be a source of revictimization, even though they do not intend to be, may be supporting to the survivor. If returning to the church or synagogue, especially if it was where the funeral was held, is more upsetting than comforting, they may appreciate the caregiver's support in deciding to take a sabbatical from their own worship service or to visit another faith community for awhile. Developing a good referral list of spiritual advisors or clergy with expertise in trauma will be worth the effort.

TIME

Most research about anticipatory grieving and death following long illness or injury tells us that the expected recovery period ranges from two to four years, based on numerous variables. Research about sudden, violent death tells us to expect a four- to seven-year recovery period, acknowledging that recovery is never complete. (Lehman & Wortman, 1987; Mercer, 1993). Many have found that the pain of mourning increases during the second and third years (Rinear, 1988; Ditchick, 1990), possibly because much of the first year is spent psychologically numbed to the reality of what happened.

Mercer (1993) found that the greatest time of unmet support needs was at the first-year anniversary, when reality was setting in but support was nonexistent. Caregivers should keep a monthly tickler file of death dates, especially if the death was sudden and violent, and remember survivors at anniversary time with a call, note or other remembrance.

Mercer's study (1993) of 1447 survivors of drunk driving crashes found that, even after five years, they were still significantly more stressed than non-victims on measures of well-being, somatization, obsessive-compulsive disorders, depression, anxiety, hostility, self-esteem and post-traumatic stress disorder. They were significantly more likely than non-victims to report poorer health, particularly high blood pressure. They were also more likely than non-victims to be taking sleep medication or anti-anxiety drugs.

WHAT HELPS?

Numerous studies have shown us what victims of sudden, violent death need (Wortman, 1985; Weinberg, 1985; Weiss, 1988):

- To talk about what happened time and time again as different aspects of their victimization surfaces;
- To have all their personal reactions accepted and believed;
- To be with others who have been through it.

We also have learned what they don't want (Wortman, 1985; Weinberg, 1985; Weiss, 1988):

- To be told they need medication (They will know themselves if their symptoms are frightening to them);
- To be told not to think about it;
- To be referred to support groups prematurely (If they have carefully selected a particular counselor, clergy person or other caregiver as their confidante, they resent being passed off to a group. *Later,* the caregiver may ask if they would find it helpful to be with others who have had similar experiences.

Grassroots groups such as Mothers Against Drunk Driving, Parents of Murdered Children and Compassionate Friends can offer extremely valuable support and opportunities for those whose loved one was killed. It is impossible to know how many survivors may not have needed professional counseling because of the support they received in these groups. While it is recommended that professional caregivers visit their local branch or chapter before referral to assure that the group would be useful for their client, most survivors who attend these groups say they serve as a healthy supplementary support to professional counseling. In fact, Mercer's study (1993) found the survivors reporting that they found their MADD victim advocate or support groups significantly more helpful than mental health counseling or clergy counseling.

All three organizations mentioned above have excellent print resources for bereaved families. MADD, in particular, has numerous useful publications for crash survivors and most MADD chapters offer support groups for those who wish to attend them. After survivors have received assistance and wish to do something to stop drunk driving, MADD offers many programs for them to choose from. One of the most promising is their Victim Impact Panel program in which a panel of three or four survivors tell their "straight from the heart" stories of what happened to them and how it has changed their lives, never in a blaming or accusing way. The audience is first-time drunk driving offenders, sent to the panel as a condition of their sentence.

Based on research suggesting a positive correlation between the opportunity to tell one's story and successful resolution of crisis, Mercer (1994) compared more than 1,500 drunk driving crash victims who do and do not speak on Victim Impact Panels. Preliminary findings indicate that 87 percent of the panelists report being helped by speaking on panels. Ten percent said they felt neither helped nor hurt by speaking on panels, and three percent felt it had been hurtful for them.

The success of panel participation was supported by pre- and post-psychological testing. There was a significant relationship between increased frequency of panel participation and overall psychological well-being of the panelists, including decreases in anxiety, somatization, depression and avoidance. Furthermore, intrusion and overall post-traumatic stress disorder scores also improved significantly. Panelists reported that participation helped because they believed they were changing others' attitudes and behaviors about drunk driving (attribution of meaning) and preventing future victimizations. The three percent who said speaking on a panel had been hurtful were found to still be needing avoidance defenses to protect them from the pain, having numerous nightmares, taking anti-depression or anti-anxiety medication, feeling angry and feeling generally stressed. This research has led to Dr. Mercer's development of a screening tool for selecting panel members who are not likely to be harmed by participation.

Few things in life are more profound than standing with someone who has had a soul-shattering experience with a sudden, violent death as a result of a vehicular crash. Your authority and status as a counselor, clergy person or victim advocate offers you an unparalleled opportunity to offer support and guidance over the years the survivors make their pilgrimage toward a recovery that is never complete. You can support them as they carve out of their traumatic experience the memories of their loved one they will cherish—memories no one can take away. While those memories hold a unique place in the heart of the survivors, very near that place are the memories of those who truly helped. Equipped with courage, compassion and knowledge about the unique nature of sudden, violent death resulting from vehicular crashes, you will be counted as one of those extraordinary people.

4. Survivors of Suicide

JUDITH M. STILLION, PH.D.

> There are always two parties to a death; the person who
> dies and the survivors who are bereaved ... and in the
> apportionment of suffering, the survivor takes the brunt.
> —Arnold Toynbee

Felicia Adams cannot seem to get over the death of her 17-year-old
son, Jerry. The older of two children born into a middle class intact
family, Jerry had always been a good student who had the mak-
ings of a natural leader. Both parents had taken a great deal of
pride in his accomplishments and had tailored their activities as a
family around his and his sister's needs and schedules. However, a
year and a half ago Jerry died. Since that time Felicia, who had
quit work to devote herself to childrearing when her second child
was born, has become increasingly withdrawn from the rest of her
family and from social activities. She cries frequently throughout
the day and explains that her feelings of sadness and sorrow
overwhelm her so often that she does not feel comfortable going
out of the house because she may break down in public. At the
urging of her husband, she has agreed to see a therapist. During
the first session with the therapist, Felicia reveals that Jerry

(a) died after a two-year bout with leukemia.
(b) killed himself after a short period of depression.
(c) died in an automobile accident.
(d) was murdered by a stranger.

Do your feelings for Felicia change depending upon the cause of
her son's death? As you consider each of the causes of death
mentioned above, do you think of different questions that the
therapist should ask? Do you see different emotional reactions
and different issues that Felicia might have to work through
depending on the cause of Jerry's death?

In fact, Felicia and her family have become survivors of suicide.
They have joined the estimated 3.68 million survivors of suicide

who exist in the United States today (McIntosh, 1993). All deaths involve loss, and grieving is the inevitable hard work that must be done to accept the loss, process its meaning in our lives and be able to involve ourselves once again in the world with renewed energy.

The depth of an individual's grief depends on a variety of factors, including the quality of the relationship with the deceased, the support system that survivors have and the nature of the death. Evidence is beginning to accumulate that suggests that those who experience the death of a friend or loved one by suicide (i.e., suicide survivors) are more likely to experience different, perhaps more complicated, grief reactions than those whose loved ones die from natural causes or from accidents (e.g., Allen, Calhoun, Cann, & Tedeschi, 1993; Van Der Wal, 1989-90; Calhoun, Selby, & Selby, 1982).

Historically, there has been little systematic study regarding the effects of suicide on survivors. At least three reasons for this dearth of research have been suggested. First, it has been difficult to identify samples of suicide survivors large enough to be representative of the total population of those bereaved by suicide. Second, few valid and reliable tools have existed for examining differences between those bereaved by suicide and those bereaved by accidents or illness. Third, many researchers have felt uncomfortable asking survivors about their feelings following suicide, fearing that such questions would intrude on their privacy or prolong their grief by making them revisit the pain involved in such sudden, unexpected and perhaps shameful deaths. Individual counselors, psychologists and members of the clergy have, of course, always worked with such survivors and discussed with each other and in professional meetings their observations of grief reactions among suicide survivors, but little empirical evidence has been available.

Beginning in the mid-seventies, however, and continuing until the present, we have begun to develop a body of research that is shedding light on the experience of suicide survivors as well as highlighting their needs for support through the grieving process. The research is divided into three major areas: attitudes toward suicide survivors; reactions of suicide survivors; and postvention approaches to suicide survivors.

Attitudes Toward Survivors

What does recent research tell us about how suicide survivors are viewed? There have been many studies that have compared attitudes of people responding to death by suicide as compared with attitudes toward death by accident or natural causes (e.g., Calhoun, Selby, & Faulstich, 1980; Calhoun, Selby, & Selby, 1982; Gordon, Range, & Edwards, 1987; Rudestam & Imbroll, 1983; Gibson, Range, & Anderson, 1987; Calhoun, Selby, & Walton, 1995–96; Calhoun, Selby, & Abernathy, 1984; Range & Thompson, 1984; Calhoun, Selby, & Steelman, 1988–89).

Most of these studies have varied the cause of death in much the same way as we varied the cause of Jerry's death at the beginning of this essay. Researchers have presented the deaths in written vignette form, in the form of a "newspaper story," and through the use of an audio tape. In general, these studies have shown that respondents view suicide survivors more negatively than survivors of natural death or of accidents. For example, one study showed that respondents viewed the parents of the child who was portrayed as a suicide as less likable, more blameworthy and less psychologically healthy prior to the death than the parents of the same child who was portrayed as having died from illness (Calhoun, Selby, & Faulstich, 1980).

A second study, presented as a newspaper account, described the death of an adult. Spouses of adults who completed suicide were seen by respondents as being more to blame, being more ashamed of the cause of death and as having been more able to prevent the death of their spouses than were individuals whose spouses died of leukemia or by accident (Calhoun, Selby, & Walton, 1985–86).

A third study asked respondents to listen to identical tapes that featured a middle-aged woman describing her grief at the loss of her husband. Once again the cause of death was the only change in the tapes. Causes included death from a heart attack, from an accident or by suicide. The results showed that respondents rated the survivor of suicide as more psychologically disturbed than the accident survivor and more ashamed than both the heart attack and the accident survivor. They also felt that the suicide survivor could have done more to prevent the death than the survivors in the other two conditions could do (Allen, Calhoun, Cann, & Tedeschi, 1993).

The Experience of Suicide Survivors

As we have seen, there is a body of evidence accumulating that supports the notion that survivors of suicide are viewed more negatively in a variety of ways than are survivors of other kinds of deaths. But how do survivors of suicide view themselves? We will examine the conclusions of four authors who have reviewed the literature on survivors of suicide at different times. The first author reviewed the literature that existed before 1982 and made three tentative generalizations about suicide survivors' experience (Calhoun, 1982). He suggested that survivors of suicide experience greater guilt, that they enjoy less social support, and that they feel more of a need to understand why the death occurred than survivors of other types of death.

In a second systematic review of the literature, Van Der Wal (1989) concluded that the available evidence suggests that bereavement following suicide is qualitatively different from other causes of death in at least six ways. Those bereaved by suicide may experience a prolonged search for motives, may more often deny the cause of death, may more often have to deal with feelings of rejection by the deceased, may raise religious questions concerning the afterlife of the deceased more often, may more often conceal the cause of death from others, and may experience heightened fear of being susceptible to suicide through heredity.

A similar review of the literature published two years later pointed out that in the United States, survivors of suicidal deaths may view the social environment as "less supportive and more rejecting than persons coping with deaths from natural or accidental deaths" (Calhoun & Allen, 1991, p. l02). These authors also concluded that the body of existing research shows that suicide survivors often absorb the same type of social stigma that is carried by the act of suicide and that survivors of suicide are regarded as "more psychologically disturbed, less likable, more blameworthy, more ashamed, more in need of professional mental health care, and more likely to remain sad and depressed longer" (p. 100).

A final review of the literature published in 1993 raised questions about the degree of difference between suicidal and accidental death survivors (McIntosh, 1993). This author, citing his own research, indicated that both accident and suicide survivors reported equally high feelings of stigma and a greater need to understand the death of their family member than did survivors of natural death (McIntosh & Kelly, 1992). However, his research also showed that suicide survivors, more often than other survivors, blamed more people and groups for the death, re-ported more stigmatizing events, and felt more strongly that they could have done something to prevent the death.

Within the published research there is also some evidence that the relationship with the person taking his/her life and the age of that person as well as the age of the survivor affect the grieving process. For example, Range and Calhoun (1990) carried out a study with 57 university students who had experienced the death of a friend by suicide, accident, homicide, natural anticipated death or natural unanticipated death. Interviews with each of these students showed that those who were bereaved by suicide lied more often about the cause of death, reported that they were expected to explain the nature of the death to others and that they received less positive support following the death than did students in any of the other conditions. Another study supported the idea that friends and acquaintances of adolescent suicides were likely to show significant psychological problems, including depression and post-traumatic stress disorder, than were peers who had no friends who had completed suicide (Brent, Perper, Moritz, Allman, Friend, Schweers, Roth, Balach, & Harrington, 1992).

Reed and Greenwald (1991) conducted a large study of relatives of suicidal and accidental death. Their study, carried out by questionnaires mailed to respondents an average of 280 days after the deaths of their relatives, revealed that the manner of death is significantly related to death. Specifically, survivors of suicidal deaths reported experiencing significantly greater guilt, shame and rejection than did survivors of accidental deaths. In a somewhat surprising finding, these authors reported that suicide survivors experience less emotional distress and shock than do survivors of accidental deaths. They explained this finding by indicating that 79 percent of those who took their lives had given some warning prior to their deaths. Such warnings often were a part of other disturbed behaviors including drug abuse, spouse and child abuse, marital discord and mental illness, which may account for another finding of the study. Suicide survivors in this study tended to view the suicide as a relief more often than did those whose relatives died by accident. However, feeling relief may in itself increase already heightened guilt feelings accompanying this type of death.

Two studies have specifically addressed the grief of parents of accidental and suicidal deaths. Kovarsky (1989) found that although survivors of accidental deaths showed higher initial grief reactions, those reactions diminished over time while the grief reactions of those surviving suicide remained level or increased over time. Miles and Demi (1991) also studied the grief of surviving parents. They found higher levels of guilt among parents of suicides who listed guilt as the most distressing aspect of their grief. Parents of children who died from accidents or from illness listed loneliness as their most distressing symptom.

Several studies have examined the grief of spouses of suicide. Saunders (1981) found that such spouses experienced greater rejection from friends and from the deceased mate's family. Another study found increased health problems among spouses whose mates had died either by suicide or by accident (Pennebaker & O'Heeron, 1984). Demi (1984) found few differences in bereavement outcome for those widowed by suicide, accident or natural deaths. She did, however, note that suicide survivors showed more guilt and resentment during the second year after bereavement. Barrett and Scott (1990) conducted two studies that were designed to assess both general and specific grief experiences of suicide survivors compared to survivors of accidents, natural expected and natural unexpected deaths. They found few differences in recovery between the groups. However, they noted that survivors of suicide experienced more rejection and felt the need to conceal the cause of death than did survivors in the other groups.

One longitudinal study of elderly spouses exists in the literature (Farberow, Gallagher, Gilewski, & Thompson, 1987; Gilewski, Farberow, Gallagher, & Thompson, 1991; Faberow, Gallagher-Thompson, Gilewski, & Thompson, 1992a, 1992b). In this study, researchers interviewed surviving spouses of natural and suicidal deaths as well as members of a non-bereaved control group at four intervals following the death. During the first two interviews, at two months and four months, both groups of widowed people showed higher levels of depression, psychological distress and more negative appraisals of self than did the non-bereaved group. At 12 months, however, the suicide survivors reported that their mental health was poorer and that they were experiencing higher levels of depression than the natural death survivors. Moreover, at two and one-half years after the death, the suicide survivors continued to rate themselves more poorly on measures of mental health than did the other two groups. The authors of the study concluded that suicide survivors received "significantly less emotional support for their feelings of depression and grief than the natural death survivors, and that they did not confide in the persons in their network any more than the non-bereaved controls did" (Farberow et al., 1992a, p. 107).

In contrast to the studies reported above, some available studies show few or no differences between those bereaved by suicide and those bereaved by accident or natural causes. Range and Niss (1990) found only one significant difference among groups bereaved by suicide, accident, natural anticipated, natural unanticipated and homicide death survivors. That difference involved a stronger feeling among accidental death survivors, compared to the two groups of natural death survivors, that the death did not seem "real." In addition, McIntosh (1993) ended his review of the existing literature by observing that there are "many more similarities than differences between suicide survivors and other bereaved groups, particularly other sudden-death survivors such as by accidental death" (p. 158). Moreover, he called for better, more finely tuned research to determine whether real and substantive differences exist between the grief of suicide survivors and that of survivors of other types of death.

It is true that the state of current research is far from conclusive. Much more remains to be done before we will have a full picture of the ways in which the grieving process following suicidal deaths differ from that following deaths from other causes. However, it seems to this writer that the preponderance of available material shows that people in society view survivors of suicide more negatively than they view other survivors and that the survivors themselves have more issues to struggle with than do survivors of other kinds of death. What, then, should be done to help the survivors of suicide—people who, like Felicia Adams, are having trouble working through their loss?

POSTVENTION WITH SUICIDE SURVIVORS

For over two decades, helping professionals have attempted to meet the needs of suicide survivors through approaches that have come to be known as postvention programs (Shneidman, 1971; 1975; 1981). Postvention activities are generally organized by communities and school systems. Frequently, they are staffed by interdisciplinary groups of professionals and volunteers who are prepared to react as a crisis intervention team as soon as a suicide occurs within a community.

A well planned and immediate reaction is especially important when the person taking his/her life is an adolescent, since "cluster" and "copycat suicides" are more prevalent in this group (Stillion & McDowell, 1996). Cluster suicides occur when a group of people who live in the same geographic location commit suicide over a relatively short time span. Highly publicized cluster suicides have occurred in places as diverse as Plano, Texas; Westchester, New York; Omaha, Nebraska; and Bergenfield, New Jersey (Stillion & McDowell, 1996). Copycat suicides occur when people, generally adolescents and young adults, take their lives using the same methods that have been used in a publicized suicide. Both cluster and copycat suicides have been referred to as evidence of a "contagion effect" in adolescent suicide (Carter & Brooks, 1990). Perhaps because adolescents and young adults are in an impressionable period that is marked by extremes in mood, this age group seems more reactive than others to deaths by suicide. In addition, many adolescents attempt to cope with the turbulence of the period by using imitation and modeling behaviors. Suicide of peers may also have the effect of "giving permission" to others who are unhappy.

In order to counteract the contagion effect, schools have begun to develop organized suicide prevention programs (Smith, 1991). Wenckstern and Leenaars (1991) have suggested that postvention work in the schools has much in common with treatment of post-traumatic stress victims and have extracted eight principles of positive postvention programs as shown below:

1. Begin as soon as possible after the tragedy.
2. Expect resistance from some, but not all, survivors.
3. Be willing to explore negative emotions toward the victim when the time is right.
4. Provide ongoing reality testing for the survivors.
5. Be ready to refer when necessary.
6. Avoid clichés and banal optimism.
7. Be prepared to spend significant amounts of time (generally several months) in one school.
8. Develop the postvention program within a comprehensive health care setting that also includes prevention and intervention.

Although these principles were intended for school personnel, they seem equally as applicable to community-based programs. The first response, regardless of the situation, is to advertise the availability of counseling personnel. The second step should be to identify all the people who think of themselves as suicide survivors. This will include relatives, close friends and acquaintances, of course, but it may also include members of clubs, organizations and institutions such as churches or synagogues, who may be affected by the loss and need some help in coping with feelings of guilt and regret that are so common in deaths by suicide.

Because of the sense of shame that some still attach to death by suicide, counseling personnel may find that they need to be more proactive in reaching out to survivors than is generally the case with other kinds of clients (Carter & Brooks, 1990).

Hazell and Lewin (1993), recognizing that it is difficult to identify people who may be at risk after a suicide, have devised a risk index for suicidal behavior among exposed adolescents and have also begun to test out a brief screening questionnaire that can be used in schools within days of a completed suicide. Following the identification phase, group and/or individual counseling should be offered.

Trolley (1993) has described the role of professional helpers following a suicide. Flexibility is an essential hallmark of helping professionals throughout the grieving process. She has suggested that the initial contact with a suicide survivor should be as a crisis counselor offering support reassurance and perhaps gentle affirmation of the reality of the death to the bereaved person. As the period of shock and denial following the death begin to recede, helpers can move into a role of information giver and can also give assistance with practical matters and serve as mediators between the bereaved and medical and funeral personnel. Empathic listening is another important role of helpers, who should be prepared to witness violent emotions of guilt, shame, anger and depression.

As the therapeutic relationship matures, helping professionals can move more fully into a teaching role, sharing resources such as books and the names of other suicide survivors (always with their permission, of course) which might be helpful to the survivor. Helpers may also find themselves filling other roles, including serving as a family mediator, a group facilitator and modeling acceptance, caring and understanding that may enable others to show such characteristics to bereaved people. Simply listening and accepting the emotions of the survivor are important since catharsis or "giving voice to the loss" can have curative value in itself (Alexander, 1991). Finally, Trolley points out that it is important for therapists to examine their own values and biases regarding suicide as well as to help survivors become aware of the attitudes toward suicide that they have brought with them into the grieving process. Caregivers need to maintain a non-punitive attitude toward both the deceased and the survivors as well as to help survivors of suicide to assign the responsibility for the suicidal act to the deceased.

SUMMARY

Many survivors of suicide carry a special burden throughout the process of grieving. Higher levels of guilt, shame and anger are just three of the emotions that such survivors may experience. In addition, those grieving loss by suicide often are left with questions such as why their loved ones killed themselves, and what, if anything, might have been done to prevent the suicide. Such questions, generally unanswerable, may prolong the process of grieving and condemn suicide survivors to live in the shadow of that suicidal death far longer than is healthy. Moreover, survivors frequently struggle with such issues as how others will view them and their remaining family members and, if religious, what the fate of their dead loved one might be in the hereafter since suicide is still considered a mortal sin in some religions. Research to date seems to indicate that suicide survivors are viewed more negatively than survivors of other types of death and that they, like Felicia Adams, may have complicated and extended grief reactions. Such survivors need support from the community and may well need additional help in the form of individual or group therapy.

5. Sudden Violent Death

Lula M. Redmond, R.N., M.S.

When death occurs from sudden, unexpected circumstances such as accidents, suicide or murder, bereavement reactions are more severe, exaggerated and complicated. The mourner's capacity to use adaptive coping mechanisms is overwhelmed. This is not meant to indicate that grief is not painful regardless of the type of death or that one bereavement reaction is worse than another, but that other factors impinge on the mourner, leading to a more complicated bereavement in sudden violent deaths. There are many variables that influence the individual's reaction to bereavement. However, those who mourn the willful, intentional act of murder of a loved one—bereaved homicide survivors—experience the unique intrusion by many outside forces in our society. We shall explore some of the factors which complicate the bereavement reaction for homicide survivors.

COMPLICATIONS OF BEREAVEMENT

There are varied reasons for the delayed, exaggerated and complicated bereavement reactions experienced by survivors of homicide. Major characteristics experienced by survivors are cognitive dissonance; disbelief and murderous impulses; conflict of values and belief system; and withdrawal of support due to the stigma of murder. Survivors must deal with feelings of fear and vulnerability, anger, rage, shame, blame, guilt and emotional withdrawal. The lack of familiarity and support by law enforcement, the criminal justice system and media intrusion also complicates bereavement. The delays in resolution of the murder conviction, lack of adequate punishment for the crime and lack of acknowledgment by society increases the feelings of loss of control.

Each of these is present as a treatment issue in working with the homicide survivor. There are other issues not addressed here, which do not negate their importance. The ones selected for this discussion are those most commonly reported and presented by survivors in individual and group therapy and in support groups.

Cognitive Dissonance

At news that someone you love was murdered, the first reactions of disbelief, shock and numbness are apparent in the inability to accept the news as real. Remarks such as, "It can't be," "Oh, my God, no," are indicative of the denial. There may be claims that the informer must have made a mistake, denying that this could happen to a loved one. There is no preparation for this sudden onslaught. There is no comprehension that death could come so swiftly, and in a violent, degrading, brutal manner at the hands of another human being.

The death does not make sense; the mind cannot comprehend or absorb the meaning. The mind demands more information than can be processed or stored. Questions about events leading up to the murder will be asked repeatedly, over and over, seeking both understanding and confirmation that it is not true! Nothing in our coping mechanisms prepares us for this level of psychological trauma.

Jim, a father, had been part of the search party looking for his missing 14-year-old daughter for over 24 hours. Later, the fire department discovered her body in a burning shack, stabbed viciously. Months later after the funeral, investigations, arrests and pretrial hearings Jim continued searching. He circled the same locations covered in the original search. He intellectually knew that his daughter was dead, and that her body had been found, but he said, "I could not believe that she was really gone."

The mind is overloaded with the events prior to, during and after the murder. There is a constant rehearsal of events: what happened; when; how; where; who did what; and the unanswerable, but *why*? There may be questions that have been answered in a logical sequence by law enforcement officers, victim advocates and other officials. None of the answers are "good enough." The mind is searching to understand something that's incomprehensible. The act of reordering the events in order to understand takes much longer than we may expect.

This cognitive dissonance may continue for months or years, and may be triggered by the court proceedings and other events relating to the murder, lasting for years in the form of a delayed grief reaction.

MURDEROUS IMPULSES AND ANGER

One of the most difficult emotional reactions for survivors, family members, friends, therapists and others who serve the victimized survivors to understand is the intensity, duration and frequency of anger and rage. Anger is a normal healthy emotion. Lifton (1979, p. 147) describes the paradigm of the emotional state of anger on a continuum from anger to rage to violence. To fantasize acting out rage is normal. To act out rage becomes violent behavior and must be prevented.

For the homicide survivor the normal anger of grief is compounded by the rage and desire to violently destroy the murderer of the loved one. The psyche is dominated by images of what the survivors "would, could and should do" to the murderer. Elaborate plans of torturous treatment may be devised. The images of seeing the murderer suffer in a more horrendous manner than one's own loved one suffered are normal reactions for bereaved survivors.

Frequently the survivor is ashamed to tell anyone of the horror of their retaliatory thoughts. It is not unusual for the victimized survivor to fantasize painful castration of a rapist-murderer followed by a slow bleeding death. Lifton (1979) explained that anger has to do with an internal struggle to assert vitality by attacking the other rather than the self in order to prevent a sense of inner deadness.

A 68-year-old father whose son had been murdered fantasized the opportunity to slice the accused murderer's body just enough for him to bleed lightly, then trolling him as bait through shark-infested waters. He was so ashamed of these retaliatory thoughts that he withdrew from his family in a deep depression.

Survivors are frightened by their murderous impulses and their sense of rage. They ask themselves, "Am I no better than the one who killed my loved one?" "If I know myself to be a good person, yet I feel the desire to castrate, mutilate or degrade another human being, can I really be a good person?" Further, "If I could do such harm or think of such savagery, am I safe around my own family?" This can lead to emotional withdrawal and deep depression. "I must be going crazy" is a common response of survivors. The survivor should be reassured that he is not "going crazy," that such retaliatory thinking is quite typical and expected under the circumstances. The internal conflict with one's own sense of values, beliefs and sense of justice is overwhelming. The murderous impulses to attack the other in retaliation for the pain suffered by the murder victim and for the pain of grief of survivors must be explored, exposed and understood to be dealt with in therapy.

It is in venting and verbalizing the murderous impulses that the anger begins to lose some of its intensity and power. The thoughts do not have to be acted out when one can tell the fantasy and the therapist listens with acknowledgment, understanding and nonjudgmental acceptance. Verbalization and ventilation provide a path to reframe the scenario. It is a way to rehearse what in effect could, should and would be done. The imagery serves to define one's troubled existence. The discussion of violent imagery serves as a form of restraint against it's being transformed into actual violence. As therapists, we must not be frightened of listening to the imagery of rage! We understand this concept as crucial to the therapeutic process.

The release from the anger, rage, violence paradigm will be dependent on the capacity to accept one's inactivation under the circumstances (Lifton, p. 151). Most survivors are able to release anger, bitterness, despair, helplessness and frustrations as they become aware of what can be accomplished. The most profound sense of power can be fueled by the energy of directed anger. This becomes a focus of the therapist's work in empowering the survivor. The survivor is empowered through knowledge of the normal and expected symptoms of grief, by gaining knowledge of the entire circumstances of the case and knowledge of what can be expected of the criminal justice and other related systems. The painful reactions become understood and normalized through verbalization and expression. Others must acknowledge that the sense of powerlessness and frustrations are real, painful and common.

It is not unusual to see survivors displace anger. The anger may not be directed at the criminal but at others who surround homicide survivors. Targets of this displaced anger may be family members, friends, coworkers, strangers in the street or even those who are trying to assist. The threshold level of instant irritation and self-control is low and survivors do not have the internal controls to endure even slight irritations.

In a "stranger-to-stranger" crime, the survivor and defendant have little to no contact. Anger, pain, fear and violation become more real when the offender is caught and brought to trial. Survivors during the trial are amazed at their own restraint. They must endure the pain of seeing this human being face-to-face. In contrast, if the offender is never apprehended, then he or she becomes a "mystical figure," elusive and not entirely real to the survivor. There is greater cognitive dissonance because there are more unanswered questions to internalize, questions that can only be answered in the imagination.

A young woman, whose mother was murdered four years ago by an unknown killer, recognized her anger and irritations over the slightest offenses. She said, "I see the murderer in every place I go, in the mall, driving down the street, in the grocery store. I was getting mad and taking it out on everybody. Once I was able to understand the anger I began to direct it. I don't have to be mad at everyone else, just the invisible killer."

In therapy groups survivors are asked, "What do you want to do with your anger?" It is the survivor's emotion that has the powerful ability to transform negative trauma into positive accomplishments, but the choice must be up to the survivors.

This technique is not useful until the anger has been verbalized, explored, reframed, rehearsed and exhausted. It must be the survivor's choice whether it will be part of an internal dialogue for the rest of one's life. By offering the survivor this choice in decisionmaking it adds to a sense of being in control and reaffirms one's power.

FEAR AND VULNERABILITY

Survivors express a pervasive sense of fearfulness and apprehension, feeling vulnerable to further psychological or physical assaults. The fears are not irrational. The world is no longer safe as was previously believed. Parents restrict remaining children from playing out of sight, worry about business or personal travel of other loved ones and restrict their own activity. A mother of a 10-year-old murder victim reported that five years after the murder of her child, her two elderly aunts, who live together, will not answer the telephone after 3 p.m. They no longer go to concerts or social events, and live in fear of someone else in the family being murdered.

Frank, in his mid-forties, finds he must search through every room of his home when he returns from work daily. His father was killed in the family home. Jeff, another survivor, bought a gun after the murder of his daughter. He had never used one before but slept on it under his pillow for months. He said, "I simply cannot let anything else happen to my family. I'm scared to death, but if I am going to be killed, I must protect the other children."

Chronic phobic reactions can develop and lead to total dysfunction due to paranoia and a sense of vulnerability. Following a presentation on normal grief and bereavement to a self-help support group for agoraphobia, a young 18-year-old came up afterwards with tears running down her cheeks. She said she had been in a mental hospital for over a year after her brother's murder. She felt it was the first time she could understand what may have happened to her. She described her paranoia, depression, suicidal ideation and subsequent emotional withdrawal. We can only question if grief therapy may have changed the course of this young life. Fear must be expressed and examined for an orientation to reality. Bard (1986) relates that the therapist can help to diminish the intensity, duration and frequency of these feelings.

Conflict of Value and Belief System

Murder violates our belief that we have a right to life and is in direct opposition to the high value we place on life. Think for a moment about our use of high medical technology and how we strive to maintain life at almost any cost. Then think how, as a nation, we have tolerated the murder of over 20,000 persons a year for the last 10 to15 years! This is a clear conflict. In other types of death the crisis may unite a family of supportive survivors. Frequently in homicide, however, murder results in explosive reactions destroying relationships among survivors. Each family member searches for a reason for the sudden, unexpected, intentional act of destruction of life of their loved one.

This is a personal violation of each one's value and belief system. We value life and believe that, if we are good people, do not hurt others and practice our Judeo-Christian beliefs, life and God will be fair to us. Murder is a violation of everything we have been taught to be right, honest, fair, or expected in life. We search to understand an act committed against our individual beliefs. When unable to comprehend, we feel powerless, frustrated and without hope. We may question what is of value, if not life? "What other parts of my belief system are false?" It is a lonely, elusive, individual search for understanding. There is a loss of trust in the world as it was believed to be.

Members of the family withdraw from one another, each nursing his or her own level of psychic pain and grief. The level and intensity of grief will differ for each. Individuals experience feeling states unique to their personality, coping mechanisms, previous crisis experience, support and individual relationship with the deceased and relationships within the family.

Each experiences emotions of guilt, anger, fear, anxiety and vulnerability. The anxiety in the system is turned up full blast, similar to the volume on a radio, and the noise ricochets in every thought, feeling and behavior of each family member. Anxious systems do not behave like calm ones. Anxious systems can become destructive.

In an effort to regain some sense of control, survivors experience guilt, blaming themselves or others for some word or deed that was done or undone. The thought that one may have changed the situation, time, place or circumstances to prevent the murder is a thundering, intrusive image. When the family system blames one of the surviving family members, either verbally or non-verbally, or when one member accepts blame, the entire relationship system may deteriorate.

Guilt and Blame

Guilt is intricately embodied with a sense of control and the search for a reason for the death. An understandable explanation is necessary for the mind to absorb the meaning of the victimization. The assault is internalized and the barrage of "if only. . . ." is endless and treacherous. We seek to blame ourselves or others in order to make sense of the tragedy and to confirm a sense of control over our life. In our homicide survivor therapy groups we provide a pre- and post- grief experience inventory test. In one post test after therapy 13 group members out of 18 showed a marked reduction in guilt; seven who showed a reduction of guilt revealed a marked increase in the loss of control components. Although this sample is too small to confirm a definitive correlation, it is indicative of the relationship between guilt and loss of control.

We have been taught to be responsible for our lives, activities, careers, care of our children, care of ourselves and those we love, and to believe we have the power to control the destiny of those responsibilities. Survivors express guilt and feelings of responsibility because they believed themselves to be in control and were, in fact, in control prior to the tragic event. There is incongruity in this belief as it is proven invalid after the murder of a loved one. The criminal has erased the power and control exercised in carrying out the daily functions of living. The murderer not only took the life of the victim, but plunged the lives of the survivors into excruciating painful grief.

Frequently one parent will blame himself or herself for any deviation that may have taken place in an otherwise normal routine. What the survivor is saying is, "I am responsible for this, I made this happen." If the survivor does not think of this primarily, someone else may direct blame either verbally or non-verbally. At times the survivor assumes he or she is being blamed by others, when this is not true. However, to verbally confront the issue with significant others becomes an overwhelming burden.

In the death of a child, one parent may go to great lengths to assuage the guilt of the other parent. But the sense of being protected from blame is a heavy burden for the one who feels guilty. This is a major cause of marital-relationship problems following the death of a child. Expressed feelings of shared guilt have a therapeutic value.

Jane allowed her 15-year-old daughter off disciplinary restriction to attend a neighbor's party. She finished the dinner dishes, primped, and as she was leaving, her father grinned and kidded about, "how easily she could convince Mom to have her own way." Mom did not tell Dad she had also granted an extra 30 minutes at the party. Their daughter was assaulted, robbed, raped and brutally killed that night after she left the neighbor's home. Father silently blamed mother for allowing her off restriction and himself for not demanding compliance with the disciplinary decision. Mother blamed herself for the 30-minute extension. Neither parent ever spoke of their inner feelings to one another. It was not until Jane sought professional help for her suicidal ideation three years later that she revealed this burden of guilt. She had been so ashamed it had been impossible to reveal it to anyone.

Family members may give and accept unrealistic responsibilities for a crime. A husband or father may assume an inordinate level of blame because he failed to protect his family. Survivors may also blame the victims for "allowing" themselves to be murdered. In our society men have been raised to be protectors. One of the crucial differences in the grieving process for men and women is how much greater the level of unspoken guilt is in males.

The degree of blame and guilt can be intensified if the murder occurred during the time the relationship was undergoing a stressful period or incident. If the murder occurs immediately following an argument or family altercation, the magnitude of unresolved grief will be more severe.

Even when no blame exists within the family, each family member may begin a process of withdrawal from one another, protecting one another, the youngest members or the elderly, from the gruesome facts of reality. Communications become inhibited and strained as each feels isolated and a deep sense of personal emptiness.

Stigmatized Death

In our society, we have held the belief that those who are murdered have in some way led to their own death. Members of a community in which a brutal murder has taken place will often blame the victim or survivors. This is, again, the same search to comprehend the horror. By these explanations, a protective shield is set up within the minds of observers that a similar tragedy would never happen to them. Everyone is, in reality, vulnerable to victimization but will seek security in finding components of the criminal activity that "could never" occur in their life. A superficial aura of personal security is established to counteract this real vulnerability.

An internalized sense of personal security is exhibited by onlookers as victims are labeled bad, drugged, careless, seductive, promiscuous, with the wrong crowd or, in some manner, "asking for it." Families of victims are also stigmatized because it is believed that they should have stopped the behaviors blamed on the victim or at least have expected the traumatic outcome. It is as though what is being said or thought is, "If I blame you for 'letting' your child be killed, how can I still be your friend?"

This is irrational thinking on the part of others to prevent acknowledgment of their own vulnerability and the randomness of murder. Evidence of this fact becomes apparent when it is the murder of an innocent child or an elderly woman or gentleman.

In order to prevent our own loss of control and gain understanding, we project blame on the lack of parental care, other caregivers, or the system within which the victim was a member. The mind continues to search for explanations until it becomes accommodated. In this projection of blame, the observer finds comfort and accepts that one's family is exempt from such a horrendous tragedy. This type of rationale provides emotional distance and exclusion, protecting those who are neighbors, friends, coworkers and other community members. This type of thinking and reactive behavior by others leaves the survivors alone in their sorrow.

It is the emotional distancing of others and stigmatization that leaves the survivors of homicide feeling abandoned, ashamed, powerless and vulnerable. Survivors report not receiving sympathy cards, the inability of others to even say "I'm sorry," or co-workers inability to acknowledge absence from work. Examples of this type of sensitivity to the needs of others are acknowledged freely in other types of deaths. Survivors report the sound of whispers among coworkers, and recognition that the murder case is the subject, but lack of acknowledgment that it is their murdered loved one under discussion. Friends, who do not know what to say or do, become uncomfortable and withdraw emotional support. Many survivors report that cherished friendships become dissolved at the time of murder of their loved one.

When the surviving family members acknowledge there were predisposed circumstances such as drug abuse, family violence or other recognizable fears they lived with for years that may have led to the murder, this does not lessen the intensity of loss to the survivor. Ambivalence creates the opposite effect. Those who have opposed parental or spousal wishes do not deserve to be murdered! The survivor must subsequently endure not only the loss of the loved one, but the death of personal hopes, dreams and unfulfilled expectations that perhaps someday the son, daughter or spouse would have functioned in a more productive lifestyle. The survivor experiences a greater sense of personal failure when there is ambivalence in the relationship, and the process of bereavement becomes more exaggerated and complicated.

We note less stigmatization of survivors when the murders are high profile media cases such as the murders of Nicole Brown Simpson, Ronald Goldman and the victims of the Oklahoma City terrorist bombing. To be supportive of the victims and survivors of these murders may signify an awareness by the American public that the possibility of murder is a reality of our times.

INTRUSION BY OTHER SYSTEMS

The raw wound of the grieving homicide survivor is overtly and covertly affected by the performance of law enforcement officials, criminal justice practitioners, media personnel and others after a murder. Prior to the murder, there is a lack of knowledge and familiarity with the functions of these systems in the normal, everyday life of victim survivors. After a murder, each system intrudes in the most personal matters in one's life at a time of great emotional turmoil. Many survivors describe secondary victimization as more severe than the psychological trauma of murder. This is due to the intrusion by outsiders, lack of respect for privacy, and the previous belief that the systems will represent the rights of crime victims. This often does not materialize.

Law Enforcement

Law enforcement officers may be sensitive and gentle but, as part of their duties, bring the most devastating news one can ever imagine. The message that someone you love was murdered is so harsh, ugly, devastating and unthinkable, that notification of next-of-kin is a horrendous task. No matter how the message is conveyed, the memories of those moments will be etched in the minds of the survivors forever. Surviving family members frequently remember the exact words used, how the officer looked, the number on the police badge, the way one stood or even held his or her hat. Some survivors physically attack the newsbearer, scream, run or faint. The desire and need to lash out in rage at the bearer of bad news is more than understandable.

Recently, the mother of a 17-year-old son who was killed in a pass-by-shooting said, "It was the way the victim advocate sat on my couch and said, 'He didn't make it,' that tore my heart out. It was said like he was some kind of stray animal. . . . I will never forget her look and the way she spoke of my son."

Previous personal experiences with a police officer may be only limited to receiving a traffic ticket. Suddenly law enforcement takes on a different meaning and unfamiliar impact in the survivor's life.

The griever is in shock and may not understand the words. Survivors may want more information than the investigating officer can share at that time. The survivors' defense mechanism of denial may be shattered by an officer who does not understand the psychological protection of the denial mechanism. The event is not only fraught with anxiety and psychological trauma, but is an intrusion into the personal, private, inner core of one's existence. In order to assist those who must provide death notification, Janice Harris Lord (1988), Director of Victim Services at MADD National Headquarters, has outlined excellent suggestions for death notification to be used by police officers and others. The newsbearer must slow down, as though he were walking hip deep in molasses, to be sensitive to the impact of every word and action on the survivors.

When one or more family members are suspected of the murder, there are additional complications in the mourning process. The family system is shattered by the incongruency of grieving for the victim and loyalty to the defendant. There is the compounded loss of the loved one to murder, and loss of the accused to a term of incarceration.

CRIMINAL JUSTICE SYSTEM

There appears to be an endless list of new words, phrases and roles in the unfamiliar world of the criminal justice system. The majority of people have never dealt with an attorney in their lives. Suddenly thrust into the role of victim survivor, they must learn the meaning of related terms such as investigations, hearings, pretrials, plea-bargain, continuances, court dates set and postponed, and learn the roles of personnel such as victim advocates, prosecuting attorneys, defense lawyers, judges, court reporters and others. And they must learn that their sense of time will not be valid in the court system.

The survivor finds out the charge of murder is a crime against the state, not against the husband, wife, mother, son or other for whom the survivor grieves. In order to keep the family out of the courtroom, they may be required by the defense attorney to give a deposition on the pretense of being a witness. In fact, this may turn out to be a ploy by the defense. The prosecutor may plea bargain, allowing reduction of the charge to a lesser offense in order to get a conviction, and this may not have been discussed, explained, understood, or agreed to by surviving family members. Victim survivors often have to face the defendant in the courtroom or in the corridor or waiting room. It is traumatic to come face-to face with the murderer. There may be numerous trips to officials' offices requiring days off from work, lost wages and the ire of a perhaps less-than-understanding employer.

Families may travel long distances incurring expenses to attend a trial that has been delayed with no notification to the family. I have witnessed one family who gathered for court on five different occasions, left jobs and arranged flights into the area, only to be told of a continuance hours before the scheduled trial.

Exclusion from the courtroom or remarks such as, "You should just get on with your life," "Leave this to us," or "Why put yourself through that?" discount the importance of the role of the victim and survivors. Survivors who are not present at any of the hearings or proceedings feel left out and abandoned by the system believed to provide justice for those who suffer at the hands of criminals. They must know they had the opportunity to represent their loved one and made their own choice to do so, or not, no matter how difficult the court experiences. We encourage our survivors to attend and actively participate in every phase of the criminal justice proceedings. Those who are able to do so appear to resolve the conflicts of the tragedy in a more positive manner.

In court, survivors may hear reports of early "good boy" school records, testimonials from teachers, principals, church leaders, boy scoutmasters, neighbors, friends and family members who testify for the defense of a known killer. It is not unusual to observe a jury, judge and society as a whole adopt the attitude that the victim must be to blame for his or her own death. Victim survivors may have to contend with the release of the criminal, light sentences, the crime never being solved, the crime not prosecuted for lack of sufficient evidence, or presented to a grand jury and not taken to trial with subsequent release of the murderer.

The murderer, whom one testified against in a trial, may be released on a work-release program unknown to victim survivors. The fear of retaliation for testimony that led to a conviction is real, and retaliation by the perpetrator occurs with great frequency. The list of secondary victimization by the criminal justice system appears endless. As a professional therapist, one may hear bizarre accounts of insensitivity and incredulous stories of victimization by the courts.

The mother of a 36-year-old daughter who was murdered said, "I could deal with the murderer. I knew he had to be sick to do such a terrible thing to my daughter. What I have had the hardest time accepting is the way the system has treated us. There's more frustration and pain in dealing with the system, than with the murder. There's one closed door after another. Everyone tells you what you can't do: can't come into the courtroom, can't show any emotion in the courtroom, can't get a trial date set, can't get a first degree murder charge. My worst victimization was by our criminal justice system. I needed to be in that courtroom. I needed to see the pictures of her body, and understand how she fought him off. They wouldn't recognize my ability to make those decisions for myself." It has been repeated many times, "The first rape was by the rapist, but the worst rape was by our system we call justice."

MEDIA

Although a large portion of crimes such as child abuse, sexual assault, rape and spouse abuse are under-reported crimes, when they are reported, victims have the privilege of being treated in a confidential manner. This is not true for victim survivors of homicide. Murder is an act against the state that usually does not go unreported, and survivors are identified publicly. There is no code of confidentiality for homicide survivors.

The sensationalism used by the media makes the stories of murder commercially viable. The sight of a body bag has a different meaning to surviving family members than it does to the majority of the viewing public. A reporter thrusting a microphone into the face of a grieving mother and asking, "How do you feel" does not indicate sensitivity, care or concern of an interested person. The media may ignore murder of low-status victims and exploit stories of high-profile victims. Imagine what the other 100,000 newly bereaved homicide survivors have felt during the year of the televised proceedings of the Brown and Goldman murders.

Watzlawick (1988) wrote of French sociologist Jean Baudrillard's description of the obscenity of television. Baudrillard spoke of the brutalizing effect of pools of blood, pictures of beheaded accident victims and violent crimes that have become the essential, if not the sole ingredient, of newscasts—scenes like the shameless and disrespectful closeups of people in desperate and tragic situations: the mother holding the body of her dead child, the moronic questions fired at someone who really needs to be left alone. This is followed by the idiotic banter of a commercial and defended as the citizens' right to be kept informed under our constitutional law.

Mrs. Caesar watched the scene of her 17-year old daughter on television. Janie was missing and later found murdered with her ravaged body in a ditch. The shock and numbness of grief did not protect the mother from the scene. She could not believe this was her child. She said, "Television is for entertainment and for celebrities—Janie would have loved to be on TV!" Other pictures of the high school beauty queen appeared counterfeit in the mother's eyes. In her stunned state her child's photos appeared unreal. The nightmares became a daytime horror. After all, she questioned, "Janie had never been on television during her life; why must she be in her death?" Survivors may not know they have the right to refuse interviews by the press and television media. They may be incorrectly quoted. Also, they may find out details about the case that they never knew from the six o'clock evening news.

More than one survivor has reported finding out about the murder of a sister, daughter or husband from the telephone call of a news reporter. Others found out their missing loved one was dead after reading a daily newspaper. Other systems of health care may also be a source of secondary victimization to survivors. Victims may have survived for hours requiring extensive emergency surgery. Hospital personnel overloaded with their medical duties, dealing with the intrusion of law enforcement personnel into their system, often have difficulty providing compassionate care to families.

Even after the death has occurred, survivors report lack of knowledge of the patient's condition, being closed in a waiting area for hours with unanswered questions. Later, they find that the death of their family member occurred hours earlier, and they were not informed. One family reported that the hospital personnel denied that the patient had died. Two hours later they were questioned about still being there, since the body of their father had already been transferred to the medical examiner's office!

This in no way is meant to indicate that there are not kind, considerate, sensitive and caring personnel in law enforcement, the criminal justice system, the media and healthcare systems. Many were taught to use emotional distancing in order to handle the trauma and stress of their daily jobs. Some are seeking education in victim issues and sensitivity training, in order to prevent secondary victimization to those they serve. The need to educate and train a vast public is evident in regard to these issues.

Loss of Control

Americans and individuals in most western cultures cherish freedom and the right to control their own lives. It is believed that in order to succeed individuals must be in control. People make choices: where to work, live, worship, play; what education level to attain; how to raise their family; what rules and structure are most appropriate within their family; and how to achieve defined goals in life. Free cultures possess this defined right of freedom and members expect to be able to direct their lives within the confines of the laws. We have referred earlier to how guilt correlates with loss of control. It is as though one says, "If I had not done something wrong, this would not have happened, because I am a responsible person." We cannot be responsible for the actions of others. However, when one believes he or she is in control and this is violated, feelings of powerlessness ensue.

When a crime occurs, the victim survivor becomes frustrated and powerless and control of one's person, property or possessions is lost. A criminal takes command of the very personal and private right to control one's own life, possessions and lives of those whom one loves.

First, the criminal violated the inalienable right of the human body to life. This represents and endangers everything the victim meant to every one who knew him and loved him.

Then law enforcement and criminal justice systems control one's right to information, to search for the accused, to defend the honor of a loved one in court, or to seek justice through punishment of the perpetrator. Whatever level of justice is achieved is arduous and slow, and requires constant vigilance on the part of survivors.

Loss of control becomes even more pronounced when the perpetrator is never apprehended, punished or acknowledged as at fault. In this event, the level of psychological trauma has no closure for survivors. The normal state of confusion experienced by all who grieve is complicated by the introduction of unfamiliar roles, legislative rules, court activities and unfulfilled expectations. Homicide survivors consistently report feelings of abandonment, loss of control and powerlessness in greater frequency, intensity and of longer duration than in any other type of bereavement reaction. They are more often required to put their grief "on hold" until they have learned to cope with the intrusions of the outside world.

EMOTIONAL WITHDRAWAL

Lindemann (1944), Krystal (1968), Lifton (1979) and van der Kolk (1987) have described the experience of uncontrollable severance of affective ties in psychological trauma. In the acutely traumatic state, one stands alone and loses all sources of feelings of security. There is a break with the continuity of life, an emotional separation from all one's emotional connections and experiences that have preceded the traumatic event. The bonds linking people are shattered with a loss of the sense of commonality. This leads to disorientation, demoralization and loss of connection. Survivors are often ashamed of their own fears and vulnerability. Erickson (1976) suggests that they become enraged about the lack of help from outside systems, and lose faith in the possibility of meaningful and mutually beneficial relationships. Survivors ask, "How could anyone ever understand how I am feeling?" "Who knows or cares?" and "Why should they care?" There is a discounting of one's feelings as being unimportant, insignificant and without value. A survivor said, "I feel as though life has been crushed out of me. I do not belong to anyone now. Even my husband can't understand me, and I can't explain it."

The survivor withdraws to make sense out of the tragedy. There is no emotional energy to direct to others. And, if there were, the survivor questions being worthy of assistance. The state of the survivor is analogous to the wounded animal who withdraws to lick one's wounds, retreating deep in the forest of self imposed isolation. The senses are constantly overwhelmed with guilt, shame, blame, anger, murderous impulses, fear, vulnerability, intrusive thoughts of the deceased, physical aching and longing, nightmares and loneliness.

When Betty came to group therapy, she had not been out of her upstairs bedroom except to bathe and eat for over a year since the murder of her youngest son. She had seen a psychiatrist twice who prescribed major tranquilizers. A year later she painfully began to resolve many of the issues of her son's death through the Homicide Survivor's Group Therapy program. After the treatment program she became a major fundraiser for a children's organization, which required contacts throughout the community in schools, churches and other organizations. This case illustrates it is possible to integrate the trauma and reconnect with one's other loved ones and the community.

A major goal of therapy is to build a bridge back to the living, recreating a sense of interdependency, so that survivors may reconnect with their families, social world and community. One cannot accomplish this goal without integration of the experience into one's own psychic framework.

It is important to recognize that the emotion of grief is a normal reaction to the loss of a loved one. There are normal cognitive, physical, emotional and behavioral characteristics of grief experienced by all bereaved. When the death is due to murder, providers and caregivers must recognize that the mourning process will be affected by systems and events outside the control of survivors. The complications that have been discussed do not indicate a pathological reaction. On the contrary, the reactions discussed in this section are normal and expected in homicidal bereavement. Untreated, the normal reactions to the abnormal event of murder may lead to psychopathology. With treatment, survivors of homicide ensure their right to an emotionally healthy, functional life. The work of the therapist is in preventive psychiatry. The focus of the work is to prevent normal reactions to psychological trauma from becoming a pathological pattern and a dysfunctional way of life.

6. Complicated Grief in the Military

BONNIE CARROLL, LISA HUDSON AND DIANNE RUBY

TRAUMATIC LOSS AND AMERICAN PRIDE

There are many types of loss in America, but none are treated so differently as a sudden, violent death while serving in our nation's armed forces. When a citizen is murdered, society as a whole condemns, prosecutes and punishes the vicious attacker. The trial is often sensational, with every detail replayed on the evening news. When an elderly person dies after a long illness, society accepts this as the normal course of events, as God's will, as out of our scope of mortal control, even a welcome relief when someone in pain and suffering is released and passes away. When a young person dies in a car accident, those are viewed as statistically improbable events that "happen to other people." We mourn the loss but don't allow ourselves to feel that this could happen to us. Lightning strikes *other* people.

But in the military, we ask the best of the best, bright, healthy young men and women, to fly faster than the speed of sound, handle weapons ranging to nuclear, operate heavy equipment through mine fields and go about the business of war, which is the business of being trained and equipped to kill. When one of these highly trained, perfectly fit young people is killed, we as a society praise their bravery with Presidential proclamations, salute their courage with 21 guns and honor their lives by carving their names on granite walls. We have even designated national days of remembrance in the spring and fall.

America has lost an average of 2,000 service members *each year* for the past 15 years (according to Defense Department statistics). That's roughly five of these bright young soldiers, sailors, airmen and Marines each day. Now, that's nothing compared to the mortality rates on our highways and in our hospitals, but let's take a closer look at the vastly different experience of the surviving military family.

In every other type of loss, the bereaved are encouraged not to make any sudden decisions. Not to move. Not to attempt major financial transactions. To rely on the support systems around them, including family, friends, coworkers and church. To stay put and let the healing take place.

In the military, however, the family *must* make sudden decisions. They are often living in government housing and *must* move out. They usually receive large serviceman's group life insurance payments and government compensation and *must* quickly make financial decisions that will impact the rest of their own lives and the lives of their children. And the very support systems that most survivors would normally rely upon may be continents away. There is no long established group of parishioners who were there for the weddings and births and are now there at the death. The fellow servicemembers of the deceased are them-selves struggling to continue on after losing a comrade in arms, yet most military spouses haven't lived in one place long enough to have a job, much less establish their own support system of coworker relationships.

Let's compound this scenario with the events surrounding the death itself. What America saw in the bombing in Oklahoma City was fairly typical of the military loss. In fact, later in this section is an article by Lisa Hudson, whose husband was among those killed in the bombing of the Marine barracks in Beirut in 1983. Violent, traumatic, sudden, devastating. The issues these survi-vors are dealing with include burnt dog tags, bent wedding rings and mangled body parts. These are not quiet deaths between clean sheets. These are sudden, violent losses in often horrid conditions a long way from home.

When a commercial airliner disintegrates into the ground or a bomb blows chunks of rubble into the air, we are horrified—and that horror is on the front page of every newspaper in America and becomes the lead story on every evening newscast. We cannot escape the images, and we are forced to feel the pain that each surviving family must be facing.

But in the military, when a bomb blows up or a plane crashes, we see only the flag-draped coffin and hear the echo of taps. We as a society are not thrust into the chaos, nor do we feel the intense pain and sudden shock of the loss. In the first hours and days, the family is supported by the military with assigned "casualty assistance officers" and told reassuringly that they will "not be forgotten." But after the funeral, they are moved from government housing (the military will pay for their moving expenses, but will do so only once, so they must choose carefully), and these survivors must then take what is left of their shattered lives and struggle on alone.

Further complicating the loss is the fact that information about the death is contained in investigative reports that are often classified and not available to the family. The most detailed information they may ever have of the death may be from media accounts, which are sketchy at best. Unlike civilian "accidents," there is no recourse for legal action as government employees and their families are prohibited from suing the federal government or its contractors, regardless of the circumstances.

So, the family is wrapped in "casualty assistance," bundled up in a moving van and transported out of sight and out of mind into the middle of America. There, they will eventually come out of their shock, fall into depression and eventually struggle to heal. How much easier it would be if the uniqueness of this phenomenon were recognized! If the caregivers, the support groups and the counselors could be aware of the complicating factors surrounding a loss in the military. How much quicker the healing would be if the compounding circumstances of the death and the loss of the survivor's own identity could be recognized and dealt with. The following is a series of three articles by military survivors with insights into their own coping and healing.

—Bonnie Carroll

THE AFTERMATH OF BEIRUT

The death of a spouse is said to be the most emotionally devastating event of one's life. Coping with this loss is difficult enough in any situation, but a military loss is complicated by factors unlike those of civilian loss. I know—I've been there. October 22, 1983, I was the wife of Lieutenant John Hudson, Battalion Surgeon of the 1st Marine Division, 8th regiment, Camp Lejeune, North Carolina. Within 24 hours, I became the surviving widow of Lt. John Hudson, and I was soon to become known as Lisa Hudson, somebody I'm not sure I really knew.

Widowhood itself casts you abruptly into this terrible place that feels (and is) unfamiliar, insecure and inhumane. You have lost your partner, and now you find the safe world you knew so well shattered and unsafe, melting before your eyes. The military widow is coping not only with grief but her "new" life outside the confines and security of the military safety net, which once provided structure and emotional safety to her world.

The civilian world, along with grief, is foreign. And she does not speak the language. In addition, deaths in the military are often violent, traumatic and sudden. The surviving widows are usually young (under 45 years of age), with small children under 18. These are factors documented to predispose the survivor to a more complicated grief.

John's traumatic death was so grotesque that I also lost my mental health for a while. Knowing what I do now as a psychotherapist, I believe I must have suffered from post-traumatic stress disorder for nearly a year and didn't know it due to the violent, mutilating and sudden nature of his death. I was depressed for several years, finally getting treatment and medication, which literally changed the course of my life. Therefore, I speculate that military loss may increase the risk for complicated grief and mental illness in survivors. You feel like you have lost your mind.

Since my husband had only been on active duty 15 months when he was killed in the bombing of the Marine barracks in Beirut, Lebanon, my experience with being a military wife was brief—only about a year. For me, therefore, the adjustment back into civilian life—and civilian grief—was perhaps not as complicated as it would be for someone whose entire married life had revolved around the military service of her husband. For these women, the transition is complicated and compounded by multiple layers of loss.

The world of widowhood is a dark, lonely tunnel complicated by layers of loss through which one must dig to begin seeing the light of day. The military widow must immediately face the loss of her status and role after being thrust into civilian life overnight. She may face moving—and knowing the military will only pay for one move, she must make the decision when she can barely think. Life in base housing shifts to a private dwelling— maybe for the first time in her life. Her identity changes as she will no longer be accepted on the basis of the status of her spouse. Her community of support, friends, an active social life and network of social contacts that often revolved around the military career and life of the spouse are gone as she is thrown into the world of singleness. She no longer participates in the wives' club since she doesn't "fit" there or feel comfortable even if asked to come. Over time, she loses contact with her husband's friends and coworkers because the person through whom the connection existed is no longer there. The military life ends the moment their life ends.

I shall never forget the hassles and heartaches of facing these losses and changes. When John died, I was miles away from the base where we had been stationed. There was no opportunity to commune with the other military widows, go to the support group or process my grief with those who truly knew my pain. The only contact I had with the military was the uniformed officer who gave me "the news" and a casualty assistance officer who so kindly and patiently guided me through the overwhelming tasks and changes. But all too soon he too was gone.

Having had little experience with the military, I found myself struggling, often lost and alone in the system, ignorant of its benefits (now greatly reduced to me and my son) and starkly more aware of its limitations (which seemed many). My husband had been the doctor for his battalion. Ironically, now I couldn't even seem to get one!

The system that upheld me seemed to be the one destroying any sense of familiarly and security I once had. I was often lost in my grief and lost in the maze of reformulating my world outside the boundaries of marriage and military life. Financial loss was immediately a grim reality. My income was cut in half overnight, my medical benefits seemed minimal at best, and I seemed no longer eligible for things that made my life comfortable. Even my ID card had to be remade to label me as the "unremarried widow." It was as though everywhere I turned, parts of my life and my identity were being ripped away. The isolation and

loneliness were often excruciating. I had no idea where I be-
longed.

Even going on base evoked a profound sense of loss for me.
Seeing uniforms like the ones he wore was so painful that I
avoided looking at them. My knees buckled when I saw camou-
flage. My eyes filled with tears if I saw a white navy uniform with
epaulets on the shoulders. I needed to shop at the PX, but could
hardly bear to be there, seeing men with their strong shoulders
(shoulders on which I could no longer lean) and strong hands
(hands reminding me of the ones I longed to hold me).

Seeing other couples and families still intact while my family lay
splintered was emotionally intolerable—reminders of what I used
to be. Hearing from other wives what tour was next and how
they were making plans together was unbearable, as my life
seemed directionless and empty. Their life was going on while
mine had come to an abrupt halt. I could hardly listen as they
would share their everyday life with me, for mine seemed an
unformed substance. I had nothing to say, except that my tears
consumed a large part of the day.

Does it ever get better? Yes, for me it eventually did. I adjusted to
the new life and the new world, making a new identity for myself
apart from my former life. This involved constructing new directions, patterns, habits and customs of everyday living, new social
structures and contacts, a new home and living environment and
a lot of learning. I learned that security is not found in another
person, their rank, position or job. It is found in me.

I now have my own identity for which I am most proud. The
painful reminders of the past are etched in my memory, but life
has a new look that I can call my own. When I go on base now, I
often look wistfully at the uniformed soldiers and remember my
former days as a military wife—a woman who is long gone now. I
belong in my new world now and it is familiar and secure—after
a decade of work to find my way there. It is a journey laced with
tears. Arriving at its destination has been truly a triumph.

—Lisa Hudson

SENSITIVITY IN TRAUMATIC DEATH CASES, FROM A SURVIVOR'S PERSPECTIVE

On December 7, 1993, my world collapsed into ruin when my unborn daughter's father, a soldier in the U.S. Army, was killed. No one—neither chaplains, nor military officials, nor friends, knew what to say or do to help me in the ensuing agony and turmoil. Many said or did things that only added to the pain, whether out of well-meant ignorance, or due to their own shock and loss. They didn't know how to respond to the death, let alone to me; nor could they begin to truly comprehend the tragedy that had devastated my life and erased my future.

In any death, a great deal of compassion and sensitivity on the part of those who support survivors is required. In cases where death has been violent, or when survivors have been traumatized by witnessing a violent death or having seen its aftermath, there are special issues that demand an even greater sensitivity.

While the support person may be struggling to process the violence and senselessness in his own mind, s/he is thrust into a role of providing support and counsel to the grieving and traumatized family, significant others, friends and coworkers. The community may also be impacted by the traumatic nature of the death. Support personnel must be aware of special issues as they extend to anyone who is grieving and traumatized, and exercise sensitivity toward each one, even as they cope themselves.

A traumatic death produces many of the common reactions of grief, for any death is still the loss of a spouse, a child or parent, fiancee or friend, coworker or fellow servicemember. Loss affects the whole person, the whole life of the survivor. In traumatic cases, grief reactions may be more intense or exaggerated.

In addition, there are several factors in traumatic deaths that complicate the grieving process. Loss is sudden, unexpected and unforeseen. The body may not be recovered, and often cannot be viewed, as the manner of death is horrible or involves mutilation of the body. Death that seems preventable, like an accident or murder and unfamiliarity with the military's procedures following a death, all serve to complicate grief and sometimes delay the manifestations of mourning.

Given the often horrifying nature of such cases, many people are surprised at the survivors' intense need to know the manner and the details of their loved one's death. As survivors, we struggle to piece together what has happened and come to terms with the loss. It is common to imagine what the death was like for our loved one, and we need to know how much s/he suffered. Frequent recounting of the known details is normal, especially initially, and is important as survivors move from denial to the reality of what has occurred.

Support personnel may feel that this need to know is morbid or abnormal, or that the actual details may be too much for the survivor to handle. It is important that survivors not be shielded from the truth. Many times, witnesses and others in the chain of command are instructed not to discuss the death with survivors. The media, however, print misleading and often vivid accounts of the traumatic death, leading survivors to question the allegiance and trustworthiness of those who won't tell them what really happened to their own loved one, while the whole world seems to know.

After a traumatic death, the survivors' world is spinning out of control. Knowing all the details gives a crucial sense of control as they struggle to learn what they're dealing with, so they can begin to heal. Questions should be answered as they arise, gently, sensitively and to the fullest extent possible. Speculation should be avoided. If an answer is unknown, offer to find out; if the information cannot be released because of an ongoing investigation, explain this and assure that it will be disclosed as soon as possible. Although the details may be painful, the worst blow—the loss—has already been struck. Without having survivors' questions answered to their satisfaction, the death is incomplete and healing is drastically complicated.

Many, even those whose professions place them in a role of support, distance themselves from survivors due to their own discomfort: the survivors are a bad reminder of the violent event. While those providing help and support strive to cope with their own traumatization, they may pass moral judgment as they rationalize the event and seek to establish reasoning, for themselves and to impart to others. Sadly, the survivors often become secondary victims, at the time they most need help and acceptance, and when their only connection with the death began with a uniformed soldier who broke the news that shattered their lives.

It is crucial that those of us providing support for traumatic death cases get past our own awkwardness, so that we can better meet the intense needs of those who have suffered such a brutal loss. To understand the special issues facing trauma survivors, it is helpful to know the spectrum of emotion and behavior they are traversing.

Immediately following the trauma, survivors experience shock, which includes a numbing toward the world and events around them. They may have a "flat," unemotional appearance, or seem too calm and detached. This numbness is normal in the early stages, and the person who seems very calm and "together" needs continuing support and the presence of others just as much as the survivor who is initially hysterical.

As the numbness gradually begins to wear off, survivors experience a surge of emotion as the trauma impacts, and their world spins deeper out of control. The normal grief responses of anger and blame are intense, and often irrational, as they struggle with the senselessness of the act. Some reexperience the trauma when they see or hear something that triggers the memory, and will avoid such things. Others are hyper-alert, easily startled, have trouble sleeping or eating, and have difficulty remembering or concentrating.

Many feel guilty for surviving when their loved one did not. Fellow servicemembers may also experience guilt over behaviors that enabled them to survive while a comrade perished. Compassionate help is needed to help the survivor dispel his or her guilt.

Following traumatic death, the world no longer makes sense. The anguished cry, "Why?", reverberates through our being. We think about the tragedy and try to find some rationale or meaning, however remote. The more we search, the more incomprehensible our loss becomes. The irrationality of a sudden, traumatic death makes it harder to process the loss. Identifying a cause, whether or not it is entirely rational, enables a survivor to regain some desperately needed sense of order and control in the early days. If a survivor is somewhat irrational as the impact of the trauma is felt, don't insist on rationality. Listen supportively to his or her ideas, and understand the need they fulfill.

Regardless of one's religious orientation, anger toward God is also a very common reaction. In a world that no longer seems just and fair, God is usually ultimately blamed for the injustice: for not intervening and preventing the tragedy, or for seeming not to care. We pray and beg and bargain, but heaven seems not to answer. A crisis of faith, and a reevaluation of beliefs, often ensues: If God is good, why did this happen? Although trauma can push some people to the extreme of rejecting their faith, many embrace it even more strongly. Faith not only offers a source of comfort in present sufferings and hope for the future; it also helps survivors as they search for meaning and try to establish some reasoning, and provides a constant in a world that has completely and irrevocably changed.

After what can seem like an eternity, acceptance of what has happened, as it affects the whole person and life of the survivor, does come out of the desperate search for meaning. We realize that we are not, and can never again be, the same people we once were. I often felt as though I were grieving the loss of myself almost as much as I grieved the loss of my truest and closest friend. Only accepting the full impact of the loss has opened the door to discovering the new self that I am becoming.

It may take years, but it is possible to find fulfillment in living once again. As a result of the trauma we have experienced, we have new insights and new skills. New relationships and perhaps even new careers may be a part of the new life purpose we find. It is vital to remember that there is no chronological schedule to the traumatic death grief experience. People process trauma in different ways, and at different rates. Couples are often out of sync in this process, and marital stress results. Reactions to the trauma may also go in cycles; seeming regression is usually part of the normal journey of adjusting to the trauma.

There are no quick-fix techniques to help a survivor cope with a traumatic loss. Sensitivity to the trauma experience, compassion and enduring support from immediate family and larger groups, such as church groups or support/therapy groups, will help survivors develop a new life strategy and heal.

People in roles of support often feel powerless to assist those who have witnessed or been traumatized by violent death. In striving to be sensitive to survivors' unique needs, it is helpful to bear the following in mind:

Don't underestimate the value of human touch. Reach out—your efforts at contact mean much. So do your hugs.

Listen, supportively and endlessly. Survivors need people who are not afraid of their intense outpourings of emotion and who can provide a shoulder to cry on, whether a week after the loss, or two years later.

Show your emotions—weep with us. Identifying with our grief imparts more strength than does stoicism.

When we discuss our loved one, don't change the subject. Share memories and reminisce with us. It's okay to express your feelings of loss, too.

Be courteous. Avoid phrases or clichés that might bring graphic reminders of the death, such as, "Don't lose your head," "It costs an arm and a leg," "It all went up in a puff of smoke," "He didn't meet the deadline," etc.

Don't encourage us to avoid dealing with our grief. It is ironic that avoidance is reinforced by others as a preferred coping mechanism by statements like, "Keep busy," "Don't think about it," "Take your mind off of it," or "Get back up on the horse and keep going."

Don't put a timetable on grief. It is not a matter of weeks or months—it is a matter of years. My own feelings are still strongly manifested, nearly two years after the murder, and I am often told by others that I should be "better" now. Traumatic loss is neither a disappointment to be gotten over, nor an illness from which one recovers. It is a deep wound that must heal slowly, from the inside out.

Don't be overprotective. Survivors need to make the decisions that affect their daily lives. Regaining a small sense of control helps them to rebuild their self-identity. At a time when they are feeling powerless and paralyzed by the destruction of their world, survivors should find something they *can* do, and do it every day.

Survivors need to face their feelings of guilt and failure. The best advice I was given was to stop asking, "What if. . .?" Forgive yourself if need be, and stop blaming yourself.

Ultimately, we can help ourselves tremendously by helping others. One of the best ways to deal with trauma is to help others work through it. Find those who share similar pain, and help each other heal.

Many military personnel in supporting roles are present at the initial stage of impact following a traumatic death. Sensitive help and support at this time can leave a survivor more receptive to continuing help in the future. Those who will not be able to follow up with survivors should provide referrals to professionals, support groups and other resources who will be able to provide needed help on a consistent basis.

December will bring the second anniversary of Greg's death, and I will struggle painfully through this poignant reminder of all that was lost: my best friend and mate, my daughter's father, the future that would have been—mine, his, ours—and the woman I once was. The phone will most likely not often ring to connect me with kind and supportive words this year. Yet, when the jagged sobs subside, a soothing flood of happy memories will come, and, when they have played lovingly through my mind, a very bright and shining future will again become visible on the horizon. It is a new future for the new woman I am becoming, and still learning to know—one day at a time.

—Dianne Ruby

Turning Bitter into Better, TAPS Created

An average of almost 2,000 servicemembers make the ultimate sacrifice *each year.* Many die in sudden, violent and often well publicized events. And while conventional wisdom dictates that the newly bereaved not make any quick, dramatic, permanent decisions in the first year, the military survivor must face moving from base housing, and the men and women who lose a fellow servicemember must continue to fly, fight and function without pause.

The wife who spent 22 years shopping at the commissary and volunteering in the post hospital must now quickly leave all that and choose where in the world she will begin a new life. The children of the hottest fighter pilot on base must leave their friends and begin a new school as kids who no longer have a dad to come and watch their baseball games. But even if they remain in the same community, they become invisible: the bad reminder of the ultimate sacrifice, not included in social activities, no longer asked to volunteer, moving unseen through a world in which they no longer belong.

I was a busy military wife, mother to three active teens, extremely happy with every aspect of life. Then, in one day, one moment, that life was shattered. At the hangar that morning I had seen Tom off, along with seven other soldiers going on a routine flight. Two hours later the pilot called in his approach to the tower. But they never broke out of the clouds that hovered low above the airstrip. Instead, their instruments had deceived them and they descended not onto the runway but straight into a jagged mountain peak at 200 miles per hour.

A uniformed soldier came to my office and told me very gently that the plane was overdue and that I should come to the armory to stand by for more information. I prayed. I *knew* that Tom would be safe. There were so many options and so much hope at that early moment. Diverting. Emergency landing. Water landing. It was a great airplane. They were the best pilots. This was a commercial airport, not the dirt strips out in the rural areas where they often flew at great peril.

The news finally came that the plane had been located and the fuselage appeared intact. My hopes soared. But the rescue workers lowered to the scene found no survivors. That's all they said. *No survivors.* People were screaming and crying and looking so terribly pained. CNN was already reporting the tragedy involving, among others, two Army generals. Yet I was serene, my heart protecting my head from news it could not possibly comprehend. My closest friend took me aside and said, "the next 10 days are important" and that gave a purpose to movement. I reassured the children that life would continue. I tried desperately to gain control as the universe spun hopelessly out of control.

When I went on television the following day as the "general's widow" to publicly comment that the pilots were the best, the aircraft solid and the families grateful for the immediate outpouring of support from the community, people were stunned at my composure. When I spoke at the funeral, the faces in the chapel told me that they were more shocked at my ability to stand and speak than touched by the words I had worked so hard to compose. When the children chose to remain in school surrounded by their friends rather than staying home, people questioned my ability to parent.

But six months later, when those who expected anguish in the first moments after the crash had disappeared back into their own safe lives, I had fallen so far into despair that I begged for my own life to end. I was paralyzed by fear, overcome with pain and lost in a monochromatic world. I explored every resource imaginable to find relief for this disabling pain.

Then a turning point came. While one is certainly cursed in a mass casualty, those remaining are blessed with fellow survivors. Misery loves—no, demands—company in order to heal. Seven months after the crash, on Memorial Day, I got back in touch with the other women made widows on that fateful day. We discovered that we shared identical patterns of pain, fear, sadness and emptiness. But more than that.

We could say things to each other that we hadn't said to anyone else. Not the therapists who patiently listened. Not the doctors who wrote prescriptions for antidepressants. Not the family members who felt so helpless. We could talk to each other about why we all left the insurance checks on our dressers for weeks. We could share feelings of wanting our lives to end so that we could be with our loved ones again. We shared our dreams and visions and visitations, and hung on every message from the "other side." We behaved outrageously (we made woolen hats for the headstones), laughed hard (no one else found our black humor particularly funny nor allowed us the luxury of laughing when it failed to meet their perceptions of grief), cried until we were sick (because we felt safe enough to do so), and lived life (after all, we had seen death and were no longer afraid of it).

Nine months after the accident we flew to the city near the crash site, flying over the wreckage and, doing what our husbands could not, and landed at the airport. We chartered a helicopter to go up to the wreckage. It was a powerfully healing time, to see physical evidence that the crash had occurred and finally *know*, for ourselves, that it was real.

On the one-year anniversary, we went together to the hangar they had flown from at the hour of their departure and prayed to go back in time and alter the course of history. Eighteen months after the accident we traveled from our respective corners of the country and went on a vacation to recapture the freedom and safety that being together gave us.

Out of that healing came an organization called the Tragedy Assistance Program for Survivors, Inc. (TAPS), a national network of peer support for military survivors, a referral point for grief counseling options around the country, a crisis intervention team whose members have critical incident stress experience, and case worker assistance to help families find answers to complicated questions in a complicated bureaucracy long after their official file has been closed.

TAPS offers another dimension to trauma recovery. Survivors reaching out and helping each other heal. If you have ever been affected by the loss of a loved one in the military, please give us a call at 1-800-368-TAPS. Together we can help each other heal.

—Bonnie Carroll

Intervening in Sudden and Traumatic Loss

KENNETH J. DOKA, PH.D.

It is one thing to recognize the particular problems and difficulties of sudden loss; it is quite another to intervene and counsel those who have experienced sudden loss. From the emergency room doctor to the policeman at the door, the very act of informing someone of sudden loss causes intense stress and grief for all of the involved parties.

The articles in this section try to provide some tools and sensitivities for those who have to assist survivors. Charles Figley begins by reminding grief counselors and traumatologists about the dangers of overspecialization. He emphasizes that each approach offers unique strengths that should be synthesized. Vanderlyn Pine, one of the earliest sociologists writing about disaster, explores the types of reactions and feelings that may be common in survivors. His chapter provides a good theoretical background for understanding the types of clinical interventions that would be helpful.

These are explored quite fully by Dana Cable and Therese Rando in their respective chapters. Cable provides a detailed description of critical counseling interventions such as critical incident stress debriefing. Rando offers a succinct summary of complications that can arise in sudden and traumatic death. And, as is her style, she provides concise clinical interventions for caregivers assisting survivors of sudden loss.

In Terry Martin's and my chapter, we draw from our emerging work on masculine grieving patterns. That work reminds us that there are different patterns of coping with loss. Many men and some women tend to exhibit more cognitive, solitary and active expressions of grief. We emphasize that there is no one way to cope with loss and that interventions need to be tailored to an individual's grieving style.

Lois Chapman Dick echoes some of these points in her approach to emergency personnel and offers two significant contributions.

First, she reminds us that sudden loss may affect many of those who may never have known the deceased, but are involved, in one form or another, in the death. Her chapter provides a detailed description of the many ways that crisis workers may be troubled by loss. Second, Dick's chapter emphasizes the critical importance of self care. Not just crisis workers but anyone involved in these situations may experience vicarious grief and shock. It is critical then that caregivers develop ways to nurture themselves.

Duane Weeks' contribution goes beyond simply reminding us of the need to consider the role of the funeral and the funeral director in situations of sudden loss. Weeks makes a poignant plea for developing meaningful rituals that are participatory and personal. My own research has found that this is critical, especially when loss is sudden. For, in such situations, the funeral service provides special opportunity to expiate guilt and bring a sense of closure that would otherwise be denied.

Finally, Rabbi Earl Grollman finishes this section underlining that spiritual care is part of the process of healing. It is suggested that one of the tasks of grieving is "to reconstruct faith and philosophical systems challenged by loss" (Doka and Morgan, 1993). This may be especially difficult in cases of sudden loss, for here the very nature of the death may challenge one's faith in a loving God or assumptions of a benign universe. Reconstructing one's faith in the face of sudden loss can be an extraordinary challenge. And it is not simply a task of clergy and spiritual advisors. It is a task that is shared by all caregivers. Grollman's chapter offers his own brand of gentle wisdom to assist us in this process.

7. Traumatic Death: Treatment Implications

CHARLES R. FIGLEY, PH.D.

On December 21, 1988, when John Cummock was murdered, with 269 other people, on Pan Am 103, I lost not only my husband, but my best friend and the father of my three children . . . It was on that day that my world was totally shattered. Not only had I lost John, but everything about my life from that point on changed forever.

—Victoria Cummock

Mrs. Cummock's story has educated people from the Oval Office to Main Street about the challenges of bereavement caused by terrorist murders. In addition, she provides an inspiring perspective for professionals by focusing a giant flood light on experiences previously hidden in the dark of silence or ignored. Her message is an important one for all of us.

My own interest in the impact of death on the bereaved began shortly after my service in Vietnam. I was introduced to war on the evening of our landing in Hue, South Vietnam. The first shot with me as a target was a rude awakening. By the time I got home, I found that death was no longer frightening.

Vietnam, and its aftermath, was, in many ways, a turning point for others as well. The field of traumatology has grown since my initial interviews with Vietnam veterans in the mid–1970s. It never occurred to me then and does not now to separate the stress associated with the death of another and the stress associated with being scared to death. Recent use of PET scans demonstrate what Selye said long ago: A stress is a stress (Selye, 1950).

In 1978, a chapter by Spilka, Friedman and Rosenberg in my book, *Stress Disorders Among Vietnam Veterans*, (Figley, 1978) noted that a majority of Vietnam war combat veterans indicated that their war experiences had increased the value they placed on their own lives (53 percent) and that 85 percent had witnessed the death of someone. The book helped usher in the diagnosis of Post-traumatic Stress Disorder (PTSD).

Those few of us in the 1970s studying traumatic stress were drawn together by our interest in the impact of death and dying on the functioning of the survivors. Lifton (1969) emphasizes that death imprint (the radical intrusion of a memory of an image or feeling) and death anxiety occur across traumatic events.

Yet, unfortunately, when the diagnosis of PTSD emerged from the 3rd revision of the DSM-III (APA, 1980), death, grief and bereavement were missing from any discussion of what constitutes a traumatic event. Perhaps it was an effort to avoid the appearance that death of a loved one was, automatically, traumatic and not a natural part of the human experience. Most of those who work in the thanatology area adopt this view.

Irrespective of the reasons, the field of traumatology quickly evolved into a field of its own (Figley, 1988; Donovan, 1991) and now claims an impressive body of literature, several journals and international associations. Clearly, the gulf that separates it from the field of thanatology is largely artificial.

My work in the 1970s shifted from war veterans to war veteran families (Figley, 1978; Figley & Southerly, 1980; Hogancamp & Figley, 1983), including POW families and families of others in harm's way. This included the families of the hostages (Figley, 1983), crime victims (Figley, 1984) and emergency workers (Figley, 1985), and, eventually, to the study of traumatized families as a unit (Figley, 1982; 1983; 1986; 1988; 1989a; 1989b). My emerging conceptualizations of individual and systemic traumatic stress always viewed death of a person or persons as a significant stressor that could be traumatic to both individuals and the entire family system.

EVOLUTION OF MODERN THANATOLOGY

Then during the decade of the 1980s an appreciation for wide variations in the grief process emerged. Even though Lindemann (1944) identified "uncomplicated bereavement" as having a predictable course, his clients were far from "normal." They were clients who had suffered from the death of a loved one who died unexpectedly and often in a frightening manner, as a result of the burning of the Coconut Grove restaurant. Yet, for nearly 30 years the prevailing depiction of the grief process has been reduced to stages or phases of recovery.

The 1980s, thanks largely to the innovative work of Therese Rando (1983;1985;1989; 1993) and Beverley Raphael (1983; 1986) building upon the innovations of Lehrman (1956), Parkes, C. M. and Brown, R. J. (1972), and Parkes and Weiss (1983), a much more complicated view of bereavement emerged that was informed by the traumatic nature of the circumstances of death.

For example, *complicated mourning* (Rando, 1993), is characterized as ". . . morbid, atypical, pathological, neurotic, unresolved, complicated, distorted, abnormal, deviant, or dysfunction." She suggests later that reactions to loss can only be interpreted within the context of those factors that circumscribe the "particular loss of the particular mourner in the particular circumstances in which the loss took place." Thus, the experience of bereavement and mourning is especially subjective. Thus, what is a "normal" death of a loved one to one person may be extremely abnormal and consequently extremely stressful to another.

Rando (1993) provides a useful description of the symptoms of complicated mourning that is strikingly similar to the description of PTSD:

> ...the grief symptomatology persist much longer than usual, and mourners typically remain socially withdrawn, developing a sense of the deceased's continued presence. The sense of continued presence binds them to the deceased and hampers their ability to function socially and occupationally (p. 175).

She suggests that there are five types of death that are highly associated with complicated mourning. Among them are such traumatic circumstances as sudden, unexpected, and traumatic circumstances; death of a child; and preventable death.

Yet, other than some isolated efforts (Redmond, 1989), there is no model that has emerged to treat traumatic bereavement within a systemic context: To treat the entire family that is traumatized simultaneously as a result of the death of someone valued by a family.

GRIEF COUNSELING

The specialization of grief counseling includes bereavement and death studies. As noted above, this literature has always focused on traumatic stress, though the concept is rarely used. More important, the field of thanatology has always concerned itself with family and other systems and how they cope with death. Although rarely using systems or family social science concepts, grief specialists have always been concerned about the consequences of survivorship within a family or system.

Although some view "normal bereavement" as the absence of a traumatic stress reaction, little research has focused on differentiating between normal and abnormal. Glick, et al. (1974), for example, found that within eight weeks after the death of their husbands 40 percent of their sample of widows consulted a physician for various somatic problems. This confirmed previous studies by Parkes and Brown (1972), who found half the widows had such complaints. They also found that 28 percent increased smoking, 28 percent increased alcohol consumption and 26 percent increased tranquilizer usage. It is not surprising that Raphael (1983) found that such major problems as depression, neurotic disorders, phobias, obsessions, hypochondriasis and various conversions follow the death of a loved one.

Redmond (1989) is the first grief therapist to acknowledge that PTSD is an expected outcome of death of a loved one, at least in the case of survivors of murder victims. In a study similar to Redmond's, though not acknowledging the similarity, Cook and Dworkin (1992) suggest that PTSD should be viewed as a form of grief reaction and that therapy should be on "resolving the tasks of grieving" (p. 25).

TRAUMA COUNSELING

Surprisingly, the traumatology literature rarely notes the traumatic nature of surviving the death of a loved one. Thus, neither literature references the other in spite of the fact that bereavement so closely parallels traumatic stress reactions; and various forms of dysfunctional/abnormal bereavement parallel PTSD.

Perhaps the diagnosis of PTSD applied to death and bereavement is discouraged by the very document that helped begin the field of traumatology: the *Diagnostic and Statistical Manual.* In the 1980 document, "simple bereavement" is specifically excluded as traumatic. Perhaps this exclusionist note was an effort to avoid the appearance of suggesting that since nearly everyone experiences the death of a family member, friend or acquaintance, the inclusion of death as a stressor for survivors would appear to trivialize PTSD. But after a decade of use, that argument seems erroneous at best and at worst irresponsible.

This is unfortunate for two reasons: First, simple bereavement may not be "outside the range of human experiences," but it is extremely stressful and rarely lasts less than one month, the minimum period of "normal" traumatic stress reactions before it is classified as a disorder. Nowhere is "normal" quantified. Second, non-simple, or dysfunctional bereavement, is quite common but has never been classified as PTSD, perhaps because of the apparent perceived exclusion of surviving the death of a loved one as a traumatic stressor. Even the most cursory review of research provides considerable evidence of the overlap of symptoms between PTSD and bereavement; that the experience of surviving the death of a loved one—especially the death of a young child or a child as an adult—is extraordinarily traumatic.

DEATH AND TRAUMA

Given the parallel development of the fields of thanatology and traumatology, Brian Bride and Nicholas Mazza produced a book that attempts to link them in four ways. First, the book provides a theoretical bridge between the two fields by providing the conceptual terminology, such as defining "normal" versus "dysfunctional bereavement" and defining the meaning and range of death-related PTSD. Second, the book confirms and illustrates the identical patterns of reactions between those who survive the death of a loved one with those who survived other types of traumatic events. This effort is part of the natural development of a field, or, in this case, fields of study. Third, the book applies the most useful theoretical models to the bereavement experience and, in turn, acknowledges the utility of generalizing bereavement models to other traumatic experiences. By doing so the best of both fields can enrich each other. Similarly, the fourth purpose of the book is to identify and apply the most useful, effective approaches in the traumatology literature to the study, diagnosis and treatment of bereavement. And, in turn, acknowledge the utility of applying the most effective approaches in the bereavement literature to the study, diagnosis and treatment of traumatic stressors other than the death of others.

GENERIC TREATMENT APPROACHES

In addition to the standard procedures followed by mental health practitioners and paraprofessionals, we have been searching for generic treatment approaches that appear to work with any traumatized person or personal relationships. Such approaches have promise irrespective of their focus on grief and bereavement.

FAMILY TREATMENT APPROACHES

Family Guidance and Therapy Model: Baker (in press) has described a promising program for helping grieving families. He says that it not only helps parents traumatized as a result of the death of a child, but his model is applicable to any tragedy or major, shared traumatic experience. His approach builds upon those offered in both the fields of parental guidance and family therapy. After noting the assessment process he suggests effective methods of intervention within the contexts of both parental guidance *and* family therapy.

The Rochester Model: Horowitz (in press), a longtime member of the University of Rochester Medical Center's Family and Marriage Clinic, has described the Rochester Model as adopting a purely family therapy approach for dealing with traumatic events including, but not limited to, the death of a family member. The Rochester Model of treatment is very brief (10-session average) and can be applied to any one of a number of systemic presenting problems, including grief work. She also discusses the context of training family practitioners at the Center and how this activity keeps the team fresh and the model constantly evolving.

INDIVIDUALLY-ORIENTED APPROACHES

However, both of these approaches help entire families. Traumatized people often seek help just for themselves. In Victoria Cummock's case, for example, she sought treatment separate from and also with her children in efforts to recover from the death of her husband. There are several individually-oriented brief treatment models for traumatized people.

Eye Movement Desensitization and Reprocessing (EMDR): One is EMDR, developed by Shapiro (1995). Recently Solomon and Shapiro (in press) discussed and described the treatment of several people who were traumatized as well as grieving. Similar to the Rochester Family Therapy Model, EMDR is proving to be effective with any one of a wide variety of presenting problems, including traumatic grief/bereavement. They begin with a case study of a client whose sister was killed in an auto accident. They then describe the major features of EMDR, along with the emerging research proving its effectiveness. They emphasize that EMDR is used within the context of an effective treatment plan, though the procedure is extremely powerful and efficient in uncovering and resolving trauma-induced anxiety. Though not fully developed, they discuss a theoretical framework [the Accelerated Information Processing (AIP) Model] that accounts for and guides clinical treatment using EMDR methods.

EMDR has the client first identify the traumatic death and related traumas and assign a subjective unit of distress (SUD) rating from 0 (no stress) to 10 (highest amount of stress) they are experiencing at that time. Then the client is asked to think about his or her emotional and cognitive themes during the traumatic experiences, and finally his or her wish for replacing those emotions and thoughts (solution-focused approach from strategic therapy). They are to think about all of this while they follow an orienting reflex generating stimulus (Denny, 1995), such as the therapist waving fingers/hand from left to right. The therapist pauses at strategic times (indicated by the client's emotional responses) to allow the client to cognitively process the information generated from the exercise. The EMDR therapist continues this strategy until all of the stressful memories are fully processed for that session. Interestingly, there have been a number of cases in which client have not disclosed any information about the traumatic event. There is a growing body of research that supports the effectiveness of this extraordinary approach (cf., Shapiro, 1995). EMDR was one of four highly powerful and efficient treatments for PTSD and grief that were studied at Florida State University's Psychosocial Stress Research Program in the fall of 1994 (Figley & Carbonell, 1995).

Thought Field Therapy (TFT): Another brief treatment approach studied by Figley and Carbonell (1995) and found extremely promising in treating traumatic stress associated with grief and bereavement is Thought Field Therapy (TFT) (Callahan & Callahan, in press). They describe a potentially revolutionary way of reducing traumatic stress. TFT includes such innovations as "psychological reversal" (PR), a procedure that helps clients to reverse their disinclination of reaching a certain clinical goal, and "perturbations" (P), the sensation of traumatic stress experienced not only cognitively, but also kinesthetically, emotionally, neuro- logically and biologically. The approach uses procedures used by acupressure specialists, but applied to psychological, in contrast to physical problems. Callahan and Callahan note that it is not unusual for those grieving the loss of a loved one to not, at one level, want to recover enough to not feel traumatic stress. Social pressure, for example, requires a certain period of mourning and sadness. If the client chooses, however, TFT can even overcome this problem using the PR procedure and go on to significantly reduce the suffering.

TFT practitioners, similar to EMDR, have clients first focus on the traumatic death and related traumas and assign a subjective unit of distress (SUD) rating from 0 (no stress) to 10 (highest amount of stress) they are experiencing at that time. Then the client is asked if he or she wishes to reduce the stress to a 0 SUD rating. If so, the therapist leads the client in an exercise that includes a sequence of tapping the upper torso in ways that appear to activate various acupressure points and neurological centers that apparently disrupt the way our bodies respond to active memory. Though the procedure takes minutes, with 2 or 3 tapping sequences, the therapist takes SUD ratings with each sequence. At the end of the session, the SUD ratings most frequently are reduced to a score of 2 or less. Figley and Carbonell (1995) report that most clients were successfully treated (i.e., low SUD scores). However, most assumed that they simply forgot what was bothering them (e.g., the "distraction" hypothesis), discovered that it was not as important as once thought (e.g., the "unimportance" hypothesis), or professed both shock and delight in being free of the stress (e.g., the "cure" hypothesis). Denny (1995) has promoted an "orienting reflex" theory to account for the success of both EMDR and TFT. Again, clients do not need to describe any aspects of their traumatic experience for either approach to work.

Visual/Kinesthetic Disassociation (V/KD): A third approach studied by Figley and Carbonell (1995) is V/KD, first described in the literature by Koziey & McLeod (1987), though invented and then incorporated into Neurolinguistic Programming (NLP) by Richard Bandler (1978).

Bandler and colleagues developed NLP and other approaches based on the writings and methods of master clinician Milton Erickson. Erickson was a master at helping the client recover lost memories, develop an alternate view of the more troubling traumatic experiences and, as a result, at least find a significant reduction in traumatic stress, if not an elimination of it entirely. Although the NLP approach was formalized in the late 1970s. It took many years to become acknowledged in psychotherapy (Andreas & Andreas 1992; Einspruch & Forman, 1988; MacLean, 1986). Like EMDR and TFT, V/KD is very brief, powerful and apparently successful in reducing subjective distress, yet without requiring grieving clients to describe their traumatizing experiences. The theory behind its effectiveness is accelerated cognitive processing of the traumatic stress-inducing experiences by shifting the point of view (POV) of the client from the first position (viewing a scene through the eyes of the traumatized person) to either the second position [viewing a scene through the eyes/perspective of the particular stressor agent (i.e., natural disaster, attacking shark, speeding train, perpetrator, enemy soldier)] of most concern to the client, or the third position (viewing the scene through an observer of both the "victim" **and the stressful aspect of** the traumatic experience). Thus the client is guided to disassociate herself or himself from the troubling traumatic situation while, at the same time noticing her or his kinesthetic reactions, and confronting all of this as an observer who is not in any harm.

Clients being treated with VKD are then asked to speed up the tape at any point in which it is scary or uncomfortable. Within a relatively brief amount of time, the client becomes comfortable in the Third Position POV. At a point in which it appears that the clients have "learned all they can" from the scene, they are asked to imagine that the person in the video (themselves at an earlier age) is sitting in a chair in front of the TV set. The client is then asked to tell his or her younger self what he or she has learned. This completes the cognitive reprocessing. Trained VKD practitioners are able to establish trust and rapport quickly, get on with the traumatic scene visualizations that yield additional information to the client from which the client forms new assessments of her or his behavior and responsibility. VKD apparently achieves all of the advantages of success of various exposure treatment methods but without the unwanted time requirements and emotional distress.

Traumatic Incident Reduction (TIR): One other potentially revolutionary approach to treating traumatic stress was developed by Frank Gerbode (1992). Yet, the roots of this approach can be found in the early writings of clinical innovator, Carl Rogers (1951). Similar to the other brief treatments of PTSD, TIR appears to be very promising for enabling clients to make significant progress in only a few sessions. In contrast to the treatment approaches noted earlier, TIR depends upon the client retelling his or her story over and over until the client finds an "end point." It is a perspective that enables the client to feel great emotional relief, though he or she experienced intense traumatic stress in reaccounting the traumas. In this approach the therapist would help the grieving person by bearing witness to the person's accounting, but nothing else. Therapists applying TIR refrain from any unnecessary comments and avoid at all cost interpreting what the client is saying. This witnessing has been found to be extremely powerful, for example, in helping torture victims recover, including and especially those who lost loved ones through murder (Agger, 1992).

Thus, the TIR practitioner would first ask the client what the client wishes to discuss (i.e., what they are "interested in focusing on"). Once that focus is declared, the therapist establishes a SUD rating and asks the client to identify when the incident started and stopped. Next the client is asked to think about the beginning of the incident and, silently, to think about what happened from beginning to end and let the therapist know when he or she is finished. At that point, the therapist would ask the client to describe the event from beginning to end. The therapist listens intently without distracting the client. "Be interested but not interesting" is the common instruction to TIR therapists. After the client has completed his or her description, the therapist says, simply: "Thank you. Now return to the beginning of the event and think about the entire event to yourself and let me know when you are finished." After the client has finished, the therapist simply says,"Thank you. Now describe the event from beginning to end." Again, the therapist listens intently without distracting the client. For many clients it is the first time they have had an opportunity to fully describe their traumatic experience with anyone. As a result, they are asked to see the events from the Third Position in order to describe it to the therapist. The therapist directs the client to describe the event until the client reaches an "end point" (Gerbode, 1992). This is indicated by several conditions: The client appears relaxed, insightful, realistic, satisfied, unburdened, and generally pleased with the progress. It is at this point that the TIR therapist stops the session (not after the typical 50 minutes are up). At times, the session can last four hours (Figley & Carbonell, 1995).

Conclusion

Buffeted by the winds of managed health care and shaped by the many emerging journals, Internet special interest groups and associations that interest them, the numbers of professionals identified exclusively with thanatology or traumatology are dwindling quickly. The trauma experienced by survivors is inescapable. The challenge of the millennium for professionals who care about survivors is to work collectively toward a common goal: To gather together the most efficient and effective tools of our collective trade to ease the pain of grief and promote the natural process of bereavement, no matter how traumatic the circumstances. The extraordinary, powerful and efficient treatment methods described in the latter section of this chapter are illustrations of the byproducts of cooperation.

Finally, if brief treatments of death-related PTSD show great promise, it is wise to consider treating ourselves. Figley (1995) has recently discussed how traumatic it is to work with traumatized people—as therapists, researchers or as funeral directors or hospice workers. "Heal thyself" is a motto we should first apply to ourselves in overcoming the most common challenge of working with the bereaved: compassion fatigue.

8. Social Psychological Aspects of Disaster Death

Vanderlyn R. Pine, Ph.D.

Dying and death give rise to personal, emotional responses, which set in motion culturally oriented reactions, which in turn elicit specific death practices. In this way, people use traditional customs for handling death, and, in general, societally based reactions guide our behavior. Ideally, such practices should provide socio-emotional support as people pass through the difficult period surrounding death and dying. Hopefully, these supports provide some measure of consolation and ease the transition caused by the needs following death.[1]

Coping With Loss

It is important for the disaster worker to understand three psycho-social terms that are frequently confused. These terms, their manifestations and their practical implications are crucial from the standpoint of providing compassion, making competent diagnoses and decisions and, in general, helping people cope with dying and death. The terms are bereavement, grief and mourning.[2] Bereavement is an *objective* state or condition of deprivation which is followed or accompanied by the process of grief.[3] Grief is a *psychic* state or condition of mental anguish, and it is a result of or in anticipation of the bereavement. Mourning is a *social* state or condition expressing the grief because of the bereavement.

Two underlying psychological factors that contribute to grief are loss and loss threat. Loss occurs when a person is deprived of something and may take place due to death or may result when something of importance is irretrievably lost. The loss may be of simple, material possessions; it may be physical, as in the amputation of a body part; or it may involve less tangible emotionally based phenomena such as a friendship or love relationship.

It is important to distinguish between *actual* loss and the *potential* for loss. The potential for loss often creates the anticipation of future deprivation. In terms of death, the potential for loss is 100 percent in that someday everyone will die. However, the abstract possibility of loss is not as powerful a force as the predictive threat of loss. An imminent negative future can create a loss-threat situation that may have serious repercussions. For example, when a physician tells a patient that a lump in the leg is malignant cancer and that the leg must be amputated in order to prevent the disease from spreading, the loss threat that occurs is qualitatively and quantitatively different from the abstract potential that cancer is a disease one conceivably could contract. Communicating such information triggers loss-threat, and a series of behavioral changes may be set in motion, and this may lead to what is called "anticipatory grief," that is, grief in anticipation of a potential loss.[5]

GRIEF POTENTIAL

As the potential for loss may vary, so may the potential one has for grief, for it, too, is influenced by both past and present events. Grief potential may be subdivided into many levels, ranging from high grief potential to low grief potential. In the abstract, the eventual death of a person who has been in a nursing home and failing steadily for several years is likely to have a low grief potential for the family. In many cases they have had time to come to terms with the idea of the death and to some degree have been able to replace their relationship with the dying person with new or different ones.

In a sudden, unexpected accidental or disastrous death, survivors have had no opportunity to accustom themselves to the idea of that person's actual or anticipated death. Additionally, accidents involve what most of us believe are inappropriate deaths in that the victims are disproportionately in the young category. Under these circumstances, the grief potential following such a death is likely to be high.

Disaster workers should recognize that a type of anticipatory grief occurs after the fact in the case of unexpected deaths.[6] When someone dies suddenly, it is common for people to mentally experience anticipation after the death has occurred. To accomplish that, people unconsciously reconstruct reality and place things in an historical perspective. For example, it is common for such people to say, "I knew something was wrong because he's been acting so strange lately," or "You know, he never was very careful about such things." This kind of historical perspective allows the "mind's eye" to recall a somewhat altered reality so that we "see" past events and occurrences differently. Disaster workers can help bereaved people in this process by giving them a chance to talk about the dead person.

The ability to reconstruct reality grows out of the social psychological principle that maintains that the human mind is capable of reconstructing past social reality over and over again in order to fit present social facts. We select from our memory those incidents that are most "satisfying" for our current personal needs and in this way are able to cope with the tension and strain of pain by recalling that which is understandable or which "makes sense" given what has happened. There is an important difference between objective chronological time and subjective social-psychological time, so the reconstruction of reality following a death may take only a few minutes. Yet it may take events from the past months, or even years, and cast them in a new light relating them to the death. The significance of such instances is that they allow retrospective grief at their occurrence, and disaster workers can facilitate this process just by recognizing the importance of what may appear to be repetitious or reminiscing conversation.

RESPONSE TO LOSS IN DISASTER

Two kinds of behavior generally arise in response to the psychological factors of loss and loss threat. First, there is reactive behavior, referring to the way people "automatically respond" immediately following the news of loss or loss threat. It results from either direct verbal communication about a death or personal observation that a loss has occurred or the awareness that loss threat exists. The extent and nature of reactive behavior often depends upon the mode of death.

Second, there is adjustive behavior, referring to the way people accommodate a loss or loss threat situation over the long haul. It differs from reactive behavior in that it occurs during a pro-tracted period of time. Adjustment refers to coping with the conditions of a given situation, coming to terms with them, and modifying one's personal behavior to suit the circumstances. Once an individual receives a loss threat stimulus, a rearrange-ment of temporal, spatial and social orientations begins to occur. Temporal rearrangement involves a sense of emotional or psychological time rather than chronological time. The projected life expectancy of a dying person may involve different views of what is reasonable after as opposed to prior to the diagnosis of dying. Some people adjust to their dying status or to the threat of loss by setting short-range goals rather than long-range goals. Rearrangement of temporal orientations also may involve the manipulation of time in one's mind. For example, bereaved people often remark that "time stood still," or "I saw my entire life pass before my eyes." Here the distinction between emotional and chronological time is of great importance in the overall grief process, for chronological time is not necessarily a meaningful measure when dealing with someone who has experienced a loss or loss threat.

Adjustive behavior is also involved with spatial changes and the rearrangement of one's sense of space. Spatial changes can create critical problems and may have a powerful impact on grief, bereavement and mourning. Disaster workers must be aware of the psychic support provided by familiar surroundings and be prepared to understand when people are hesitant to leave their home, even though it is necessary. Recognition of the tie to grief can assist one's patience and facilitate helping people through emergency situations.

Finally, adjustive behavior involves the psychosocial concept of coping. To cope means to manage, handle or deal with a prob-lem, and, among other things, it involves the way we try to control things such as fear, denial, loss and loss threat. In gen-eral, grief is just such a coping mechanism.

There are many manifestations of grief, and we could devise an exhaustive list of possible types or stages. It seems more useful, however, to capsulize a few main components of grief that may

have a direct relevance for the disaster worker. The way people
cope with their own dying has been described by many. There
are many reactions to the grieving process, but for our purposes,
here are five that are important to understand.[7] An initial reaction
of grief is disbelief. It can be compared roughly to reactions of
denial often experienced by dying people. The main difference is
that disbelief occurs after the death when the mind must come to
terms with the actual loss. It is common for disbelieving people
to talk to themselves. They may mumble, "It can't be, I just saw
him a few minutes ago." or "It's not possible. You must be wrong.
She couldn't be dead." People seem to try and convince themselves that their disbelief is legitimate and that the death really
has not occurred.

A second common reaction of grief is questioning. This refers to
a grieving person's seeking reasons for the death. During this
period of questioning it is common to hear such comments as
"What happened?" "How did she die?" "Why did she have to die?"
In general, a cause for death is sought. It seems that the etiology
of the death is important for making the loss believable, and
bereaved people often seem pathetic in their fruitless search for
answers to unanswerable questions. For the disaster worker,
patience is called for in helping a bereaved person who is asking
unanswerable and/or repetitious questions.

A third reaction especially found in disaster death is anger. Anger
often is expressed by such statements as "Why did this have to
happen?" "I can think of a number of people who deserve to die
more than she did." "You can't love a God who lets somebody
like him die." The anger may be nondirected and emotional,
people may kick at immovable objects, bang their fists against a
wall or demonstrate other forms of semi-violent behavior. For
the disaster worker dealing with the anger of a bereaved person,
it can be frustrating and at times downright dangerous. The
anger may be directed at the nearest person, regardless of
responsibility. Direct eye contact and honest explanations
rationally offered are especially beneficial in dealing with very
angry bereaved people.

Another typical response of grief is guilt and/or blame. This
refers to the tendency to seek a source of responsibility for the

death or the disaster. Guilt may be presumed of one's self or of some outside "responsible" disaster cause or agent.

Following human-responsible disasters there is a strong tendency to place blame. This differs from natural disasters, which often are attributed to God or fate, thereby increasing the nondirectional anger so often observed.

Desperation is also a common response. Characteristically, the grieving person avoids eye contact with others and may look upward and downward rapidly and appear to be overwhelmed by resignation and dismay. A sense of hopelessness, despair and resignation to a death often is displayed through the inability to maintain eye contact. It is as though concentrated attention on one living human triggers the realization that another important person is gone. Gentle understanding and quiet assistance is the disaster worker's best approach.

Following any death, bereaved people have many personal needs that must be addressed. Dealing with grieving people often is not easy, and in accidental, disaster or violent deaths, the problems become even greater. In most instances of accidental or violent deaths, there is a tendency to "blame" the death on something or someone.

In events that can be attributed to social rather than natural forces, bereaved survivors often choose to believe that they resulted from human or organizational fallibility. As a result, human-responsible deaths often cause the bereaved to decide who should be "blamed" for the death that has occurred. On the other hand, in natural events it is more common for bereaved individuals to consider the event "an act of God." Rather than react with anger and hostility directed at a particular person or organization, the bereaved often respond to the death with remorse and shock.

A further complication is caused by the multi-emotional response characteristic of people's reactions to accidental or violent deaths. Specifically, bereaved survivors may demonstrate simultaneously or sequentially multiple feelings of fear, hostility, love, guilt or hate. Since survivors may suffer the frustration of having been powerless at the time of the event only to find they are equally powerless following it, their emotional responses may be intensified.

THE PROBLEM OF UNEXPECTEDNESS

Life events can generally be divided into those that are expected versus those that are unexpected. The distinction between the two takes on greater importance when the event involved is someone's death. At the abstract level of expectation, most people understand that all living things eventually will die. At a practical level, when diseases or conditions that can be expected to lead to death occur, they set in motion death expectations that can lead to anticipatory grief. Remember, so-called anticipatory grief actually is grief in advance of an expected death event, and it is a social psychological buffer to the impact of the eventual death. Expectation enables individuals to construct a new view of reality that will include the death of the person defined as dying. To some extent, then, expectation may assist at least the beginning of the grief process.

Since most accidental disaster deaths are sudden, there seldom is a clearly defined, delimited notion of death. Thus, such deaths often cause especially painful shock, commonly accompanied by an inability to believe that the event has happened and that someone close has died as a result of it. In the initial moments following death, the major consolatory strategy is to provide empathetic strength and understanding. This can be done by maintaining direct eye contact, firmly holding the bereaved person's hand(s) or shoulders, speaking clearly and slowly, answering questions briefly and with quiet control, giving firm physical support for someone seemingly "weak-kneed," and any intuitive socio-emotional skill that the disaster worker might draw upon.

The need to deal with the physical shock that results following accidental disaster deaths is an important one. In an effort to cope with reactions to "natural" death, some modern facilities for dying people have a "screaming room" in which people can release their feelings. For the surviving relatives and friends of accidental disaster deaths, it would be especially beneficial to have a room available or to give sufficient "social space" in order to encourage "purging" emotions of anger and frustration. Since such facilities are not ordinarily available, people often suppress feelings of anger, and unfortunately, they may be repressed for long periods of time. Such undealt-with emotions can induce serious mental health problems or manifest themselves physiologically in the form of ulcers or other somatic illnesses.

The second important emotional/physical reaction is psychic shock. Psychic shock should be met with gentle attention to reality and by attempting to assist the bereaved in coming to grips with the death. One of the best ways to accomplish this is through sensitive communication with the bereaved. Discussing the death-related event and the resulting death can be helpful in assisting the bereaved to start the process of accepting the death. In light of this recommendation, the common practice of heavily sedating someone who is in deep psychic shock often is inappropriate as a therapeutic solution to the problem.

Part of the problem is the dilemma of care vs. cure. While sedation may "cure" the immediate shock symptoms, it may not provide adequate care for the bereaved person. In general, a more effective treatment is to foster and retain mental alertness throughout the acute grief process.

Another important psychological process following an accidental disaster death is the need to reconstitute one's personal identity in the absence of the dead person. While this is an almost universal component of grief reactions, most normal deaths are relatively private and allow for some personal readjustment time. However, news about accidental disaster deaths generally is public. This means that a person bereaved through a disaster must attempt to reestablish his or her identity based on instantaneous public knowledge and perceptions of the event, as well as the personal reality of the death.

Bereaved people usually have many serious needs that should be taken into account. For example, they should be (but seldom are) accorded consolation, care and consideration as usual features of organized disaster activity. Bereaved people at the scene of a disaster are engulfed with questioning behavior to an often extraordinary degree. Moreover, they often seek answers that customarily cannot be provided. Their questioning seems directed at an attempt to have some party admit responsibility for the event or to discover magically that the event has not occurred and that their family member has not been involved.

Another problematic element is the simultaneous impact of a crisis (the death event) and loss (the death of a specific person). This dual difficulty exists in most disasters, but there is the compounding problem of loss threat. When individuals are missing but definite notification of death has not yet occurred, those close generally experience great difficulty because of the possible but unconfirmed loss. To further complicate matters, confirmatory evidence in the form of a dead body may not exist. Adding to the problem is the fact that an individual's death is especially difficult to accept when identification is based on partial or nonrecognizable human remains. A hope often persists that the entire disaster is not true, and this makes it difficult for any level of understanding between the disaster organization involved and the bereaved people. Even when the death is confirmed by expert identification, the nature of the death is such that the dead body may well be severely injured, mutilated or destroyed. The bereaved are then unable to confirm the reality of the death visually. Under these circumstances, there is a greater likelihood that the death will be denied.[8]

A further problem is that accidental and violent deaths often seem "inappropriate" to bereaved people. In one sense, no death is appropriate except when it ends a meaningless, painful or problematic life. However, here "inappropriate" represents a more expanded socio-economic judgment. Specifically, the "inappropriateness" of the death may be due to the timing of the event in relation to an individual's life, the age of the victim or other specific circumstances surrounding the event.

People seem to have at least two different philosophical outlooks toward accidental disaster deaths.[9] A traumatic death may be seen as (1) one that did not have to happen, but it did or (2) one that had to happen because it did. From a psychological perspective, those views are differentially used by individuals to help the unexpectedness of an unintended event. Regardless of which view is held, accidental disaster deaths usually remain "inappropriate," especially for younger people.

Social Support in Disaster

Calamitous death events can have an impact on an individual, a community and/or an entire society. People responding to such events on the individual level from an outside location may be unable to recognize the unique social-structural or social psychological components of the event. Thus, a serious lack of understanding of the realities and difficulties of the situation may result because of one's location vis-à-vis the death event itself.

Serious dysfunction between the expectations and responses of the disaster workers and those of the community may occur. The extent to which a community as a whole can respond to a death event depends upon the number of members of the community involved, the willingness and ability of the community to respond in a cohesive fashion, and the extent to which individuals within the community recognize the event as a psycho-social occurrence that merits some form of unified response. For example, when a natural disaster or one confined to a specific geographical location takes place, it is common for the community as a whole to become involved in the social organization of the aftermath in both a formal and informal fashion. However, when scattered locations are involved, concerted community organizational activity is seldom possible.

Regardless of how people react as individuals, major traumatic death events often serve as reference points in time for the people who experience them. Using the event as a benchmark in time enables people to evaluate life experiences in a temporal perspective. It acts as a means of understanding personal circumstances vis-à-vis community responses to a set of powerful death events. While this use of an event may or may not make it more compatible with everyday reality, it does serve as recognition that the community or social group survived a particularly difficult situation. Taken together, accidents and disasters comprise a large number of deaths annually. Each one has a relatively small impact on a societal level, unless, of course, it is the death of a prominent person. At the individual level, however, each such death is very important. Again, taken collectively, accidental disaster deaths create serious societal consequences, and they represent a real threat on the community and societal levels. Thus, the federal government, state and local governments, private companies and other concerned groups often have elaborate plans and systems for dealing with such events. Clearly, the serious social-psychological, physical and financial consequences of such events have brought about a high degree of social awareness. However, the societal organizations that may be involved seldom address themselves to the repercussions which they can have on the surviving friends and relatives.

One of the most important social processes following accidental disaster deaths is communication.[10] The process of communication allows for the formal and informal transmission of information about the event from one source to another. Formal communication originates from a "proper" source. Since the source seems "proper or official," there is an assumption of "correctness" concerning the facts and, given their origin, it is *implicit* that the facts are *known*. Unfortunately, however, this is not always the case. The confusion surrounding the scene of most disasters is such that even formal communication often is misleading and at times totally incorrect. The sometimes contradictory information disclosed by officials contributes to the problematic aspects of death-related communication.

Informal communication is an even more difficult problem because it may be transmitted by anyone about anything at any time. It often contains rumors, gossip or information with no factual basis. Understandably, when communication contains contradictory statements and impossible promises, bereaved people may experience severe emotional reactions. For example, someone may know that someone close has been involved in the disaster event and may be dead; however, the process of identification often does not allow definite "official" confirmation of the death for an extended period. Such rumor-like knowledge may create great emotional difficulties for the bereaved.

Social support becomes especially important following a disaster death. The possibility of strong social support is largely dependent upon the circumstances surrounding the event. For example, in cases where the victims are from a limited geographical area rather than from a diffuse geographical area, the potential for social support in the form of a single unified community response is much greater. Although the events surrounding a disaster may hinder it, social support should begin immediately after a death event has occurred. The evidence demonstrates that the sooner the grieving process begins, the better the chances are for resolving grief.

Purposive, instrumental activity by bereaved people often helps to initiate the process of grieving. Generally, such post-death activity is beneficial for bereaved people, and survivors may be adversely psychologically affected when deprived of such activity and responsibility. Put differently, bereaved people should be encouraged to "do" things they feel are meaningful and discouraged from becoming immobilized and "stuck" in a mood of inactivity.

The post-death activity of making funeral arrangements can be an important element in the grief process of those bereaved by disaster. Generally, in deaths resulting from natural causes, the funeral director serves in an advisory capacity to the immediate relatives who make the final decisions about the many alternatives available. However, in many disaster deaths, it is common for the sake of expediency and in the belief that it is more humane that the funeral arrangements be made by well-meaning others. This often deprives the family of the opportunity of working with the reality of the death and limits their area of decision-making concerning how the funeral should be handled. Additionally, the mourning period may be abbreviated if there are many deaths for which arrangements must be made. This is unfortunate, since it usually is beneficial for "normal" arrangements to be carried out by the bereaved family and for their personal needs and desires to be addressed through appropriate funeral customs and practices.

Social support is an important component in aiding bereaved people.[11] It is most effective when the bereaved are treated honestly and with willingness on the part of friends, relatives and others to communicate openly. The surviving relatives and friends of disaster victims often need the opportunity to relive the experience in order to better understand it and the deaths involved. One of the keys to communicating with people surviving such a death is to be a good listener. Allow the bereaved to work out their grief both emotionally and verbally. It is important for your reaction to be nonjudgmental; and when bereaved people seek your consolation, it should be given with empathy and sincerity.

Funeral behavior should be carried out as soon as possible after identification has occurred. This does not mean having a funeral ceremony abruptly; however, it calls for family and friends to be encouraged to plan and arrange the most appropriate activities that they wish to carry out in the funeral. Delays to allow injured survivors to attend the ceremony are advisable because the needs of the bereaved and the injured may be considerable.

The best manner of handling disaster death funerals is openly and with whatever level of public involvement the family desires. As a guide in this regard, it is advisable to encourage public visiting and public ceremonies because, in many disasters, the community shares in the sense of bereavement and grief. Furthermore, the feeling of collective loss is an important ingredient in helping individuals to know that others care. An important aspect of disaster death is the impact that it has on the people involved. On one level, this involves the bereaved and others personally affected by the event and/or the death. The complications of experiencing many deaths can lead to "death overload."[12] Death overload is a psycho-social crisis response that occurs when someone becomes overwhelmed by the sheer quantitative and qualitative excesses of deaths. This may result in an inability to deal effectively with them, and "burnout" may result. Burnout is a psycho-social reaction and may range from apparently absent grief to a complete breakdown from grief. Death overload burn-out has the potential of affecting one's life adversely. For example, it may lead to ongoing denial of the event and the deaths accompanying it. Death overload also may manifest itself in less obvious ways. It can take the form of death denying behavior or death-avoiding behavior. It may manifest itself physiologically, leading to ulcers or other somatic illnesses.

SUMMARY

There are many dimensions of disaster death that influence the social-psychological reality of people touched by the events. An informed awareness of the social-psychological aspects is an essential part of carrying out effective disaster work. Even so, a critical caveat is necessary. Each individual reacts uniquely to a given event and a person working professionally in disaster must be prepared to deal with a wide range of responses. Using various points raised in this lesson may facilitate sensible actions, although there is no guarantee that people will behave in a perfectly predictable fashion. Understanding this complication may help disaster workers deal more effectively with its occurrence. Above all, each person's unique type of behavior should be considered.

9. Grief Counseling for Survivors of Traumatic Loss

DANA G. CABLE, PH.D.

Providing appropriate counseling for those who have experienced a traumatic loss requires special understanding and skills. Whether we are dealing with family members and loved ones, or those whose occupational roles expose them to traumatic loss, the grief experienced in such situations goes beyond the norm. Although in general traumatic loss involves many of the same issues and needs as any other loss, there are some significant differences.

CRITICAL INCIDENT STRESS DEBRIEFING

In doing post-trauma intervention to help post-traumatic stress in high-risk occupational groups, the most often used technique is Critical Incident Stress Debriefing (CISD) (Mitchell, 1983). This technique, although thought of primarily for the high-risk professionals (police, firefighters, military personnel, emergency medical technicians and disaster workers), has much relevance for professionals and paraprofessionals working with the victims of disaster. Such recent tragedies as the fires at Storm King Mountain, the bombing of the Federal Building in Oklahoma City and the hurricanes in the Caribbean Islands are excellent examples of times when CISD would be relevant.

Critical Incident Stress Debriefing is a part of the model of crisis intervention or preventive intervention (Caplan, 1969). Crisis intervention involves the undertaking of activities to reduce the incidence of a disorder. It focuses on factors that may lead to psychological illness. By reducing the anxiety or tension related to an event, we are able to assist individuals in resolving the immediate crisis.

The concept of CISD was first proposed by Jeffrey T. Mitchell (Mitchell, 1983, 1988; Mitchell and Everly, 1995). Its initial use was for professionals in emergency services. Today, hundreds of

CISD teams in the United States and elsewhere stand ready to assist victims of such disasters as well.

Mitchell and Bray (1990) have outlined the phases in facilitating the debriefing process. They provide a useful guide for all those who work in the area of traumatic loss. The team involved may consist of several members, including a mental health counselor and a peer counselor. The role of the peer counselor is important because he or she is a member of the same professional group being debriefed, but has not been directly involved in the trauma. The peer counselor provides credibility regarding the job-related aspects for the group, and also serves to show that the process is not meant to be group counseling. CISD is usually used between one and three days after the incident has occurred.

Critical Incident Stress Debriefing consists of a series of seven steps or phases. In the first or *Introduction* phase, the facilitator establishes the ground rules and gives an overview of the process. Issues of confidentiality can be discussed, as well as making it clear that one should feel free to talk or to not talk. It is also important to explain that part of the goal is to talk about what happened at the workplace rather than taking it home. The facili- tator should also let people know that he or she will be available after the session for anyone who needs to talk individually.

The second phase is known as the *Fact* phase. The participants are asked to describe the facts about what happened. Open- ended questions are helpful at this time. We are trying to get the participants to focus on the facts of the event, rather than their reactions.

In the third or *Thought* phase, the mental health counselor will begin to elicit information about the first thoughts the members had during the event. This begins the shift from facts to thoughts and provides a good transition to the following phases.

The fourth phase is the *Reaction* phase. Since one of the goals is to help participants avoid stress-related illnesses, it is important to encourage them to talk about emotions. By asking questions such as, "What was the worst part of this experience for you?", the group members have an opportunity to express their feelings of sadness, helplessness and the like. As always, participants should not be forced to respond, but rather feel free to do so if and when they desire. The group setting offers a secure environment in which the members can disclose their reactions.

During the fifth or *Symptom* phase, the mental health professional helps the participants discuss the signs and symptoms of stress, both emotional and physical, that they have been experiencing. It is often helpful to present some of the most common symptoms and ask if anyone has been experiencing them. This stage also serves as another transition point to move the group back to a more cognitive level. It must be remembered that the goal of CISD is to provide stabilization for the participants, but not counseling. The information provided by the participants in this stage will help identify those who need more intensive individual counseling.

The sixth phase is the *Teaching* Phase. Here one tries to help the participants see that what they are feeling and experiencing are normal reactions. They need to learn that these reactions are temporary. This fact can, in turn, help reduce their anxiety. It is also important that participants learn to recognize reactions that go beyond the norm and that may suggest deeper difficulty. Information on community resources can also be given.

Finally, we reach the *Reentry* phase. At this point, we are trying to reinforce constructive coping mechanisms. We also want to make participants aware of inappropriate or dysfunctional mechanisms. We try to provide some closure and answer questions. Participants may have additional questions to ask. Often, handouts can be given to participants so they have material to review and refer to as necessary. The facilitator can summarize the content of the session and bring it to closure.

The CISD process will usually take no more than two to three hours. During that time, we have enabled the participants to express their thoughts, fears and concerns in a nonthreatening supportive environment. By conducting the CISD soon after the disaster, we may well prevent significant psychological problems, or identify those individuals who need more individual support.

Critical Incident Stress Debriefing represents one intervention approach in traumatic loss. It is not, however, a counseling technique per se. Rather, it represents a crisis intervention approach to assist the professionals who deal with traumatic loss.

The approach does, however, have merit for other situations of traumatic loss. It can be adapted to communities that have experienced earthquakes, fires, etc. Members of the community who have been part of the disaster and the rescue efforts could greatly benefit from such an approach.

IDENTIFYING TRAUMATIC LOSS

As mentioned before, CISD was designed for special types of traumatic loss. But many death situations may be seen as trau- matic to the individual. Rando (1993) has suggested five specific factors that may cause us to see a particular death as traumatic. These include: 1) the fact that the death is sudden and we have had no opportunity to anticipate the loss; 2) deaths that involve mutilation, violence and the like, such as homicides; 3) the sense that a death was preventable or was random in nature; 4) mul- tiple deaths, whether in a car accident, bombing or other situa- tion; and 5) the mourner's personal encounter with death, which may include the discovery of the death and mutilation of others, or where there has been a significant threat to one's own per- sonal survival.

Given this context, one can easily recognize that a large number of deaths fit the description of traumatic. Whether the loss occurred in a fire, bomb blast, murder, suicide or automobile accident, many of the above factors are present.

With this in mind, we need to identify what the grief counselor, or other helping professional, can do to facilitate the grief process.

GOALS OF GRIEF COUNSELING

Worden (1991) has proposed four goals for grief counseling. The first goal is to increase the reality of the loss. The grieving indi- vidual must accept the fact that the death has occurred. In many grief situations, this is accomplished in part by a viewing of the body. This forces the griever to admit the fact of the death and begin the more involved aspects of grief. However, in many traumatic death situations, viewing may not be possible. Without the body, it becomes easier for the griever to deny that the death has happened. There is acceptance at the cognitive level, but denial at the more visceral, emotional level.

In such cases, it is important to use the language of death. Expressions such as "passed away," or "lost," only serve to maintain denial. The counselor must not fall into the trap of supporting this type of denial. The griever must learn to deal with the more painful aspects of the loss.

It can also be important in traumatic loss to assist families in getting accident and autopsy reports. These provide a reality to the death. Arranging for the griever to speak to those who were on the scene of the accident or tragedy may provide an opportunity to get questions answered and confirm the death. This author has had the experience of a griever bringing photographs, taken of the body at the accident scene, to the counseling session. At the request of the griever, we have looked at the photographs together. Although this was not a pleasant experience, after the tears the griever made statements to the effect that now the death had been confirmed. This served as the bridge to allow the griever to move on toward recovery.

Worden's second goal is to assist the counselee in dealing with expressed and latent affect. For most grievers, the expression of sadness and related emotions is not difficult. However, to admit to other feelings is equally important. With many death situations, there is anger, guilt and other intense emotions. Grievers need the encouragement to express their feelings without value judgment. In traumatic loss, anger and guilt may be very common. For example, if the loss was in a car accident, there may be anger with the fact that the deceased was speeding, drinking, etc. Guilt over having sent the individual on an errand may also be present. Grievers must be in a permissive environment where they can feel free to express all of these emotions.

Having the counselee write letters to the deceased can be a helpful technique here. Role play and the empty chair approach can also be useful. This author has found that giving the counselee a blank tape and letting them record a message to the deceased in the privacy of their home will often allow more expression of the seemingly taboo feelings than can occur in the presence of the counselor. In a later session the tape can be played and discussed. The griever is often surprised by what they have been able to voice on the tape.

The third goal in grief counseling is to help the counselee over-come the impediments to readjustment. The griever often at-tempts to continue living in the pre-loss world. Grievers become reluctant to take on new roles and make necessary changes. The counselor can assist them with both the practical and emotional aspects of this goal. From the smaller task of managing the finances to larger issues of dealing with other people, each aspect of readjustment must be faced.

It is sometimes within this goal that the issue of what to do about physical reminders becomes significant. The question of when to pack away or give away clothes and other objects is a difficult one for many survivors. It is important to help the griever find ways to make changes that are not irreversible. For example, packing things away means that they are still available if later the griever has regrets and feels that there is still a need to look at and experience those objects.

The author once dealt with a patient who was having great difficulty with her grief several years after her husband's death. It became evident that her house was just as it had been the day he died. With some time and effort, the griever finally decided to move things around in her home. Although all the objects were still present, they were no longer in the same place and did not evoke the same painful memories. With these changes, she proceeded to continue her adjustment to a world without her husband.

The last goal is to aid the griever in saying good-bye and to begin a reinvestment in life. For many grievers, this is the most difficult issue of all. The griever often feels that in saying good-bye, they will be forgetting the person. The counselor must assist in helping the griever to understand that they may give up the pain, but they never have to give up the memory. This last goal involves helping the griever recognize that the person is gone from their physical world, but not gone from inside them.

TECHNIQUES FOR GRIEF COUNSELING IN TRAUMATIC LOSS

In the case of traumatic loss, all of these goals are just as appropriate as in any other type of loss. However, traumatic loss may require some special techniques to help the griever resolve his or her feelings (Rando, 1993). A traumatic death tends to live on longer in the memory of grievers. They need assistance in re-thinking and reliving the experience over and over until it is no longer the powerful force that it once was. This means the griever needs permission to retell the story again and again until it no longer evokes the intense reactions it once did.

The griever needs an opportunity to work through all the emotions of the traumatic event, such as the sense of terror and helplessness. Often, the griever needs to find a way to turn the emotions into action. It is not unusual to find a griever who, in dealing with a death of a child caused by a drunk driver, turns his or her energy into fighting for new laws and punishments for drinking and driving. This becomes a healthy outlet for one's emotions. This ultimately gives a sense of meaning to the death.

With traumatic loss comes a feeling that one will never feel better again. There is a need to educate the griever about the facts of recovery from such loss (Scurfield, 1985). We must help the griever understand that this type of loss would produce extreme reactions in almost anyone. This reassures them that they are not different or alone.

The griever needs to be helped to understand how important counseling is to recovery. Without such intervention, the griever may continue to experience symptoms for many years, making daily functioning more difficult. They need to be aware that their feelings may get worse before they get better. One of the reasons that many individuals experiencing traumatic loss do not stay with counseling is that they feel they are not getting "better" as fast as they thought. By alerting the person from the beginning of what to expect, it is far more likely that he or she will continue in the counseling relationship.

Finally, we need to help the griever understand that the grief associated with traumatic loss can be treated. This does not mean that memories and thoughts of the event will never occur again. Rather, it suggests that the daily feeling of grief and loss will dissipate. But from time to time, certain cues may recall some of the feelings. If appropriate coping techniques are developed, the griever will be able to manage those occasions.

It is useful to review some of the strategies for intervention that may be used with grievers (Sanders, 1989).

Medication. In traumatic loss situations, as well as in normal loss, some therapists, or even family members, may believe that medication is a necessity. In most cases, using antidepressants for grievers is not advisable. They tend to dull reactions and often result in delayed grief.

In the early days following a death, grievers usually have the best support system they will ever have. This is the time for the griever to experience and express all of the pent-up emotions, while good support is available. With antidepressants, by the time the full impact of the death is felt, the support system may no longer be as present. Only where extreme anxiety, pre-existing conditions or deep depression exists should medications be used.

Client-Centered Therapy. This represents a nurturing approach to counseling. It is particularly useful when the griever's emotions are still very strong. It entails a sense of acceptance, empathy and genuineness. In traumatic loss, there is often a sense of lack of safety on the part of the griever. The client-centered approach helps meet this need.

Gestalt Therapy. In Gestalt therapy, the counselor assists the griever in focusing on the here and now. In traumatic loss, there is often a great deal of unfinished business. The griever must learn to let go of the past and stop punishing himself or herself. The counselor becomes the guide for this task.

Psychoanalytic Approach. Perhaps the most useful aspect of the psychoanalytic approach in grief counseling is the fact that it allows the griever to use transference. This provides the griever with an outlet for some feelings, particularly in regard to unfinished business.

Behavior Therapy. In traumatic loss, behavior therapy may prove particularly useful in helping the griever become desensitized to the anxieties they feel in regard to the death situation. However, other approaches must also be used to ensure that personal and social adjustment are facilitated.

Peer Support Groups. To aid grievers in recognizing they are not alone and that their feelings are not unusual, peer support groups can be very helpful. By bringing together grievers who have experienced loss under similar conditions (e.g., murder), it is easier for grievers to recognize the same feelings and behaviors in others that they find in themselves. With members of the group at all different points in the grief process, it also provides a point of reference. A griever can usually see someone who is further along than he or she may be, and also see those who have further to go. The griever has an opportunity to direct attention to someone seen as worse off and to feel as though they must have made progress if they are able to attend to the needs of another.

Whatever approach we choose to use, we must be careful to never lose sight of the griever as an individual. We must adjust our treatment approach to meet the needs of the person, not attempt to fit the person into a treatment that is not appropriate for them. We must also remember that grief takes time. The timetable of grief cannot be set by the counselor, but must fit the framework of the griever.

OTHER ISSUES IN COUNSELING FOLLOWING TRAUMATIC LOSS

Finally, it may be useful to consider some issues related to counseling. The author believes it is often valuable to have at least one counseling session with the griever in his or her own home. This gives the griever an opportunity to share the environment of the deceased and show all the objects that were important in the life of the deceased. Moreover, the counselor will get a better picture of how the griever is functioning and what steps they are taking to help themselves in their own environment.

Grief counseling is often done by professionals who are well trained in the dynamics of loss. However, this does not preclude the use of trained volunteers to work with grievers. Hospices are becoming an increasing source of volunteer support for grievers. The important thing is to recognize when one is dealing with a grief situation that is beyond his or her expertise to assist.

There is no absolute rule as to when grief counseling should be done. Once we have performed crisis intervention, counseling can occur only when the griever is ready. Sometimes encouragement must be given to get the griever to actively seek help, if the grief seems to be going on too long and interfering with daily functioning. But the reality is that some individuals are ready to enter grief counseling soon after the death, while others will need time before acting.

The counselor must be aware of their own reactions within the grief counseling setting. In all grief counseling, but particularly in that associated with traumatic loss, there is the possibility of the counselor finding his or her own sense of vulnerability. We are all grievers and we all must deal with death in our own lives. If the counseling situation provokes too many issues for the counselor, it is time to involve someone else in the counseling. The griever's needs must be the priority.

Traumatic loss creates special challenges for the counselor. With the appropriate techniques and time, grievers can recover from their loss and move on with their lives.

10. Using Funeral Rituals to Help Survivors

O. DUANE WEEKS, PH.D.

WHEN IS DEATH TRAUMATIC?

Roger, a volunteer fireman, was justifiably proud when his 16-year-old son, Andrew, asked for permission to join him as a volunteer. After several weeks of training, Andrew was allowed to ride on the fire truck his father was driving to a small house fire. As they reached the fire scene, Andrew was somehow thrown from the truck and his father, unaware that Andrew was no longer on the truck, backed over and killed his oldest son.

A recently-married couple had just moved into their new home when the husband awakened to a noise downstairs. As he went down the stairway, he confronted an armed robber and was shot to death. His wife, hearing the gunshots, called 911 and was ordered to hide in the closet and wait for help to arrive.

In January, 1995, Seattle firefighters were called to a blazing warehouse fire. With the building fully engulfed in flames, several firemen were ordered into the conflagration and four were trapped inside when the building collapsed. All four were killed.

Certainly these three illustrations are all examples of traumatic death. Yet, there is some disagreement about what constitutes a traumatic death. Howarth (1993:231), suggests that all deaths are traumatic when she states that ". . . bereavement is possibly the most traumatic crisis that an individual may experience." However, a different view has been expressed by Eth and Pynoos (1985), who believe that trauma occurs only when "an individual is exposed to an overwhelming event resulting in helplessness in the face of intolerable danger, anxiety, and instinctual arousal" (Eth and Pynoos, 1985:173). Perhaps the useful perspective is to view deaths on a continuum from minimally traumatic, on the one end, to extremely traumatic, on the other.

Why are some deaths more traumatic than others?

Both the nature of the death (Raphael, 1983; Rando, 1993; Bradach and Jordan, 1995) and the circumstance of the individual survivor (Fulton, 1994) are variables that help determine the extent to which a death is traumatic. Thus, although some types of deaths certainly are considered more traumatic than others, varied causes, circumstances and relationships combine to determine whether or not a death is traumatic and, if so, the degree to which trauma occurs.

In addition to individual circumstances and the nature of the death determining whether or not a death is traumatic, deaths can be considered traumatic when they are contrary to the natural order, challenge our sense of control or threaten our well-being.

For example, during the early 20th Century, there were high rates of infant mortality and early childhood death. In 1900, over half of reported deaths involved persons 14 years of age and younger. Today, less than three percent of total reported deaths occur among this age group (DeSpelder and Strickland, 1992:13).

American childhood deaths have diminished to the point that the deaths of children now conflict with our idea of the natural order. In the natural order, grandparents live to be elderly and die first, then the parents, and eventually the children. We expect the deaths of our parents, we accept the death of our spouse, but we reject the death of our child. Thus, when a child dies, the natural order is contradicted.

Additionally, the death of a child challenges our sense of control and threatens our own well-being. "Parents are likely to feel they somehow failed, that society will condemn them . . . . There may be much preoccupation with possible causes, both to settle issues of fault and blame and to attempt to gain control in the future . . ." (Raphael, 1983:235).

"If I cannot prevent this death," a parent may ask, " how can I protect my other children, or even myself?" Kearl (1989) has identified the decrease in child mortality as one of three ways in which western society has reduced the threat of death and extended our control over our own mortality. He argues that we have decreased infant and child mortality to such an extent that, for all practical purposes, only the elderly die. Second, Kearl explains, we reduce the social identity of those most likely to die, the elderly, by segregating them into retirement centers, nursing homes, or hospitals. Third, continues Kearl, we have assigned care of the dying and dead to professionals (social workers, nurses, hospice workers, undertakers, clergy, and grave diggers) so that we will not have to contaminate our bodies or our minds with their care. Thus, those who are dying are, for the most part, out of sight and out of mind. Since we have effectively removed the elderly from society, we have also taken control of and removed death.

The more traumatic deaths, unexpected and unnatural, cause us to question the order of the universe and experience the discomfort that comes with loss of control. Thus, these deaths—the accidental death of our child, the random shooting of our neighbor, or the terrorist attack on the Federal Building in Oklahoma City—leave us with fear, hopelessness, despair and the sense that our lives are in chaos. It is the survivors of these very traumatic deaths that we now consider.

WHAT ARE THE NEEDS OF TRAUMA SURVIVORS?

There are six basic human needs relating to death: spiritual, financial, physical, cultural/ethnic, psychological, and social. If, as suggested above, we consider deaths on a continuum of trauma, we can understand how these needs apply to all survivors, including survivors of extremely traumatic deaths. The extent to which any or all of these needs are evident in trauma survivors depends on, again, the circumstances and nature of the death.

Trauma survivors may, for example, have witnessed the death and themselves been in danger (Pynoos et al., 1987; Pynoos and Nader, 1990; Schwarz and Kowalski, 1991). In this instance, they need to be comforted, feel protected and they need to be listened to nonjudgmentally. These needs may by considered psychological, physical, social and/or cultural.

Survivors of traumatic deaths must be assured that they are different people in different situations than those who have died and, as survivors, they will not be victims of the same circumstances. This assurance may be particularly important in the instances of suicide, where surviving family members worry that they are somehow tainted with the same self-destructive tendencies (Carter and Brooks, 1991); homicide, where survivors fear the perpetrator (Redmond, 1989); or natural disasters, where survivors experience anxiety over the possibility of a reoccurrence. These are psychological, social and physical needs.

Trauma survivors often feel victimized, feel that someone or some circumstance has wrested control from them. These trauma survivors have a need to feel they have regained control of their lives and their personal environment. This need is psychological, social and perhaps spiritual. Trauma survivors have other psychological and social needs, needs that are also applicable to survivors of less traumatic deaths, and include the need to acknowledge and comprehend the death, both intellectually and emotionally; the need to experience grief; the need to mourn; and the need for an unspecified length of time in which to adjust to life without the deceased.

How Can Funeral Rituals Help Meet Trauma Survivors' Needs?

November 22, 1963, the date President John F. Kennedy was assassinated, is a date branded unforgettably into the minds of Americans who were adults during the Kennedy administration. Each of us remembers where we were and what we were doing when we heard the President had been shot. We remember our responses when his death was reported, and we recall the days of national sadness, mourning, anger and confusion that followed, days in which the only radio music was funereal music, and all television networks and stations played and replayed each intimate detail of the Kennedys' fateful trip to Dallas.

Funeral rituals are rituals of binding and release. While they bind mourners together in their common grief, they are facilitating separation from the one who has died. It is only necessary to remember the intense sadness of those few days and the funeral rituals broadcast to millions of Americans to understand how death rituals helped the Kennedy family, and the nation, begin our grief work.

Many funeral rituals are religious—traditional, liturgical services where the bereaved may be passive observers rather than active participants. Mourners often choose traditional services because the services are predictable, familiar, and comfortable. This predictability can create structure and stability amid chaos. In addition, many choose these types of services because they do not have to participate, make any decisions, or expend their already drained emotional energy. Trauma survivors may experience such an emotional and physical numbness that they are incapable of participating in funeral rituals.

Still others select traditional religious services because they value the spiritual content or the particular ceremony involved, and they are comforted by it. And some choose traditional religious services because they are unaware that they have other options. Wolfelt (1994) expresses his concern that " . . . individuals, families and ultimately society as a whole will suffer if we do not reinvest ourselves in the funeral ritual (Wolfelt, 1994:4). He continues to encourage caregivers to create death rites that are personal and meaningful to the bereaved. Many churches have begun to initiate ritual participation for mourners participating in the death rituals. In the Roman Catholic burial mass and Lutheran burial services, two generally non-participatory examples of funeral services, surviving family members are asked to place the church's white pall over the casket as the body is moved into the sanctuary. In these services, relatives or friends of the deceased are also sometimes asked to read a scripture or provide a eulogy.

ARE FUNERAL RITUALS ALWAYS HELPFUL?

Bill, a 57-year-old airline pilot, was killed in an automobile accident. His three adult sons had been baptized as infants in the community church, but none of the family members had attended any church since the boys were very small. Because Bill's widow and sons had no other connection with a church, they asked the community church pastor to conduct a funeral service in the church. More than one hundred pilots, their families and friends, attended the traditional service but few of those attending had a religious background. As a result, the four hymns chosen by the pastor were sung only by the pastor and his wife, the organist. The scripture verses, also chosen by the pastor, had little meaning to the mourners. And the funeral message, devoid of any personal references to Bill, provided little consolation for the widow or her sons. It is important to note that too often traditional services are conducted where neither the deceased nor the surviving family members have any connection with or understanding of the rituals involved.

"I myself have attended way too many of what I would term generic funerals—cookie cutter ceremonies that leave you feeling like you may as well have been at a stranger's funeral (Wolfelt, 1994:7).

When funeral services have no personal significance to the survivors, they are of little benefit and may, in fact, be harmful. A clergyman once boasted to a funeral service class that he had conducted more than a thousand funerals, using an identical service for each except for changing the name of the deceased and the dates of birth and death. This is, of course, an extreme example of laziness and mediocrity, but caregivers are too often inclined to plan death rituals that are familiar or helpful to them, rather than to the survivors.

Inappropriate and impersonal funeral rituals are not only problematic for clergy of mainline denominations. Fraternal lodges, military service organizations, and others also bear the responsibility for sometimes providing non-helpful funeral rituals.

Glen, a retired car salesman, always had a friendly smile and warm welcome for anyone in his small town. He was known for his easygoing manner and his willingness to help others. While trying to assist a man under the influence of drugs, the man shot and killed Glen. Glen's memorial service was facilitated solely by one college professor, a friend of Glen's son, who spent less than five minutes telling stories he had heard about Glen and then dismissed those attending the service. As Glen's brother-in-law remarked, "I don't even feel like we had a service."

Funeral rituals may also complicate mourning if the most closely-related survivors have no input into the rituals. It is not unusual for friends, clergy or funeral directors to make important funeral decisions for trauma survivors in a misguided attempt to protect them. Since they have no input, the bereaved are not heard and denied the opportunity to express their concerns, feelings and opinions.

Two needs of trauma survivors, the need for protection and the need for adequate time to mourn, are not necessarily fulfilled by funeral rituals. It might be argued that participating in death rituals socially sanctions the survivor's role as a bereaved person, allowing him or her time to grieve and protecting him or her from social intervention, but it might also be argued that such participation accentuates the relationship between the survivor and the deceased, thus putting the trauma survivor more at risk for unwanted attention from a perpetrator of violence, the media, etc. (Redmond, 1989).

To be helpful, a death ritual must have some value to the survivors. To have value, the ritual must also have meaning. And to have meaning, the ritual must be personal. In a pluralistic society, there are many ways of dealing meaningfully with death. Some may choose a minimal role . . . others will seek more active participation (DeSpelder and Strickland, 1992:229).

PARTICIPATORY DEATH RITUALS

Rituals that include extensive mourner participation are, by definition, personal rituals. These rituals are oriented more around the survivors and less around religious traditions. Although there is little empirical evidence, there appears to be a positive correlation between amount of participation in funeral rituals and value derived from those rituals. When a young boy died, his family was having difficulty. . . coming to terms with their emotions and the loss of their son. Someone in their circle of friends suggested they could direct their energy into building a coffin. Soon, friends and members of the family, including the five-year-old brother of the child who was killed, were busily engaged in the task of constructing a coffin. Later, they experienced a sense of relief at "being able to do something." For the participants, building the coffin became a meaningful way to honor the dead child as well as a means of working through some of their own feelings. . . . This, then, is the real value of learning about and considering our options: finding the response that is meaningful to us personally (DeSpelder and Strickland, 1992:229).

When survivors participate in rituals, not only are they helped by others, but they are also provided with an opportunity to help themselves mourn. They often have an innate understanding of what will make them feel better, and they can participate in a way that provides that help. Thus, they are, at the same time, furnishing themselves, and being supported in, the opportunity to mourn.

Those who are participating in death rituals are, by their actions, acknowledging the reality of the death. Each aspect of involvement—planning the ritual, taking part in it, contacting others to participate—requires recognition that the death has occurred and the survivors' lives have been irrevocably altered.

Participatory tasks provide survivors with comfort. A mother whose son was fatally crushed in a logging accident is comforted by spending a few minutes alone with him and stroking his uninjured arm. A father is comforted by holding his young daughter during her funeral service. A daughter is comforted by conducting a memorial service for her mother, and a fiancee is comforted as she places her never-to-be-worn honeymoon lingerie into the coffin of her fiancee, killed in an airplane accident.

Trauma survivors who participate are listened to. When survivors participate, their ideas are acknowledged, and the magnitude of non-survivor's input is diminished. Such transitions increase the chance for those most traumatized to mourn.

What can hardly be disputed is that participation in death rituals increases survivors' sense of control. By participating in rituals, trauma survivors are more in control of that ritual and, thus, taking the first steps toward regaining a degree of control in their lives. More than observers to an unfolding drama, trauma survivors who are participating become actors in the drama and, as actors, capture the ability to help influence and control the outcome.

CHILDREN AS SURVIVORS OF TRAUMA

Within the past two decades, American children have gone from vicariously experiencing death in television cartoons and B-grade movies to personally experiencing death as part of their daily lives and environment. This societal tragedy has led to a plethora of studies investigating the relationship between children and their exposure to traumatic violence and death (Boatright, 1985; Pynoos and Eth, 1985; Pynoos et al., 1987; Pynoos and Nader, 1990; Schwarz and Kowalski, 1991). The research findings provide clear evidence that children involved in traumatic death situations experience long-lasting emotional and behavioral effects of that trauma (Pynoos and Eth, 1985; Wenckstern and Leenaars, 1993; Bradach and Jordan, 1995).

Like adult survivors of traumatic death, survivors who are children need to feel secure (Boatright, 1985), protected (Pynoos and Nader, 1990) and comforted (Nader et al., 1990). In addition, children who survive traumatic loss may experience poorer learning skills and increased absenteeism in school (Boatright, 1985), and disruption in their future development (Pynoos and Nader, 1990).

Children often witness traumatic violence and death because they are less able than adults to leave a scene of potential violence. Further, they are often powerless to deter acts of violence where, if they were adults, they might be able to prevent such violent acts. Although many children who witness or experience traumatic deaths will need counseling to reorganize their lives (Nader et al., 1990), participation in funerary rituals may help them understand the death, gain a sense of belonging and a feeling of value and self-worth. Unfortunately, most funeral rituals are designed by and for adults, so children often do not comprehend all the activities surrounding death rituals or the rituals themselves (McCown and Davies, 1995).

Whether or not children fully comprehend all death rituals, those who have experienced a traumatic death should be encouraged, or at least offered the opportunity, to attend the subsequent funeral rites. Their attendance provides support to other mourners while some of the rituals sanction and nurture their own mourning. A compassionate adult with a thorough understanding of death rituals can provide a valuable service as he or she patiently assists the child in understanding the circumstances and meaning of the rituals.

For those children who are able to participate, there are many opportunities for involvement in the funeral rites. Children can assist in making funeral arrangements. Their opinions should be considered in determining the time and place of services, the type of service, format of the service, designing the eulogy, selecting music, purchasing a casket and/or urn, and choice of a cemetery or other place of interment.

Children are often discouraged from viewing the body of one who has died. A well-meaning relative will suggest "You don't really want to see your brother, do you? Why don't you remember him as he was alive?" It is important to remember that children have vivid imaginations and what they imagine the body to be like is usually more dreadful than what they actually will see. Especially in instances where the child witnessed the traumatic death, it may be important for the surviving child to see, and sometimes touch, the dead body in order to know that the deceased is no longer in pain or disfigured. When the surviving child is young, it will be helpful for a knowledgeable and empathetic adult to explain what is happening and answer the child's questions.

There are other opportunities for children to participate in funeral rites. They may recite a poem, sing or play a musical instrument, read a special passage, lead a prayer, place a special object in the casket, carry the casket, and/or help bury the casket.

Children who survive traumatic death should not be denied the opportunity to be involved in death rituals. Such involvement will help them experience a sense of belonging and the satisfying knowledge that they have contributed to the memory of the deceased and the community weal. Most importantly, when children are included in death rituals, those rituals demonstrate the continuity of society and the reorganization of life, even thought a terrible thing has happened and an important person in their lives has died.

POST-FUNERAL RITUALS

Whether or not those who have experienced a traumatic death attend the formal death rites, or if there have been no formal death rites, there are special rituals in which the bereaved may participate and which may be helpful to them. Wolfelt proposes that ". . . if the funeral was somehow minimized or distorted . . ."

family members may want to provide their own rituals (Wolfelt, 1992). These family rituals may include commemorating the dead person on the anniversary of the traumatic death, lighting a candle in memory of the deceased, visiting the grave and recalling the person's life or by writing letters to the person who has died.

Sometimes people choose to memorialize by helping others. For example, following the accidental death of a high school student, his classmates, along with his parents, established a scholarship fund. The fund has helped dozens of students continue their education, while commemorating the young man who was killed.

Caregivers in communities across the country now provide helpful post-funeral rituals. For example, many funeral homes present complimentary holiday memorial programs for the bereaved in their communities. These programs effectively honor the memories of those who have died and help provide closure to survivors.

It has long been recognized that grief does not stop with the funeral. Wolfelt (1994:3) reminds us that ". . . meaningful funerals are doorways to healing for the bereaved." Thus, making arrangements and facilitating the memorial ritual are only the first steps. The bereaved are just beginning a long journey of coming to terms with the reality of death, a journey that can be frightening and lonely, yet enlightening and strengthening.

CONCLUSION

It is evident that further study is necessary to determine which death rituals are helpful to those who suffer traumatic loss, to what extent they are helpful and what degree of participation in those rituals is helpful. Fulton (1994) has written: Mortuary rituals, then, are a functional or a dysfunctional set of activities depending upon place and circumstance. . . . If the funeral is a rite of integration and separation, is it beneficial? The answer to that question is a contingent one. Ultimately, it is one that depends upon the individual survivor and the circumstances surrounding a death (Fulton, 1994:294-303).

This brings us back, then, to the premise that deaths range on a continuum from minimally to extremely traumatic. When working with those who grieve, we must strive to provide death rituals that are appropriate to the extent of trauma, to the degree of survivors' grief, and to their ability to mourn. These death rituals may take a great deal of imagination and effort, and they will be helpful. For helpful rituals are personal, meaningful, and valuable.

11. Complications in Mourning Traumatic Death

Therese A. Rando. Ph.D.

When the death of a loved one occurs under traumatic circumstances, the survivor's mourning is predisposed to be complicated by his or her reactions to the specific event. In such situations, the caregiver must be skilled at intervening in the ensuing posttraumatic stress reactions to the event as well as in the bereavement over the loss itself, and must comprehend the interplay between both processes. Unfortunately, however, posttraumatic elements of bereavement too often are neglected totally or are insufficiently appreciated. Posttraumatic stress is treated just like other loss-related elements of bereavement, usually to the mourner's detriment.

Relatively little has been written in the thanatological literature about the clinical combination of posttraumatic stress and mourning. It is true that in recent years there has been increasingly strong interest evidenced in those types of deaths that inherently lead to a mixture of both (i.e., accidental deaths, disaster deaths, suicides, and homicides). However, with the exception of the works of a few writers (most notably, Amick–McMullan, Kilpatrick, Vernonen & Smith, 1989; Lindy, Green, Grace & Titchener, 1983; Raphael, 1986; Redmond, 1989 and Rynearson, 1987), the interest on the parts of those in the thanatological community has been directed primarily towards the bereavement aspects, thus overlooking the posttraumatic aspects. This incomplete perspective not only has left a serious gap in the treatment literature but has contributed to the persistence of treatable complications in mourning traumatic deaths.

The purposes of this chapter are to identify and discuss those issues that generally complicate mourning after traumatic death and to delineate relevant concerns in the conceptualization and treatment of mourning complicated by posttraumatic stress. While an in-depth examination of the perspectives, guidelines, and interventions for the treatment of complicated mourning in general or complicated mourning secondary to traumatic death is prohibited here due to space constraints, it is found in my work, *The Treatment of Complicated Mourning* (Rando, 1993), to which the reader is referred for the specifics of the interventions mentioned here.

The Increasing Prevalence of Complicated Mourning

Despite many changes, today's mourner still must contend with most of the same issues, experiences, and processes as did the mourner of previous times. There still is the agonizing experience of separation pain and the often unanswerable question of "Why?" There continues to be a struggle to find expression and closure for uncomfortable psychological reactions, accompanied by anxiety about who and what one is and will become as intense and unexpected emotions are encountered. Confusion, disorganization, and depression are the results when the old world is shattered by the death of the loved one. There remains resistance to relinquishing old ties to the deceased and to forming new ones more appropriate to the present reality. Attempts to avoid changing the old ways of thinking about and being in the world keep being made. Despite all of this, ultimately, in healthy mourning, there is a yielding to these demands and resultant alterations are made in relationship to the deceased, the external work, and the self and self's assumptive world. Appropriate reinvestment stays a critically important goal.

However, while the actual experiences of mourning and its demands have not changed very significantly over time, what has changed is the potential for problems with them. In today's world, the typical mourner sustains a greater probability of being compromised in his or her mourning as a consequence of a number of sociocultural and technological trends (i.e. there is a greater chance that a bereaved individual may develop complicated mourning). Elsewhere, I have identified and discussed factors resulting from such trends that contribute to the increasing prevalence of complicated mourning in Western society (Rando, 1993). These include (1) the types of deaths occurring today, (2) the characteristics of the personal relationships severed by today's deaths, (3) the personality and resources of today's mourner, (4) present-day limitations of the mental health profession regarding bereavement, and (5) contemporary problems in the field of thanatology. Because of these developments, today's caregiver can expect to see an increasingly greater number of bereaved persons with complicated mourning.

COMPLICATED MOURNING

In order to appreciate how traumatic death specifically predisposes to complicated mourning, it first is necessary to understand that phenomenon. *Complicated mourning* is a term describing the state, wherein given the amount of time since the death, there is some compromise, distortion, or failure of one or more of the six R processes of mourning. The six R processes of mourning (Rando, 1993) necessary for health accommodation of any loss are:

1. Recognize the loss.
    Acknowledge the death.
    Understand the death.
2. React to the separation.
    Experience the pain.
    Feel, identify, accept, and give some form of expression to all the psychological reactions to the loss.
    Identify and mourn secondary losses.
3. Recollect and reexperience the deceased and the relationship.
    Review and remember realistically.
    Revive and reexperience the feelings.
4. Relinquish the old attachments of the deceased and the old assumptive world.
5. Readjust to move adaptively into the new world without forgetting the old.
    Revise the assumptive world.
    Develop a new relationship with the deceased.
    Adopt new ways of being in the world.
    Form a new identity.
6. Reinvest.

In all forms of complicated mourning, there are attempts to do two things: (1) to deny, repress, or avoid aspects of the loss, its pain, and the full realization of its implications for the mourner; and (2) to hold onto and avoid relinquishing the lost loved one (Rando, 1993). These attempts are what underlie the complications in the R processes of mourning.

Complicated mourning may take any one or combination of four forms (Rando, 1993). Complicated mourning *symptoms* refer to any psychological, behavioral, social or physical symptoms that reveal some dimension of compromise, distortion, or failure of one or more of the six R processes of mourning. They are of insufficient number, intensity, and duration, or of different type, than are required to meet the criteria for any of the other three forms of complicated mourning.

Seven complicated mourning *syndromes* have been identified. These may occur as syndromes independent of or concurrent with each other. (Also, various elements of the different syndromes may intermingle with each other to form diverse constellations of complicated mourning symptoms. The seven syndromes include the three syndromes with problems in expression (i.e., absent mourning, delayed mourning, and inhibited mourning); the syndromes with skewed aspects (i.e., distorted mourning of the extremely angry or guilty types, conflicted mourning, and unanticipated mourning); and the syndrome with a problem with closure (i.e., chronic mourning).

The third form that complicated mourning may take is of a *diagnosable mental or physical disorder*. This would include any DSM-III-R diagnostic mental disorder (American Psychiatric Association, 1987) or any physical disorder. Finally, a fourth form of complicated mourning is death. This may be consciously chosen death (i.e. suicide); death that is immediately secondary to complicated mourning reactions (e.g., automobile crash consequent to driving at excessive speed); or death that stems from the long-term consequences of complicated mourning reactions (e.g., cirrhosis of the liver caused by alcoholism). The latter two types of death may or may not be subintentioned on the part of the mourner.

There are seven generic high-risk factors for complicated mourning (Rando, 1993). These are factors associated with either the specific death or with relevant antecedent or consequent variables which would tend to predispose any mourner to complications. These high-risk factors include:

Factors associated with the specific death

- Sudden, unanticipated death (especially when it is traumatic, violent, mutilating, or random)
- Death from an overly lengthy illness
- Loss of a child
- The mourner's perception of the death as preventable

Antecedent and Subsequent Variables

- A pre-morbid relationship with the deceased that was markedly (1) angry or ambivalent or (2) dependent
- Prior or concurrent mourner liabilities of (1) unaccommodated losses and/or stresses or (2) mental health problems
- The mourner's perceived lack of social support

To the extent that any bereaved individual is characterized by one or more of these factors, that individual is said to be at risk for the development of complications in one or more of the six R processes of mourning, and hence at risk for complicated mourning.

TRAUMATIC DEATH

While it is understood that virtually any death may be perceived by the survivor as personally traumatic, the focus of the remainder of this chapter is exclusively on death that transpires under circumstances that are *objectively* traumatic. These are to be differentiated from internal subjective experiences engendering feelings of trauma (e.g., a feeling of helplessness or powerlessness, the perception of untimeliness in the deceased's death, etc.), which are not the topic of discussion here. Factors that make a specific death circumstance traumatic include (1) suddenness and lack of anticipation, (2) violence, mutilation, and destruction, (3) preventability, and/or randomness, (4) multiple deaths, or (5) the mourner's personal encounter with death, where there is either a significant threat to his or her own survival or a massive and/or

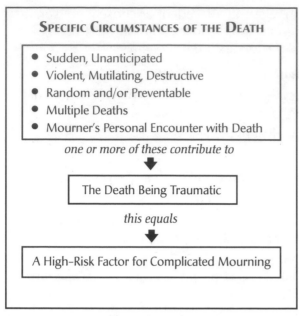

SPECIFIC CIRCUMSTANCES OF THE DEATH

- Sudden, Unanticipated
- Violent, Mutilating, Destructive
- Random and/or Preventable
- Multiple Deaths
- Mourner's Personal Encounter with Death

one or more of these contribute to

↓

The Death Being Traumatic

this equals

↓

A High-Risk Factor for Complicated Mourning

The relationship between the elements comprising traumatic death and complicated mourning.

shocking confrontation with the death and mutilation of others (Rando, 1993). In each of these situations the external circumstances are such as to engender the disorder psychic and/or behavioral state resulting from mental or emotional stress or physical injury that is known as "trauma" (adapted from Merriam-Webster Dictionary, 1987). Refining this further, the use of the concept of trauma henceforth in this chapter shall represent "an emotional state of discomfort and stress resulting from memories of an extraordinary, catastrophic experience which shattered the survivor's sense of invulnerability to harm" (Figley, 1985, p. xviii).

SUDDEN, UNANTICIPATED DEATH

Across approximately 1380 cultures studied, a sudden, unanticipated death is considered "bad news," stimulates concern about whether the loved one suffered before death, and initiates rituals to build the deceased back into the group in some form (Platt, 1991). It is a determining factor in at least three of the complicated mourning syndromes (i.e., distorted mourning of the extremely angry type, chronic mourning, and the unanticipated mourning syndrome), although it certainly often plays a part in the others as well.

Suddenness and lack of anticipation influence the mourner's internal world and coping abilities so adversely that a subjective trauma is created regardless of whether the actual external circumstances are traumatic. Raphael (1983) has termed this the "shock effect" of sudden death. With no time to gradually anticipate and prepare for the loss, the full and total confrontation of it all at once is overpowering. The mourner's coping abilities are assaulted by the sudden and dramatic knowledge of the death, and the adaptive capacities are completely overwhelmed. The sequelae of sudden, unanticipated loss of a loved one tend to leave the mourner stunned, feeling out of control and confused, unable to grasp the full implications of a loss that is perceived as inexplicable, unbelievable, and incomprehensible. The mourner becomes bewildered, anxious, insecure, self-reproachful, depressed, and despairing. He or she is in shock emotionally and physiologically, and it persists for an extended time. This further interferes with the mourner's ability to grasp what has occurred and exacerbates the intensity and duration of the acute grief symptomatology. Often the mourner engages in the avoidance of others and social withdrawal.

Although the person mourning a sudden, unanticipated death has the same six R processes of mourning to complete as does any other mourner, the devastated adaptive capacities secondary to the shock of this type of loss tend to compromise their completion. The additional intellectual confusion and emotional intensity wrought by this type of death handicaps the person. In essence, the shock effect overwhelms the ego and its resources, which then become taken up with trying to master the helpless ness and other flooding affects, the intrusion of associated traumatic memories and the resulting sense of personal threat and vulnerability – all of which interfere with the mourning that is required (Raphael, 1983).

Specifically, there are 11 issues inherent is sudden, unanticipated death that particularly complicate morning (Rando, 1993). These include:

- The capacity to cope is diminished as the shock effects of the death overwhelm the ego at the same time new stressors are added (e.g., heightened personal threat and vulnerability).
- The assumptive world is violently shattered without warning and the violated assumptions (e.g., the world as orderly, predictable, and meaningful; the self as invulnerable; etc.)

cause intense reactions of fear, anxiety, vulnerability and loss of control.

- The loss does not make sense, and cannot be understood or absorbed.
- There is no chance to say good-bye and finish unfinished business with the deceased, which cause problems due to the lack of closure.
- Symptoms of acute grief and of physical and emotional shock persist for a prolonged period of time.
- The mourner obsessively reconstructs events in an effort both to comprehend the death and to prepare for it in retrospect.
- The mourner experiences a profound loss of security and confidence in the world which affects all areas of life and increases many kinds of anxiety.
- The loss cuts across experiences in the relationship and tends to highlight what was happening at the time of the death, often causing these last-minute situations to be out of proportion with the rest of the relationship and predisposing to problems with realistic recollection and guilt.
- The death tends to leave mourners with relatively more intense emotional reactions, such as greater anger, ambivalence, guilt, helplessness, death anxiety, vulnerability, confusion, disorganization, and obsession with the deceased along with strong needs to make meaning of the death and to determine blame and affix responsibility for it.
- The death tends to be followed by a number of major secondary losses (Rando, 1984) because of the consequences of lack of anticipation (e.g., loss of home because of lack of financial planning).
- The death can provoke posttraumatic stress responses (e.g., repeated intrusion of traumatic memories, numbing of general responsiveness, increased physiological arousal).

If circumstances are such that there has been no body viewing to confirm the death, the mourner is at additional risk for complications. So, too, if there are legal inquiries and/or processes, these can complicate the mourning by forcing the need for intentional repression and/or presenting the mourner with circumstances causing secondary victimization (Redmond, 1989).

Suddenness and lack of anticipation are nonspecific variables that can be found in all forms of death. They are inherent aspects of a number of high-risk deaths (e.g., accidents, disasters, suicides , and homicides) and tend to occur concurrently with other factors known to contribute to complicated mourning, most especially the other four sets of circumstances associated specifically with traumatic death.

VIOLENCE, MUTILATION AND DESTRUCTION

Deaths involving violence, mutilation, and destruction are particularly traumatic because of the massively frightening feelings they engender in the survivors: terror, shock, helplessness and powerlessness, vulnerability, threat, anxiety, fear, violation, hyperarousal, and victimization. Ultimately, they typically lead to significant anger, guilt, self-blame, and shattered assumptions. Such deaths are particularly problematic to mourn for a number of reasons which, because of their frequent association with suddenness and lack of anticipation, must be added to the complications already delineated above. These deaths breach the mourner's senses of invulnerability, security, predictability, and control, viciously violating the mourners assumptive world and bringing all the types of adverse consequences such violations cause. Other problems stem from the fact that violence is highly associated with the development of posttraumatic stress (Rynearson, 1987), which includes among its many sequelae posttraumatic imagery that can be particularly overwhelming and recalcitrant. Additionally, because of personal attachment and identification, survivors of these types of death are compelled to work through an internalized fantasy of grotesque dying that not only increases their own fears but additionally complicates their mourning by presenting them with the task of assimilating the violence and, in cases of homicide, assimilating as well the transgression implicit in this type of death (Rynearson, 1988).

A major problem is that violence, mutilation, and destruction stir the mourner's previous aggressive thoughts or fantasies regarding the deceased, often bringing guilt as a result and linking the death with these prior thoughts (Raphael, 1983). The violence itself can cause aroused hostility in the mourner, which can contribute conflict within the conscience and lead to guilt or shame (Horowitz, 1986). Raphael (1983) has observed that violence, mutilation, and destruction fulfill the most primitive destructive fantasies and reawaken the most basic death anxiety and fears of annihilation, leaving those affected called upon to master these additional stresses along with their mourning. As well, she notes that the mourner must confront the general destructiveness of humankind and/or nature.

All of this leaves the bereaved having to contend with and work through the heightened senses of personal vulnerability and threat and the violated assumptive worlds that are left. Such deaths inevitably conjure up for the survivors images of what suffering they imagine the deceased felt at death, and this adds enormously to their distress and increases their guilt for not being present and/or able to alleviate that suffering. In homicide, and presumably in other scenarios as well, bodily mutilation appears to result in stronger identification with the deceased and in the survivor's losing more control of his or her personal life and environment (Redmond, 1989).

PREVENTABILITY AND/OR RANDOMNESS

The death that is preventable and/or random presents the survivor with distinct complications of the mourning processes. Often polar opposites, each characteristic brings its own specific problems to the mourner.

The mourner's perception of the preventability of the death often is an underappreciated factor in that individual's response. The perception of death as *preventable* appears to increase the duration and severity of grief and mourning (Bugen, 1979). This is viewed as a death that did not have to occur. It could have been avoided; it was not inevitable. Anger is intensified. The perception of preventability propels mourners to spend great time and effort searching for the cause and/or reason for the death, to affix responsibility by determining who or what is to blame, and to mete out punishment if possible. It prompts attempts to find some meaning in the death and the striving to regain a sense of control. The violations of the mourner's assumptive world make it difficult to make any sense out of the event. The fact that this was a death that did not have to occur is obsessively ruminated on by the mourner, who struggles to comprehend how and why such an avoidable happenstance transpired and to manage the outrage and frustration it engenders. The unfairness and injustice in this being a death that did not have to happen boggles the mind, begs for explanation, and intensifies the emotions.

The volition (as an act of willful, intentional killing or irresponsible negligence leading to death) and the violation (as an unprovoked, transgressive, exploitative act) of preventable deaths lead to two major compensatory psychological responses seen after these types of traumatic deaths (Rynearson, 1987). The volition, as previously observed, leads to compulsive inquiry to establish the locus of responsibility and purpose of the death; while the violation leads to the psychological reaction of victimization, including such aspects as shame, self-blame, subjugation, morbid hatred, paradoxical gratitude, defilement, sexual inhibition, resignation, second injury, and socioeconomic status downward drift (Ochberg, 1988).

Truly *random* events are especially terrifying because they are unpredictable and therefore uncontrollable: Individuals cannot protect themselves from them. Therefore, a common tendency on the parts of mourners and those who have been victimized by random events is to assume blame for them. It is relatively easier to cope with an event's being one's own responsibility—and thus potentially being within one's own control—than it is to contend with the fact that it was a genuinely random event. The assumption of blame is the price paid to maintain the needed perception that the world is not random and unpredictable, but orderly and dependable. This is similar to the psychological dynamics behind the phenomenon of "blaming the victim." In both cases, there is an attempt to take the event out of the realm of a random occurrence against which one cannot protect oneself and make it manageable by identifying elements the survivor can control or avoid in the future to forestall a recurrence.

Caregivers must be mindful that the most important point here is that it is the mourner's perception of the death's preventability or randomness that is the issue, not the objective consensus of others.

MULTIPLE DEATHS

With the increased number of traumatic, unnatural deaths occurring in contemporary society (Rando, 1993), there are greater chances for an individual to be confronted with the loss of two or more loved ones in the same event or to experience a number of losses occurring sequentially within a relatively brief period of time. Each of these circumstances can give rise to what has been termed *bereavement overload* (Kastenbaum, 1969). As applied to the topic of mourning traumatic deaths, the focus here is on simultaneous multiple deaths, such as might occur in a common accident, a natural disaster, or a murder-suicide scenario.

Essentially, simultaneous multiple deaths confront the mourner with the high-risk factor of concurrent crisis when it comes to mourning each deceased individual. Mourning for a given loved one is compromised by the concurrent crisis of the ongoing, stalled, or delayed mourning for the other loved ones. A vicious cycle often exists: The death of person A cannot be worked on in the fashion ideally desired because of the emotional press of unfinished business from, and remaining reactions to, the deaths of persons B and C; each of these deaths, in turn, cannot be worked through because of incomplete mourning and stress associated with the death of person A.

There are eight types of dilemmas in mourning multiple deaths, each of which call for specific treatment interventions (Rando, 1993). These dilemmas are found in the following specific areas: (1) the approach to be taken in mourning multiple deaths, (2) prioritization of the loved ones to be mourned, (3) differentiation among the loved ones, (4) loss of social support, (5) conflicts inherent in multiple deaths, (6) the overwhelming nature of the situation, (7) compromise of the six R processes of mourning, and (8) survivor guilt.

THE MOURNER'S PERSONAL ENCOUNTER WITH DEATH

Posttraumatic reactions are quite common following an individual's personal encounter with death in which he or she experiences a significant threat to survival or subsequent to a massive and/or shocking confrontation with the death and mutilation of others. Both scenarios bring about intense psychological reactions. Raphael (1986) notes that it should be expected that there always will be some feelings about survival when one has faced death and lived, especially if others have died. She observes that many people are psychologically traumatized by such experiences despite the support of others and their own efforts to master it. This is particularly the case when the stress and death confrontation is sudden, shocking, intense, and massive. Further, Raphael has found that cardinal reactions to trauma (i.e., intrusive repetitious images and avoidance) are always common in those experiences where there is personal threat to the self, an intense shock effect, and where the individual is rendered helpless. Issues of what one did or did not do to survive become critically important considerations.

In a personal encounter with death wherein one experiences a *significant threat to survival*, the traumatic stimulus of the event can overwhelm the ego and cause posttraumatic reactions. Examples of such events might include a mourner's surviving an automobile crash that kills other passengers or being rescued from a brutal assault right before the assailant attempts murder. The direct exposure to the threat of one's own death brings fear, terror, anxiety, heightened arousal, helplessness, a sense of abandonment, increased vulnerability, and the yearning for relief and rescue (Raphael, 1986). As with other trauma, the need often exists to relive and reexperience the event, as well as to defend against it by avoiding it or shutting it out. This undergirds the stress response syndrome (Horowitz, 1986), which is the process believed to underlie all dimensions and variations of posttraumatic stress disorder.

In situations involving the *massive and/or shocking confrontation with the death and mutilation of others*, the mourner loses a loved one in circumstances that expose him or her to intense terror, sudden helplessness, and frightening perceptions. Examples of such scenarios include mutilating airplane crashes or devastating disasters. For purposes of this discussion, included herein also are situations in which the exposure to the death and mutilation of others is on a smaller scale but still quite shocking (e.g., finding the blue and bloated body of a loved one hanging in a garage after a successful suicide attempt or having to identify the burned and mutilated body of one's kidnapped child). In both types of cases, the mourner must contend with a variety of stimuli stemming from severe injuries to other human beings. These may involve all the senses, not just vision (e.g., the smell of burnt flesh or the screams of wounded friends). The sights, the sounds, the smells—and all the other sensory images of death - become emblazoned in the mourner's mind and fuel the traumatic impact of the event. They produce reactive phenomena (e.g., nightmares, flashbacks, intrusive images, memories triggered by situations and stimulus cues similar to the original experience) that require integration (Raphael, 1986). Such phenomena complicate the mourning that must be undertaken.

EFFECTS OF TRAUMATIC DEATH

The *stress response syndrome*, as identified and described by Horowitz (1985), is accepted herein as the process underlying posttraumatic reactions. Briefly, the process commences with an initial outcry in response to a stressful event. A phase of denial and numbing is usually witnessed in reaction to the initial realization that a traumatic event has occurred. After this initial phase, the individual is confronted with phases of intrusive repetitions of traumatic memory, thought, feeling, or behavior which alternate repeatedly with the denial and numbing. Such alternation of phases constitutes a way of the mourner modulating the emotional reactions to the event by containing them within tolerable, paced doses. The processes of reliving and reexperiencing aspects of the trauma and inversely attempting to shut them out continues until the traumatic event is worked through by being integrated cognitively and emotionally, and the individual develops appropriate adaptational responses. The press for repetition of the trauma ceases because cognitive completion with affective release has been achieved and the distress stimulating it is terminated.

The stress response syndrome catalyzed by a traumatic death can produce a number of sequelae in the mourner which coexist in different degrees with bereavement reactions. These may be found in one of two forms: (1) posttraumatic stress symptomatology overlays the mourning much like a blanket and requires full-scale intervention first in order to get to the mourning underneath which is completely shut out, or (2) posttraumatic stress elements are interspersed with the mourning and intervention requires paying relatively more attention to them initially, but not overlooking those aspects of mourning that are available to be treated simultaneously. The information below is presented as if the former case were at hand (i.e., the posttraumatic stress symptomatology is preventing the mourning). To the extent that a given clinical situation departs from this, the information must be extrapolated to accommodate the treatment needs.

Posttraumatic stress symptoms may or may not meet the criteria for a full-blown posttraumatic stress disorder (PTSD) as delineated in the *Diagnostic and Statistical Manual of Mental Disorders, Third Edition, Revised* (DSM-III-R; American Psychiatric Association, 1987). According to the criteria, the type of stressor prompting the disorder must be "a psychologically distressing event that is outside the range of usual human experience. . . [and which] would be markedly distressing to almost anyone, and is usually experienced with intense fear, terror, and helplessness" (p. 247). Four types of situations are potential stressors: (1) serious threat to one's life or physical integrity, (2) serious threat or harm to one's loved ones, (3) sudden destruction of one's home or community, and (4) seeing another person who has recently been, or is being seriously injured or killed as the result of an accident or physical violence. Thus, deaths caused by accidents, disasters, war, suicide, and homicide, as well as the death of a child—which is specifically in the DSM-III-R—readily qualify as traumatic stressors. These deaths, more so than others, tend to embody the five previously identified risk factors associated with traumatic death and predispose towards PTSD and its three categories of symptoms (i.e., reexperience of the traumatic event, avoidance of stimuli associated with the traumatic event or numbing of general responsiveness, and increased physiological arousal).

As synthesized from Rando (1993), the most common generic posttraumatic stress aftereffects complicating mourning—regardless of whether they reach the criteria for formal diagnosis of PTSD—include: (1) anxiety, (2) reactions to the helplessness and powerlessness that usually constitute the central features of a traumatic experience, (3) survivor guilt, (4) one or more dimensions of psychic numbing, (5) repetitious reactions to the trauma (e.g., intrusions of posttraumatic imagery), (6) violated assumptive world, (7) the need to formulate meaning in the trauma, and (8) personality disturbances. These are the general posttraumatic issues the caregiver will have to focus on in the posttraumatic stress portions of the treatment.

For some traumatized individuals, reactions will be minimal or relatively short lived due to personal factors, a lower degree of exposure to the traumatic event, or therapeutic support from others. However, for many others, posttraumatic reactions can become entrenched and evolve into full-blown PTSD. Factors associated with more severe reactions to trauma have been identified by Raphael (1986) and include: (1) the shock effects of sudden, unexpected trauma, which leave the ego no time to protect itself; (2) the severity of the threat to life; (3) the degree to which the individual feels helpless and powerless in the face of the trauma; and (4) the intensity, degree, proximity, and duration of exposure to shocking stimuli, violence, death, destruction, mutilation, and grotesque imagery. Preexisting vulnerability from earlier trauma plays a part as well.

However, it must not be assumed that a person who has developed a mental disorder subsequent to a traumatic event is a person who was more impaired at the time of exposure (Horowitz, 1985). Psychological trauma is the type of experience that can produce posttraumatic symptomatology in almost anyone, regardless of pre-trauma characteristics. Unless there is clear evidence that there was preexisting psychopathology that has influenced the posttraumatic reactions over and above the normal responses to trauma, the caregiver must avoid interpretations of psychopathology. Especially in cases of unnatural dying (i.e., accidents, suicides, and homicides) which involve varying degrees of violence, volition, and violation, it is imperative that posttraumatic stress, compulsive inquiry, and victimization be understood as the psychologic consequences of overwhelming affect and defensive collapse, not as the reflections of unconscious conflict (Rynearson, 1987).

TREATMENT CONCERNS

As noted at the beginning of this chapter, when the death of a loved one occurs under traumatic circumstances, the survivor's mourning is predisposed to be complicated by his or her reactions to the specific event. This does not mean that complications inevitably occur, only that they are likely to do so. While there are a number of possible forms of complicated mourning that can develop, posttraumatic stress of some dimension typically is a consequence of traumatic death. As one form of complicated mourning, it may occur collaterally with any of the other forms of complicated mourning.

This requires that the caregiver be skilled at intervening in posttraumatic stress reactions as well as skilled at intervention in bereavement. After addressing the posttraumatic elements, the treatment of mourning complicated by posttraumatic stress then necessarily builds in two areas of components as found in Rando (1993). Intervention for the generic issues of complicated mourning *must* be added to the specific interventions for: (1) the type of death involved (i.e., accident, disaster, war, suicide, homicide), and (2) any other high-risk factors the death entails (e.g., guilt, anger, dependency, lack of social support, etc.).

TREATMENT OF MOURNING COMPLICATED BY POSTTRAUMATIC STRESS

Problems in treating mourning complicated by posttraumatic stress tend to fall into two main categories: (1) problems stemming from the inadequate appreciation and treatment of the posttraumatic stress and (2) problems resulting from the insufficient understanding of the nature, dynamics, and treatment of complicated mourning. Regarding the former, many caregivers focus exclusively on the loss and bereavement aspects of the traumatic death and do not attend appropriately to the sequelae identified above as stemming from the traumatic circumstances. Hence, the point of concentration tends exclusively to be on the loss *per se* and not on the overwhelmed individual who has sustained it. In their desire to arrive quickly at the heart of the loss-related issues, caregivers frequently overlook, minimize, purposefully avoid, or attempt to rush through the trauma-related ones. In such scenarios, several non-therapeutic results are know to occur. The mourner may flee treatment, be re-traumatized, develop additional symptomatology and/or defenses, or become engaged in a power struggle with the caregiver.

Problems with complicated mourning may cluster around a number of issues too numerous to mention here (see Rando, 1993). Suffice it to say that insufficient attention is paid to the *reasons* for why mourning becomes complicated to begin with and the *working through* of the resistances to the necessary six R processes of mourning which must occur if mourning is to be uncomplicated. By definition, in the situation of traumatic death, one of the complications is the effect of the posttraumatic stress on the mourner (e.g., impaired adaptive capacities after the sudden and unanticipated loss), which combines with the complications posed by the additional issues created by such circumstances (e.g., the increased guilt stimulated by the violence and mutilation). Therefore, traumatic death results in complicated mourning because of (1) its adverse impact on the mourner himself or herself and (2) the additional issues that the mourner is forced to confront as a consequence of it.

In treating mourning complicated by posttraumatic stress, the caregiver must integrate intervention directed at ameliorating the effects of the trauma with intervention focused on promotion of healthy mourning. However, if the posttraumatic stress overlays the mourning, the order of intervention is not arbitrary: Working through of the effects of the trauma and the defenses erected to protect against them must take place first (Lindy et al., 1983). Failure to do so leaves the mourner unable to progress with mourning as the self remains anxious and overwhelmed, fragmented and dissociated to varying degrees, victimized by repetitive trauma-related intrusions, fixated on particular concerns, and without full and conscious access to the ego functions.

GENERIC TREATMENT OF POSTTRAUMATIC STRESS

This section examines generic psychotherapeutic goals for intervention in posttraumatic stress. These must be embraced by the caregiver working with the mourner traumatized by the circumstances of a loved one's death, and must be incorporated with intervention for mourning. Depending on the degree of severity of the posttraumatic symptomatology, these interventions must be implemented prior to work on mourning the loss or integrated with such work as necessary to treat specific aspects of the mourner's bereavement.

A review of approaches designed to treat PTSD and its variants indicates that the broad goals are to empower the individual and liberate him or her from the traumatic effects of the traumatic event. Issues of grief and mourning are consistently mentioned as inherent aspects of healthy adaptation to traumatic stress, and an examination of the following strategies for treatment of posttraumatic stress in general reveals their similarities to the R processes of mourning. As abstracted from Rando (1993), the caregiver attempts to assist the person with posttraumatic stress to achieve the following:

- Bring into consciousness the traumatic experience; repeatedly reviewing, reconstructing, reexperiencing, and abreacting the experience until it is robbed of its potency.
- Identify, dose, express, work through and master the effects of the traumatic encounter (e.g., helplessness, shock, horror, terror, anxiety, anger, guilt).
- Integrate conscious and dissociated memories, affects, thoughts, images, behaviors, and somatic sensations from the traumatic experience.
- Mourn relevant physical and psychosocial losses.
- Discourage maladaptive processes and therapeutically address the defenses and behaviors used to cope both with the trauma itself and the mechanisms employed to deal with it.
- Acquire and develop new skills and behaviors and/or retrieve overwhelmed ones to promote healthy living in the world after the trauma.
- Counter the helplessness and powerlessness with experiences supporting mastery; a sense of personal worth and value; connectedness to others; coping ability; release of feelings in small doses; undertaking of action to give testimony, help others, or minimize the effects of similar traumatic experiences; and the avoidance of further victimization.
- Develop a perspective on what happened, by whom, to whom, why and what one was and was not able to do and

control within the traumatic experience; recognizing and coming to terms with the helplessness of the trauma.

- Accept full responsibility for one's behaviors as is appropriate and ultimately relinquish inappropriate assumption of responsibility and guilt after therapeutically addressing survivor guilt.
- Create meaning out of the traumatic experience.
- Integrate the aspects of the trauma and its meaning into the assumptive world; placing the event in psychic continuity within the totality of one's past, present and future.
- Form a new identity reflecting one's survival of the traumatic experience and the integration of the extraordinary into one's life.
- Reinvest in love, work, and play; reconnecting with others and reassuring the continued flow of life and development halted by the traumatic experience.

These goals specific to posttraumatic stress are facilitated by 11 therapeutic processes that the caregiver must integrate with interventions that either facilitate uncomplicated mourning or work through complicated mourning. Interventions which work through complicated mourning are discussed in Rando (1993) and not repeated here. Those that pertain specifically to post-traumatic stress are addressed there as well, but are also delineated below in summary:

1. Establish a trusting relationship.
2. Provide psycho-educational and normalizing information about posttraumatic stress and trauma, loss, grief, and mourning.
3. Focus interventions not only on the cardinal symptoms of posttraumatic stress, but also on (a) the defenses erected against the symptoms (e.g., distancing or distortion), (b) the behaviors used to control the symptoms (e.g., acting out or self-medication through drug abuse), and (c) the skills required to implement alternative responses to the symptoms and promote healthy posttraumatic existence (e.g., assertiveness or problem solving).
4. Intervene in denial and numbing reactions.
5. Intervene in intrusive and repetitive reactions.

6. Assist in the recall of the trauma.
7. Enable appropriate acceptance of the helplessness and powerlessness during the trauma.
8. Work to understand, transform, and, as appropriate, transcend survivor guilt.
9. Assist in the management of anxiety associated with traumatic memories.
10. Enable the individual to recollect and reintegrate traumatic memories into a new identity while adapting to, reconnecting to, and reinvesting in a revised assumptive and external world; facilitating healthy reintegration, rebuilding, and reconnecting.
11. Provide access to proper medical and psychopharmacological treatment as necessary.

A CAVEAT FOR CAREGIVERS

Treating those mourning traumatic deaths is often enormously stressful for caregivers. We are susceptible to our own posttraumatic stress reactions secondary to this work and are vulnerable to countertransference phenomena and a number of therapeutic errors in working with this population. The reader is referred to Rando (1993) for full discussion of the personal and professional pitfalls and promises of providing care to the traumatized mourner.

SUMMARY

Today's deaths are increasingly more likely to result from circumstances that are traumatic in nature. Reactions to death in these circumstances tend to complicate the normal processes of grief and mourning. Consequently, caregivers must be prepared to address both the posttraumatic elements of the bereavement, as well as its loss-related elements. Failure to understand the dynamics and complications of posttraumatic stress seriously hampers the caregiver in his or her attempts to uncomplicate the mourning and enable the mourner to achieve healthy accommodation to the loss, reintegration after it, and the resumption of appropriate investment and growth.

12. Masculine Grief

TERRY MARTIN, PH.D. AND KENNETH J. DOKA, PH.D.

Is there only one "right" way to cope with traumatic loss? If there is more than one healthy way of coping, is it based on sex differences?

Recently, differences between men and women have sparked our curiosity and our imaginations (e.g., John Gray's bestselling *Men are from Mars, Women are from Venus*). While much of the popular information has explored different ways of communicating, there has also been increasing interest in gender differences in grief.

Many authors who write about grief and many therapists have traditionally viewed men as being at a disadvantage in grieving when compared to women. Women embrace help and express emotion, both of which are viewed as essential to the process of grieving. Men, however, ignore their feelings, refuse offers of help and hide from their grief. The prevailing view has been that there are only certain ways of coping effectively with loss. Staudacher (1991) endorses this sentiment:

> Simply put, there is only one way to grieve. That way is to go through the core of grief. Only by experiencing the necessary emotional effects of your loved one's death is it possible for you to eventually resolve the loss (p. 3).

Yet, this assumption is questionable. To state that only one pattern is acceptable colors those who grieve differently as "denying" their losses. The general attitude seems to be that if you do not outwardly show intense feelings or seek help for private, painful feelings, you will most certainly encounter difficulties in the future.

In grief, we treat males the way we treat females in many other contexts—we judge them according to what is normal for the other sex. In truth, the mosaic of behaviors deemed "normal grief" is primarily based on samples of women. When men are evaluated against these norms, they are judged as not grieving as "well," as "completely." This chapter explores an alternative expression of grief. Since a preference for solitude as well as inhibited expressions of feelings are usually associated with men, the term "masculine" grief has been chosen to contrast this response pattern from the more familiar or "feminine" grief pattern.

Feminine Grief

Common views of feminine grief hold that openly showing and sharing feelings with others are healthy ways of dealing with the loss of a loved one. Feminine grievers often discuss intense, uncomfortable feelings with family and friends. When they seek understanding outside their immediate circle, it is usually in a support group of other grievers. In addition, they accept that they will undergo a period of recovery involving reduced activity levels or disruptions in daily routines. The literature on grief provides lists of normal emotional responses to bereavement (e.g. Rando, 1993; Worden, 1991).

Overall, displaying emotion and seeking and accepting help are the hallmarks of feminine grief. However, some individuals, especially men, respond quite differently to loss through death.

Masculine Grief

Outside of anger and guilt, masculine grievers, particularly men, appear to have a limited range of emotional responses. In fact, initial responses are often of a cognitive nature—thinking rather than feeling. They may first contemplate the implications of their loss, before encountering the pain of separation. For example, a psychologist and his wife each lost both of their parents within an eight-month period. While his wife described her grief using descriptions of intense feelings—"a wild roller coaster ride"—the husband intellectualized and sought to understand his new circumstances, wondering what it meant being an orphan: "Do you realize that I'm the last male alive in my family; that when I die our family name dies too?" Another couple grew embittered with each other several months after the sudden death of their 17-year old son. Responding to his wife's accusations that he had failed to share in her grief, the husband responded, "I couldn't allow myself to miss (him) until I figured out what I needed to do to help our family deal with (his) death." This suggests that some grievers initially experience their loss cognitively, rather than emotionally.

It should not surprise us that anger is easy for many men to express. More than any other trait, aggression differentiates men from women. It is the largest and most consistent psychological sex difference. Unfortunately, anger and aggression may not provide the therapeutic benefits of other forms of emotional release. For example, anger does not seem to buffer cardiovascular stress. Instead, it has been implicated in the development of heart disease, especially if it is part of an enduring pattern of personality (Friedman and Roseman, 1974). Yet, for many men, anger is the most familiar of the intense feelings.

Anger may not always be detrimental to one's health. Physicians first became interested in the Type A behavior pattern when they noticed that many patients who suffered heart attacks seemed to share certain personality traits. These individuals tended to be hostile, aggressive and impatient. However, recent findings have suggested that only those persons who fail to express their hostility are at risk (Matthews, 1988). Evidently, anger that is withheld rather than discharged is hazardous to its holder.

Many masculine grievers experience guilt, particularly right after the loss. This probably relates to assuming the role of protector. A sense of failure and feelings of guilt can follow, especially if the deceased was one of the "protected." These survivors often castigate themselves with statements like, "I should have made him/her go to the doctor sooner," or "I'm not sure I did everything I could have done." One client's guilt was almost palpable following his wife's sudden death. After working long hours as a postal employee, he spent his free time as a volunteer fireman. He kept resisting his wife's pleas to travel with her, arguing that there would be "plenty of time later." When his wife died just three weeks after he retired, the husband berated himself for putting off his wife's dreams. "I should have stopped working sooner so we could have taken some of those trips." This particular griever initially refused the many offers of social support and comfort, explaining, "I don't deserve help. My wife can't enjoy our friends' company, so why should I?"

Masculine grievers tend to be reluctant to seek help and share their grief. Men learn to hide their reactions and vulnerability from potential rivals. "Never let'm see you sweat!" becomes a way of exerting influence and control. This guise often subdues or limits overall emotional responses. Sadly, some men choose to quash all emotions; they negate the significance of the deceased and deny feeling any sorrow. In these cases, repression is the price of vigilance.

Men also value self-reliance. This masculine desire to "go it alone" may sometimes deprive them of beneficial and timely help. (Women confirm this when they become frustrated with male drivers who refuse to ask directions when they are obviously lost!) Support group facilitators can verify the poor levels of participation by men. Ironically, some men are able to cry only when they are with other men whom they trust: four brothers came together for the first time since the traumatic death of their father, a professional firefighter who was killed in the line of duty. These men wept openly, unashamedly. One said "It feels so good to have a safe place to cry. I can't do this with anyone else." Another safe place for men to weep is during the post-death rituals, where shedding tears is expected and sanctioned.

Some men resent being encouraged to express their grief emotionally. One thanatologist, Dennis Ryan (1989), in responding to the loss of his stillborn son, expressed this conflict well:

> I knew I could hide my feelings very well. I had learned that and counted it as a strength. People who thought similarly would never try to draw someone's feelings out unless they wanted to humiliate him or her. I was thankful to these, for there were times when I was very close to that fearful state of being out of control of my emotions. But I was spared that indignity (p. 128).

When men respond behaviorally to a loss, they often resort to activity. Sometimes they immerse themselves in work. Other times, they adopt an activity that is intimately related to the loss. Men may take legal or physical action in response to the loss.

For example, a young student pilot crashed his training airplane and was lost and presumed dead. His father found solace by helping in the search for his son's body. Other men may take active roles in the funeral. Ryan (1989), while supporting his wife's emotional response to the loss, expressed his own grief by carving his son's memorial stone.

Men may focus on the problems caused by the death, actively seeking solutions. After his 20-year-old daughter lost control of her car and was killed, the father spent several weeks rebuilding a neighbor's fence that was damaged in the accident. He later described this activity as crucial to "getting me through those first two months." Unfortunately, when coping mechanisms such as these do not help, men may seek escape in alcohol and drugs.

WOMEN AS MASCULINE GRIEVERS

Just as many men are comfortable in relating intimately with others and sharing emotional pain, some women view solitude and self-reliance as virtues. Though most masculine grievers tend to be men, some women respond to loss in like fashion. Recall the 1963 assassination of President John F. Kennedy. Chances are that, if you were old enough to understand the significance of that event, you have some powerful images of that tragedy indelibly etched in your memory. In particular, the image of Jackie Kennedy and her stoic behavior at her husband's funeral was an issue among some of the "death professionals" of that era. Many therapists and teachers felt that Mrs. Kennedy's muted responses reflected dignity and control and should be admired. However, other professionals maintained that her self-control established an unhealthy standard for grieving. We recall a remark made by a psychology professor in a course on death in the early 1970s: "Jackie Kennedy did a tremendous disservice to the American public when she hid her true feelings about her husband's death." Could it be that Mrs. Kennedy's expressions of grief were simply more "masculine" than "feminine?"

In an interview conducted shortly after the assassination (Stolley, 1964), a journalist reported that Jackie kept busy and stuck to a regular schedule. Mrs. Kennedy responded to the interviewer's inquiry about her recent ski trip to Vermont with the following: "I loved it. But that poor instructor who had to put up with me!" If Mrs. Kennedy's private response to her husband's traumatic death mirrored her public behavior, she would indeed have been a candidate for membership in the stiff-upper-lip crowd.

Although women seek support more often than men, some report feeling uncomfortable with openly venting painful emotions, a practice that is often encouraged by groups or individual therapists (J. A. Nichols, personal communication, April 29, 1994). One woman, after attending an initial support group meeting, said that she felt uncomfortable with the intense feelings shared by the group and the subtle pressure to share her own. Another woman reported that she felt coerced by her close circle of female friends to "open up and let it out." One group member suggested that she consider viewing tearjerker movies so she could move beyond her blocked feelings. Some women are driven to action when they suffer loss. One widow revealed how, after her husband's sudden death, she had stepped into his proprietorship and successfully negotiated several contracts. She said, "I felt compelled to carry on his work." Sadly, she reported that many of her friends and associates believed that she was cold, wooden and unfeeling. This particular woman chose action and problem-solving as a way to respond to the death. These and other stories suggest that the masculine pattern of grief is not gender-specific.

Experience vs. Expression

Although masculine grievers often react stoically to the deaths of loved ones, it is important to stress that this does not mean that they are unaffected by significant losses. Major differences between masculine and feminine grief simply resonate different ways of coping with the same thing. Understanding these differences may depend on one's interpretation of grief and mourning.

"Grief"' is usually defined as the emotional response to loss. Grieving is an internal process involving various psychic tasks, including changing our relationship to the deceased, making sense of the loss and establishing a new identity.

Grieving means confronting intense feelings. Much is written about the need to experience the pain of loss (e.g., Worden,

1991). Masculine grievers frequently contain extreme feelings by redirecting their energies. On the other hand, feminine grievers tend to give full vent to their feelings. Feminine grievers, with their open emotionality, resolve losses by sharing their feelings and thoughts with others. Masculine grievers feel the agony of loss just as surely. However, they tend to limit the expression of that pain to the period immediately after the loss. Further, they complete the psychic work of grieving, which is mostly an inner task, by privately solving the issues spawned by their thoughts and feelings about the loss. The Lone Ranger is not unaffected by the death of Tonto; he simply deals with it in a different way.

HELPING THE MASCULINE GRIEVER

In a recent episode of the hit television series, "Home Improvement," the protagonist, Tim Taylor, loses his "Tool Time" sponsor and surrogate father, Mr. Binford, to a sudden heart attack. He becomes defensive when criticized by his wife and costar for not being upset, for not crying. Instead, he repairs to his favorite watering hole to guzzle beer and throw darts. Later that same night, he whisks his young sons away to play a bellicose game of basketball. Finally, after a continuous frenzy of activity, he confides in his wife. He is afraid that there is "something wrong with me," because he's not suffering over the death. He also admits to feeling terribly guilty; his first reaction to the death was to wonder whether or not his show would be cancelled. Tim also regrets setting a bad example for his sons. He did, after all, tell them that "guys don't cry." (He does eventually cry at the funeral.) Tim's final act is to chisel a memorial from wood in the shape of a clawhammer, and give Mr. Binford a 21-nailgun salute. In these ways, he gives closure to his experience, and the story.

This story illustrates the chief elements of the masculine pattern of grief:

1. Feelings are limited or toned down.
2. Thinking precedes and often dominates feeling.
3. The focus is on problem-solving rather than expression of feelings.
4. The outward expression of feelings often involves anger and/or guilt.

5. Internal adjustments to the loss are usually expressed through activity.

6. Intense feelings may be experienced privately; there is a general reluctance to discuss these with others.

7. Intense grief is usually expressed immediately after the loss, often during post-death rituals.

Unfortunately, most grief therapies overlook potential differences between feminine and masculine grief. Traditional approaches to counseling are designed to facilitate feminine grief. While virtually all methods emphasize showing empathy, several encourage, even insist, that the griever reminisce about the loss, experiencing and then expressing painful feelings. Ironically, masculine grievers find this focus on feelings unhelpful and may even resent being urged to express them.

The following guidelines suggest ways to help masculine grievers

1. Provide the griever with basic human support and comfort.

2. Explore the individual's cognitive responses to the death.

3. Reassure the griever that crying and a temporary loss of emotional control are normal responses to losing a significant other.

4. Acknowledge all of the griever's affective expressions of grief, but do not insist that he/she cry.

5. Respect the person's need to withdraw into self, or to a private space and haven.

6. Encourage constructive venting of hostility, anger and aggression.

7. Assist the griever, when appropriate, in recovering emotional self-control.

8. Focus the person's attention on problem finding and problem solving.

9. Facilitate a rapid return to useful and meaningful routine activities previously enjoyed by the griever.

10. Be alert to self-destructive behaviors, especially alcohol and drug abuse.

11. Gently encourage the griever to seek professional help if there is a total absence of feelings and/or acknowledgment of the significance of the person who was lost. This might indicate severe adjustment issues.

Since masculine grievers are often reluctant to seek help, it may be necessary to reframe help-seeking as a problem-solving and protective action—a way to assist others in the family cope with their feelings, for example. Even professional counseling can be presented as a challenge to be mastered: "It takes courage to confront things and share them with a stranger." However, masculine grievers may choose to withdraw from everyone, to "go into their caves," (Gray, 1992). Respect this response to stress.

When dealing with emotions, use traditional counseling methods of enabling emotional catharsis (e.g., probing for feelings, recreating emotionally charged events) with caution. A suggestion to discuss "reactions" rather than "feelings" allows the griever to share in ways that conform to his/her role identity.

Since the community generally accepts, encourages and even expects outward expressions of grief immediately following the death and during post-death rituals, this may be the most appropriate time for the griever to discharge intense emotions. Later, issues of self-control and mastery will tend to dominate the masculine pattern of grief.

Because masculine grievers may see thinking as more important (and perhaps less threatening—than feeling, counselors and others should focus on thoughts about the loss as well as feelings. One system of therapy, cognitive-behavioral therapy, emphasizes thinking and its mastery, which results in emotional management and behavioral control. It is critical to accept and facilitate this traditional masculine need for emotional self-control. A temporary loss of control is acceptable to most masculine grievers; remaining at the mercy of one's emotions challenges the foundations of masculine identity and self-esteem.

It is important to encourage activity and problem-solving. Physical activity can be an effective way of coping. Exercise, for example, is often used as an outlet for anger and aggression. One woman exacted revenge on the physician she believed was responsible for her daughter's death. With each stride in her daily run, she trod on his face. While running is a solitary activity, some grievers may choose some form of organized sports activity. The playing field, baseball diamond, bowling alley or gym not only provide outlets for anger and aggression, but also opportunities for companionship and support. Bibliotherapy (directed reading) is also a useful activity; it involves thinking and is solitary in nature and may be wonderfully well-suited to the masculine grieving style.

Finally, we must respect individual needs and differences. Some grievers may wish to grieve in a way that he/she believes is not in sync with gender expectations. For example, one male client needed reassurance that his crying and his strong need for his wife's comfort at the death of his father were both normal and manly. Another man found that he could sleep through the night only as long as he was cradled in his wife's robe. He later admitted that it was the lingering fragrance of his late wife's perfume that calmed and comforted him. A female client needed encouragement to continue pulling (safely) to the side of the road and pounding her fist on the dashboard, while cursing in frustration and rage at her sister's sudden death.

MASCULINE GRIEF IN TRAUMATIC LOSS

It is no coincidence that the most widely used approach to helping survivors of traumatic loss seems tailor-made for masculine grievers. Critical Incident Stress Debriefing (CISD) addresses many of the needs of masculine grievers. Jeffrey Mitchell developed Critical Incidence Stress Debriefing to assist high-risk professionals following the Air Florida 90 disaster (Mitchell, 1983). Because men have always outnumbered women in the high-risk professions (e.g., police, firefighters, disaster workers, military personnel), CISD logically targeted a predominately male population. For instance, 96.7 percent of professional firefighters are males, as are 88 percent of law enforcement professionals. In the military, women represent 12 percent of soldiers, sailors and pilots (*Statistical Abstract of the United States,* 1995). Nevertheless, the late Secretary of Defense Les Aspin only recently removed the restrictions on women flying combat missions allowing them to regularly fall "in harm's way" (Time, 1993). The medical profession is likewise male-dominated. Less than 4 percent of physicians classified as specialists in emergency medicine are women (World Almanac and Book of Facts, 1995). We might also speculate that a certain type of individual, regardless of gender, may choose a life of risk and adventure. That type would most likely be more masculine in attitudes and behaviors, than feminine.

The basic elements of CISD mirror the reactions of the masculine griever: (a) thoughts are dealt with before feelings; (b) the expression of feelings is encouraged early in the model (after cognitions) but reasserting self-control is the goal before advancing to the problem-solving phases (4, 5 and 6, above); (c) there is sense of closure to the overall experience. Elements of the CISD model might serve as a foundation for developing other and equally effective methods for assisting masculine grievers.

SUMMARY AND CONCLUSION

Although experiencing and sharing intense and painful feelings have traditionally been regarded as the mark of the healthy griever, this chapter describes another, equally sound pattern of grieving. Masculine grief tends to be private, dominated by thinking rather than feeling, and action-oriented. While most masculine grievers are men, many women adopt this pattern of coping as well. Although traditional therapies have encouraged grievers to openly share their emotional distress and to recall painful events, masculine grievers may respond best to private, problem-solving approaches that respect and encourage emotional mastery. Critical Incident Stress Debriefing is a method of intervention that has been used successfully with emergency services professionals, and may be a useful tool for counseling masculine grievers.

Finally, there are advantages and strengths in expressing emotions and seeking help. But there are complementary strengths in stoically continuing in the face of loss and in seeking resolution in cognitive and active approaches. We can learn from both types of responses. Different ways of coping are just that—differences, not deficiencies.

13. Impact on Law Enforcement and EMS Personnel

LOIS CHAPMAN DICK, M.S.W.

Trauma is described in the dictionary as a *disordered psychic or behavioral state resulting from mental and emotional stress or physical injury.* Most Americans are spared exposure to severe and repeated or protracted traumatic events. They, therefore, have little appreciation or understanding of what law enforcement and emergency services personnel face on an almost daily basis. I have found over the years that in colleges and universities there is seldom sufficient training in the form of films/videos or presentations by law enforcement and emergency services personnel about their traumatic losses. Especially for counselors and therapists this information has much more impact when they see it or hear about it from the people involved as opposed to merely reading about it.

There are other factors that contribute to the heavy impact of traumatic loss on emergency services personnel and police. One of them is that the very personality traits that make them highly successful at their jobs can negatively impact them when they have been traumatized, particularly if the trauma has resulted in the death of someone they know. A second factor can be a lack of staff training about reactions to traumatic loss that they might experience on scene at an event or later.

Here in King County, Washington, our Critical Incident Stress Management Team, in addition to doing debriefings, provides law enforcement and emergency services personnel with training about critical incident stress. I will be discussing these factors in greater detail later in this chapter.

TRAUMATIC/CRITICAL INCIDENT STRESS REACTIONS

The traumatic/critical incident stress reactions have been detailed elsewhere in this book. Reactions may surface immediately on scene at an incident, within 24-72 hours, or days or even weeks later. When and if any of these reactions set in will generally have to do with what is going on in the traumatized individual's private and professional life. It also has to do with how much baggage they are carrying, how much loss and trauma they have experienced in the past that has not been dealt with in a beneficial manner. All too often police and emergency services personnel try to suppress their reactions to tragic events that occur both on duty and in their personnel lives. As you will see in more detail later in this chapter the very personality traits and behaviors that make them successful at work can complicate grieving and other strong emotional reactions when something traumatic happens in their lives. Traumatic events such as divorce, death of a loved one, death of a fellow officer and injury on the job can significantly impact them.

One reaction that may occur is sometimes not mentioned. It is called anhedonia (the inability to experience pleasure), and it can be confusing for those experiencing it. An example: the day before the traumatic loss or event occurred you were reading a book you enjoyed or were watching your favorite television show. Now, after the traumatic event you are thinking that the book or the television show will provide you with a pleasurable escape from the pain/stress you are feeling. You turn on the television and end up being bored and questioning why you ever thought you liked the show. Or, you discover that you have been reading your favorite book for 40 minutes and can't remember anything you have read.

Another activity that may be impacted by anhedonia is our ability to have and enjoy intimacy and sex. Yes, we do sex with our bodies, but the ability to give ourselves mental or emotional permission to do so is given by our current state of mind. If we cannot relax we probably will not be able to be aroused or achieve climax. It is important not to panic; anhedonia is usually temporary. It is extremely important to tell a loved one when you have been traumatized so that if you are unable to become aroused, your partner won't think it is his or her fault, that he or she are doing something wrong. Say something like, "Honey, I just want you to know that I've had a traumatic event at work and I may be a little out of it for a bit of time. It isn't because you are doing something wrong or that I don't love you."

Events Most Likely to Cause Traumatic Loss Reactions. There are certain events that will usually cause reactions. There are a variety of them, but most people will have fairly strong reactions that may last from 24 hours to even weeks depending upon the impact on them personally.

Human-caused events. Once when I was doing a ride-along with emergency services personnel, we got sent to the scene of an accident. A semi truck had T-boned a limousine. The drunk driver of the truck hadn't been injured. It took almost two hours for personnel to extricate the bodies of a young woman in her blood-soaked bridal gown and her husband in his equally blood-soaked tuxedo from their limousine. The limousine driver was also killed. They were on their way from their wedding ceremony to where the reception was to be held. There was a debriefing for emergency services personnel and police 36 hours after the event. So many of the personnel on scene admitted to being impacted. One man had to brush his tears away while trying to extricate the bodies . . . he had been married just a month before. We also held a partner/spousal debriefing.

I have found that the establishment of Peer Support Groups in police and emergency services personnel departments is very helpful for staff. Yes, sometimes someone will need to go to a counselor/therapist, but having the availability of peer support is additionally helpful.

Marital/Partner Peer Support Groups are another extremely important type of caring that can be given to personnel. It promotes more communication and encourages greater open-ness between personnel and their wives/partners. Events with unusual sights, sounds or smells. Years ago I was doing a ride-along with a police officer when we were dispatched to a low-income apartment building. It had been reported by neighbors that they hadn't seen one family for days and that there was a horrible odor coming from their apartment. When we got there we found the body of a 4-year-old boy. Petroleum had been poured on him by his father and then his father had set him on fire with a match. Almost three decades later I can still smell the odor of his burned, disintegrating body and still see that muti-lated little boy.

Events that are life-threatening to the worker. This past August, 1995, I was called to do a debriefing for a group of Mt. Rainier Forest Rangers. Two of their coworker rangers died in an accidental fall after two people who had been climbing in the snow and ice were rescued. The work of forest rangers, law enforcement officers and emergency service personnel has the potential to be life-threatening to them. The media graphically presented an account of the deaths of these workers. And unfortunately the number of their deaths seems to be increasing and not just here in the Pacific Northwest.

Events that violate the worker's sense of how the world is or should be. These events include the death of children and holiday disasters. A police officer told me of a horrible holiday disaster he had experienced. He and his partner were on patrol when they were dispatched to a home where neighbors thought they had heard the sound of a gunshot. When they went into the house a mother and her two teenage sons were standing in the living room crying next to the Christmas tree. The teens' father had committed suicide in the kitchen with a shotgun about 15 minutes earlier...on Christmas Eve. But, that's not all these officers experienced. The following Christmas Eve the officers were dispatched to the same house and were told by the mother and the younger teenage son that the older boy had just killed himself with his late father's gun. The officer said that nothing had ever impacted him as deeply as these two deaths, and it was due in part to the fact that the deaths occurred on Christmas Eve.

Events drawing high media coverage. High media coverage can interfere with the performance of job functions. Working under the pressure of being observed is difficult..."What if I am caught making a mistake?" And, you see over and over again the traumatic event that you were involved in.

Events that the worker can identify with. These include the death of a coworker or another rescue worker, knowing any of the victims in an event, being familiar with the event scene, and circumstances that parallel events in the worker's life. When a coworker dies one sometimes feels guilty, however irrational the guilt may be: "There should have been more I could have done." Your next door neighbors die in a fire. Not only did you know your neighbors, but now every day you will see the event scene.

Your child recently died after a short illness and now you, an emergency medical technician, are trying to resuscitate a child of about the same age and CPR doesn't seem to be working. The thought you probably will have..." I'm failing again."

Impact of CIS/Death in the U.S.

The Center for Disease Control has researched the impact of critical incident stress/death in the U.S. They have found the following:

Percent of People Affected

Within 24 hours	85%
After 3 weeks	45%
After 6 months	20%
After 1 year	5%
After 1 year of line-of-duty death/disaster	10%
Permanent profound distress	3%
Post-traumatic Stress Disorder (PTSD)	3%

Law Enforcement/Emergency Services Personality Traits

I mentioned earlier in this chapter that generally the very personality traits that make most law enforcement officers and emergency services personnel effective at their work can have a negative impact on their recovery from trauma and loss. What are these personality traits?

- The need to be in control.
- Obsessive. Desire to do a perfect job.
- Compulsive. Tend to repeat the same actions for similar events. Very traditional.
- Highly motivated by internal factors.
- Action-oriented.
- High need for stimulation.
- Easily bored.
- Risk-taker.

- Rescue personality.
- Highly dedicated.
- Strong need to be needed.

When death/loss/trauma occurs to them how will these traits go from being helpful at work to destructive in their private/professional lives?

PERSONALITY TRAITS VERSUS SUCCESSFUL TRAUMA RECOVERY

• Need to be in control	Displayed reactions show weakness. Dependence creates anxiety.
• Obsessive. Be perfect.	Something will always go wrong. The unexpected will happen.
• Compulsive.	Unusual death/trauma requires flexible reactions and new adaptations.
• Action-oriented.	Can't hurry things up and do them: trials, administrative leave, grieving.
• High stimulation need.	Trauma/loss creates numbness.
• Easily bored.	Life is on hold.
• Risk taker.	Judgment can be affected by trauma/loss.
• Highly dedicated.	Feelings of guilt...loss of job and other areas of responsibility.
• Strong need to be needed.	Loss of the person(s) who needed them.

Sometimes the experiencing of multiple traumatic events over years and the difficulties that some emergency services personnel and police officers have in expressing their pain, anger and sorrow can result their taking their own lives. The suicide rate for police officers is rising in the United States. In 1994 in New York City 12 police officers committed suicide. The police are constantly facing event trauma and criticism from the public, and this causes both acute and chronic stress. An example of this is the impact the O. J. Simpson case has had not only on the Los Angeles police department, but on departments around the country. Dr. John H. Burge in his book entitled *Occupational Stress in Policing* talks about statistics that found that "...police officers committed suicide twice as often as police officers were murdered by others." (p. 147).

CARING FOR AND COUNSELING THE TRAUMATIZED

So, given all of the above, what are good and effective ways to counsel and care for law enforcement and emergency services personnel if they are your clients, friends, colleagues or loved ones? What I have seen over the years as I have worked both personally and professionally with them, is that honesty is paramount. As friends, colleagues, loved ones or counselors we should not be aggressively confrontational. We should be gently expressive of our concerns for their health and safety. How do we do this? It may sound silly to you who are reading this chapter, but never use the "F" word, "feeling." If you ask strong and stoic people, "How are you *feeling*?" Their response generally is, "Fine, I'm fine." Because to say anything else may expose weakness or need qualities they are not supposed to have. So, either in the privacy of your professional office, home, or when the two of you are alone at work use the "R" word: "reaction." Say something like the following:" You know, Harry, I was thinking about what you experienced last night, and I had some reaction. I couldn't stop thinking about the trauma you faced and your possible reactions. I also remembered other traumas/reactions from my past. I couldn't get to sleep, and I have been unable to concentrate all day. Do you think I'm losing it? Have you had any similar reactions?"

First of all, you have said up front that you have been experiencing reactions. Therefore, they do not feel like they are the only ones who may be traumatized. And, they can now reach out and reassure you that you are okay. You have given them the chance to *help* someone. Helping is what they do for a living, and it is what makes them proud to be them!

There is a book that allows firefighters to tell their own traumatic stories about their work entitled *Firefighters* (listed in the Reference Section). It is not only informative for readers, it is helpful for the firefighters to be able to share their stories. I also highly recommend that you encourage emergency medical services departments, especially, to obtain videos from *Emergency*

Medical Update (listed in Reference Section). These are films produced to provide training for personnel. I was asked to do a segment entitled *Death and Dying* for their October 1994, Vol. 7 No 12 film. The film is about a two little children who find a gun while playing in one of the children's backyard. One child accidentally shoots himself in the head. His mother hears the shot and runs to find him. Emergency services personnel arrive and try to help the child. It is too late. In the film we talk about what to say to the loved ones of victims. For example, it is a good idea to ask any children present if they want to go and say good-bye to their friend/family member before they are taken away. All too often children are not given that opportunity. Don't make them go over to the dead one; merely ask them if they want to go over and say good-bye. The film also emphasizes the need for personnel to care for themselves during and after a traumatic event.

WHAT TO SAY, NOT TO SAY TO THE TRAUMATIZED

All too frequently people think they must stop the person who has been traumatized from feeling bad, so they will say things they hope will stop their pain/grieving. They don't mean to be unkind; they just don't understand what the person is experiencing. The sort of things they say include:

- "They are in a far, far better place."
- "They are no longer in pain."
- "Don't worry about it anymore."

All the traumatized person "hears" is "shut up" and "stop grieving" and "stop feeling what you are feeling." I once heard a loving, gentle hospital chaplain say to a young couple who had their three-year-old child die suddenly: "Well, thank God you have other children!" I didn't hit him, although I wanted to do so. I came up to him later and asked him, "How can you be so cruel?" He said, "What are you talking about, Lois?" I said, "How many children do you have to have so that the death of one doesn't matter?" He looked at me and tears came into his eyes. "I didn't realize what I was inferring. Thank you, Lois, for bringing this to my attention." He called the couple and apologized for what he had said.

WHAT DO WE TELL THE KIDS?

Very often people who are traumatized do not feel they should talk to their children about what has happened. They don't want to hurt or worry their little ones. Let's get more realistic. Think back to when you were a child. Whenever Mom or Dad was upset you could tell it when you were with them. All you had to do was look at their faces or listen to their voices. So, how do we talk to children about our traumatic loss? First of all, children cannot understand death until they reach an age when they can comprehend the meaning of "time" and "never." You can take a toddler to his or her grandfather's funeral and two weeks later he or she will ask "When is grandpa coming back?" Usually the ability to understand "never" and therefore "death" comes at about age five or six, but it can occur earlier.

Take the child aside and say, for example, "Honey, Dad has had a friend, a coworker, die and for a little while you are going to see me looking sad. If there is anything you want to ask me about this you can do so." You don't need to go into graphic detail about the death/trauma, but it is important to honor the children's questions because it will prepare them for their inevitable losses in the years to come.

I also suggest that you find a way for the children to memorialize the loved ones/friends/pets they have cared about who have died. One suggestion is to have a Christmas ornament made with a symbol of something the dead one loved and the name put on the ornament. Then, when the Christmas tree is up allow the children to choose the ornaments that they each want to hang on the tree. Yes, there will be sadness, but there will also be happiness in honoring those who have died that were loved and are now missed.

FACING ONE'S OWN MORTALITY

One of the best counseling techniques I have found for the traumatized is to get clients, especially law enforcement officers, emergency services personnel and the military, to take a look at their own mortality. I do this by asking them the following questions:

- What is important in your life?
- How many more years do you expect you have to live at the level of living you want to experience?
- How many of your dreams have you accomplished?
- Who will miss you when you die?
- What are your "dying" wishes? To die alone? Worst way to die? Views on assisted death? Are there any situations where it might be okay for you? For others?
- What kind of funeral/memorial service do you want?
- Do you want to be buried or cremated?
- What do you want on your headstone?

The result of asking these questions is that, for the first time, they may have openly/honestly looked at life as well as death. In this culture we do not usually look at or discuss death and dying. Thus, when it occurs, we are not even a little bit prepared to deal with our traumatic reactions.

THE TIME REMAINING

After we have discussed the above I will ask my clients what they want to do in the time remaining before they die. The following topics are discussed:

- Are you having a good time? How? Recreation, hobbies, risks?
- Are there high work performance expectations? Yours and/or your boss's?
- Are there difficult, nasty people you confront daily? Don't get caught up in their issues.
- Do you have someone to spend your life with? Is s/he loving, supportive, fun?
- How often do you relax? Hourly, daily, weekly, monthly, yearly? Once every decade?

Charles Figley in his book *Trauma and Its Wake: The Study and Treatment of Post-traumatic Stress Disorder* echoes my observations about assisting those traumatized in moving from being a victim to being a survivor, "What separates victims from survivors is a conception about life, an attitude about the safety, joy, and mastery of being a human being" (p. 399).

Physical Exercises to Relieve Stress/Trauma

For some people one of the best physical exercises to relieve stress/trauma can be dancing/bouncing/marching to music they love. It works for me and is mentioned in the book *Structured Exercises in Stress Management* (see References). Out here in the Pacific Northwest many use mountain climbing and skiing for pleasure and also for tension/stress release. For others, just going out into the yard/garden and working can help...doing something that allows the mind to drift off while the body works.

The Tubesings in their Volume 4 handbook, *Structured Exercises in Stress Management,* provide multiple ways to relieve trauma-induced stress.

Another book that covers a wide range of stress/trauma treatments is George Everly, Jr.'s book on this topic. *A Clinical Guide to the Treatment of the Human Stress Response* is excellent, in my opinion, and also has some of my favorite quotes about life. One is by Max Ehrmann:

> With all its sham, drudgery and broken dreams, it is still a beautiful world. Be cheerful. Strive to be happy (p. 399).

A Safe Place to Let It Out in Portland, Oregon

There is a wonderful counseling center for children who have had loved ones die. It is called The Dougy Center. Part of each child's weekly counseling is a period of time when they go with their counselor to a room where they are given a plastic baseball bat and told that they can hit the floor, hit the walls and hit the chairs as they scream, cry, yell, etc. The kids have named it *The Volcano Room*. I believe that every law enforcement, emergency services department and forest ranger station should have their equivalent of a *Volcano Room*. This probably won't happen, so suggest to your clients, friends, loved ones that they find their equivalent of a *Volcano Room*, meaning a safe place where they can let all their emotions out.

The Best and Final Advice

I also ask my clients to look at what they want to do during the rest of their lives. Are they thinking of themselves first? Generally the response is that they think of their loved ones first. This is what most of us do and particularly law enforcement and emergency services personnel. As children we are told that it is selfish to think of ourselves first. My experience, both professionally and personally, is that if we don't think of ourselves first, or take care of our needs, we will grow to resent those around us who are getting what they want. Whereas, if we take care of ourselves and our needs first, then when we do something for someone else we will be doing it because we want to do so, not because we should do it. Live life now! It could be over tomorrow, a lesson that most emergency services personnel and police officers are taught over and over again on a daily basis.

14. Spiritual Support After Sudden Loss

EARL A. GROLLMAN, D.D.

When life seems so unfair, you may feel alienated and betrayed by God. God may appear distant and removed, too far away to be of help. C.S. Lewis, a great religious writer, describes the feeling as portrayed in *Shadowlands* "Like a door slammed in your face. Where is God when you need Him?"

Spiritual beliefs are often challenged during the crisis of living with grief after a sudden loss. Some people believe that if you live a truly spiritual existence, "Goodness and mercy will follow you all the days of your life."

Not true!

Religion is not an insurance policy offering protection against the cruel blows of sudden death. Religion does not preclude grief nor inoculate you against suffering. Doubts are part of the cycle of faith.

You may ask: "Dear God, why me? Why us?"

It is natural that in your scientific world you seek answers and explanations. Know this. No one has a complete understanding of why good people go through such tortuous times. No philosopher or theologian has a cosmic computer to plug into this unknown secret formula. God doesn't hand out prizes based on your list of karmic gold stars.

"Dear God, why me? Why us?"

You may rage at God because of this lingering, crippling anguish. Honest anger could be your form of prayer. You cannot be angry at nothing. No one can hurt you like those closest to you. A stranger can not wound your emotional self as can a spouse, parent, child, close friend. To be furious at God could indicate that there may have been a God-Force in your life that was real and meaningful. Your wrath may be evidence that God was once present in your life and may be again.

"Dear God, why me? Why us?"

You may think that God is punishing you. You think 'What did I do to deserve this?' You might look inward to justify this new painful event in your life—a kind of Divine Chastisement for not attending religious services regularly and for doing things of which you are not proud.

You may feel that God is singling you out for tragedy. How many living saints do you know? Sudden loss has nothing to do with rewards and punishment. You and your loved one are not being disciplined by God. God doesn't consult a divine computer to find out who is most deserving or who can handle it best.

"Dear God, why me? Why us?"

You may be furious because life will never be the same. With such omnipotent power, why didn't God prevent this occurrence? Blaming God is a natural and normal response that helps to vent incensed pent-up emotions. Many spiritual leaders have felt this way:

> My God, my God
> Why has thou forsaken me?
>
> —*Psalms: The Bible*

It's okay then to be angry at God. God can take it.

In the book *The Dying Child*, Dr. John Easson tells of a young patient saying:

> If God is God, He will understand my anger.
> If He can not understand my anger,
> He can not be God.

What a powerful confession of faith.

"Dear God, why me? Why us?"

When a woman heard her husband had been killed in an accident, she said that her spiritual pain was so great that she felt like Jacob wrestling with the angel. Yet in the midst of suffering she found a comforting presence in a power greater than she. No longer did she have to struggle alone "in the valley of the shadows." In the dark news of her anguish she discovered a measure of peace and hope and said with the Psalmist:

The Lord is near the brokenhearted.

—Psalms 34:18

With faith and doubts, she quoted Elie Wiesel:

God is the answers . . . and the questions, too.

"Dear God, why me? Why us?"

Her prayers—simple or formal— were an effective means of communication. She could unload, express herself, rid her feelings and dare utter her secret concerns and fears, bringing solace and comfort in the face of helplessness and hopelessness.

When unexpected crises shatter life and anxiety and grief become the fabric of your days, your faith may flicker low and become extinguished. Facing illness can also be a religious pilgrimage where, however painful the spiritual struggle, your faith is somehow strengthened finding comfort in your beliefs and a holiness with deeper insights and new understandings, that even as you struggle you do not struggle alone to find out who is most deserving or who can handle it the best.

"Dear God, why me? Why us?"

Remember, three of the Psalms start with "why":

"Why do you stand far off?" *(Psalms 10)*
"Why have you forsaken me?" *(Psalms 22)*
"Why have you rejected us forever?" *(Psalms 74)*

But each one ends on a note of trust in God. The "whys" were really cries of anguish, a natural reaction to pain. There are 16 "whys" in the book of Job. God never answered Job's "Why?" Instead He answered "Who."

The statement: "Dear God, why me? Why us?" may be not only a question but your own normal cry of distress, a plea for help. As you probe even further:

"Since it has happened to me—to us—what can I—we—do now that life has changed."

PRAYER OF FAITH

We trust that beyond absence
there is a presence.

That beyond the pain
there can be healing.

That beyond the brokenness
there can be wholeness.

That beyond the anger
there may be peace.

That beyond the hurting
there may be forgiveness.

That beyond the silence
there may be the word.

That beyond the word
there may be understanding.

That through understanding
there is love.

—Author Unknown

Helping Survivors: The Role of Other Organizations

COMMENTARY BY KENNETH J. DOKA, PH.D.

Whenever there is sudden, and especially traumatic, loss, a variety of institutions, among them the media, may have roles that will either complicate or facilitate the grief of survivors. A number of chapters have emphasized that media can often be intrusive, adding to the difficulties of the bereaved. In fact, the power of media coverage is that it makes viewers virtually secondary victims, bringing the trauma of the loss right into their homes.

In a sensitive article, Brian Kates offers a balanced perspective on the role of media. Kates is a working journalist as well as a professor who teaches journalistic ethics. He also is an officer in a family-owned corporation that publishes *The American Funeral Director,* allowing him a special sensitivity to grief. Kates notes that laws do not really provide much guidance. He sees the decisions on how to cover tragedy as essentially an ethical issue balancing the rights of the public with the needs of those immediately affected by the loss. Kates points out that media coverage does not have to be divisive, but can be healing if it is reported carefully and with editors consciously monitoring the message.

Schools are critical in the healing process as well since they are often the places where children and adolescents will process losses. Robert Stevenson reminds us that schools cannot just expect to respond to a crisis, they must constantly prepare for such event. This is critical because one of the key problems in traumatic loss is a perceived lack of control. By effective and immediate intervention, school programs can diminish that sense of helplessness. Stevenson notes that many of these principles have relevance beyond traumatic loss and that proactive efforts by schools can help stem the epidemics of violence and AIDS that reach into our schools.

Laura Boyd, both a therapist and an Oklahoma state representative, provides a case study of the ways that government can respond to mass trauma. The "Oklahoma standard" showed that tough, thorough and caring leadership is essential to assist individuals in taking care of themselves. Boyd notes that the government must respond in both symbolic and substantive ways. Substantive ways in the Oklahoma City bombing included actions such as coordinating efforts and arranging assistance and compensation for victims and survivors. But equally important were symbolic actions, thanking people involved in responding to the disaster or discouraging talk shows that incited hate. And again Boyd, much like Stevenson, notes that certain actions including healthcare and insurance reform are active ways to facilitate recovering efforts.

Throughout the chapters in the book, there is a recognition of the role of ritual as a tool for healing when disaster affects a nation. These rituals have to be nationwide. As we discussed earlier, the John F. Kennedy funeral was an act of national healing. Stevenson addresses the need for commemoration. This provides a way, with media assistance, for symbolic action by government officials. The commemorative service in Oklahoma city, for example, moved us as a people, Kates affirms, from "Terror" to "Together in the Heartland."

15. Sudden Death: How the Media Can Help

Brian Kates

September 14, 1989: Gunfire erupted in the Standard Gravure printing plant in Louisville, Kentucky. When it was over, eight people lay dead and 12 more were wounded.

Within minutes, the plant swarmed with reporters and photographers from the Louisville *Courier-Journal*, located next door. The rampage, by an angry man with an AK-47 military assault rifle, was a tragedy of major proportion in Louisville.

The Courier-Journal would commit four full pages and nearly 20 photos to the story. It gave the people of Louisville what the editors thought they needed to understand the enormity of the event. But the coverage would trigger considerable controversy— and a lawsuit—in this conservative southern city.

Killings like those at Louisville's Standard Gravure plant are a regular staple of big city journalism. But even the smallest weekly newspaper must contend with sudden, violent death. Terrible traffic accidents. Drownings. Fatal fires. Teen suicides. No town is too small to escape these kinds of tragedies. Clearly, it is the duty of the news media to report such incidents. But it is also their responsibility to consider the effect their coverage will have on the public.

In dealing with traumatic death, journalists must understand— and the good ones do—that their reporting can do considerable damage as well as good. Every day, all over the country—at big papers and small, at the tiniest radio station as well as the largest TV network—responsible journalists engage in a dicey balancing act between hard-hitting, truthful reportage and the ethical responsibility to minimize harm; they must weigh the need to inform the public against the need to show compassion for those involved.

The Louisville case, cited by the Society of Professional Journalists in its treatise, *Doing Ethics in Journalism*, shows how difficult that can be and how even the best intentions do not always produce the desired results.

After the shooting, editors and reporters gathered in a conference room to map out strategy for bringing the news of the carnage to the public the next day. Reporters discussed the information they'd gathered: interviews with survivors and descriptions from witnesses, details from police officers, background information on the shooter and his victims.

The paper's coverage was complicated by the fact that, as editor David Hawpe put it, "We knew many of the people shot." In a sense, that made the reporters and photographers victims as well. But, like journalists in the aftermath of tragedy everywhere, they had to put aside their own horror and concentrate on how best to recount the terrible story. And, if possible, to find meaning in it.

"We used a process," editor Hawpe told the Society. "We asked questions like 'What is the story?' 'How to tell it best?' 'What gain and loss from using certain pictures?' 'What precedents do we have?' 'What alternatives do we have?' 'What impact will this have on the families of the victims?' 'Will too powerful a photo deter engagement by the readers?'"

They focused not only on what to put in the paper, but also on what to leave out—duplicative material, anecdotes of questionable veracity, exaggerations, marginal information, off the-wall speculations, potentially libelous accounts, material that would be hurtful to the people involved without advancing the story.

As they worked, scores of dramatic photos were arrayed before them. One stood out. It showed the body of a dead pressman sprawled across a conveyer belt in the basement of the plant. "Around the table, we heard people say, 'That's it. That's the image,'" Hawpe recalled. Not everyone agreed, of course; some saw it as too gruesome. Still, the editors decided to run it, and run it big: Page One. Four columns by seven inches. Above the fold—the most prominent position in the paper.

"We think we made a defensible action," Hawpe would say later. "The photo did what I wanted it to do by showing the reality of what assault weapons are capable of. A less graphic photograph would not have been as effective." Photo director Tom Hardin agreed. "We don't make a habit of blood and gore, or showing pictures of accidents; it goes against our tradition. But this photograph was tasteful and dramatic...in the same vein as some of the Viet Nam photos which brought home the horrors of war."

Many Louisville readers, however, were deeply offended. Soon after the paper hit the stands, the city desk switchboard lit up with complaining calls. The paper reportedly received more than 500 letters condemning use of the photo as in poor taste and insensitive to the family of the victim. Nevertheless, said Hawpe, "We provoked a very vigorous dialogue in the next session of the [state] legislature, and there was passage of a law strengthening controls on assault weapons."

To Hawpe and most of the paper's hierarchy, that end justified the means. But not to the pressman's family. They sued for invasion of privacy. Though the suit was dismissed by a state trial judge and both the Kentucky and U.S. Supreme Court refused to hear the case, it caused the paper's leadership to reexamine their actions.

After the family complained, Hawpe told the Society of Professional Journalists, he called the victim's widow and told her "about our longtime concern about the epidemic of assault weapons." But, said Hawpe: "She was not mollified." Only later did it dawn on him: "I should have called her the night *before*" the story ran.

It is, perhaps, an understandable oversight. Hawpe and his colleagues were caught up in the event, pressed by a deadline, and rightly concerned that the paper convey the full impact of the tragedy.

Should the paper have used the photo? Even hindsight doesn't present a definite answer. As the Society of Professional Journalists noted in analyzing the coverage:

> Certainly one could challenge the decision of the editors at *The Courier-Journal* to run the photo. It was invasive. It was graphic. It may have been insensitive and in poor taste to some readers....However, this photo also fulfills a primary obligation of journalism to 'tell the truth as best as possible.' ...The editors at *The Courier-Journal* went through a valid decisionmaking

process under great pressure. They asked important questions about alternative actions, about clarity of facts, and about consequences of their decision.

In other words, the editors' *approach* was responsible and ethical—even if the *outcome* was less than desirable.

Hawpe later realized that if he had called the family to warn them about the photo—not to seek their approval, but to prepare them—he would have minimized harm to them while fulfilling his duty to inform the public. And, as the Society advises, the goal in reporting traumatic death ought to be "to maximize truthtelling while minimizing harm."

A similar case from the 1980s involving a photo in the Bakersfield *Californian* remains controversial. The image is terrifying and haunting: In the foreground a child's head is seen poking from an open body bag. Next to the corpse is a man on his knees with his fists pressed tight to his head, keening. A boy at his side screams in grief. He is kept from collapsing only by the strong arms of a woman. Her face is twisted in agony. They are all wearing bathing suits; the young victim had drowned.

After the paper ran the photo, 400 people called to complain and more than 500 letterwriters protested the intrusion into the family's privacy. Eighty readers canceled their subscriptions. The dramatic photograph was picked up by the Associated Press and widely distributed. Many papers used it, including the Long Beach, California, *Press-Telegram*. Its readers were so incensed that the paper ran 70 column inches of protest letters. Syndicated columnist Bob Green branded use of the picture a "gross invasion of privacy."

Nevertheless, the photographer, John Harte, defended taking and publishing the photograph. "Our general policy is not to run photos of deceased persons, and we pay special attention to the sensitivities of both our subjects and our readers," he was reported as saying. "But special circumstances prevailed that led to the running of this photo. One, our area is plagued by an unusually high number of drownings annually. During the week this photo was taken, there were four drownings, two that day, in our area's public waters. Two, by having a policy of not running these pictures except for special circumstances, we hoped that by running this one our readers would have gotten the message that we felt it was important they witness the horror that can result when water safety is taken lightly. As horrible as it was, there was a message in that photo."

Perhaps. But the Bakersfield *Californian was* sufficiently chagrined to apologize three times in print for using it, and in a memo to the staff, top editors noted: "We make mistakes—and this was a big one."

As both these cases show, covering traumatic death is complex and complicated for reporters, photographers and their editors. That's why Kenneth J. Doka, professor of gerontology at the Graduate School of the College of New Rochelle (NY), refers to murders, suicides and violent accidents as "dirty deaths."

As Doka wrote in *The American Funeral Director* magazine: "These deaths are 'dirty' insofar as they are marked by a variety of complicating factors that may be less apparent in other types of loss....Here the loss is sudden and unexpected. Here the loss is troubled by feelings that it could have been easily prevented. Here the death reminds survivors of their vulnerability and mortality."

And there's the rub.

"We cringe from confrontation with our mortality," says Melvin Mencher, of the Columbia University Graduate School of Journalism. "Death is said to be the last taboo." But, as Mencher notes in his seminal text, *News Reporting and Writing,* inexperienced reporters too often go to the other extreme:

> Carried away by the drama of violence, they may chronicle the details of death—the conditions of bodies strewn alongside the airliner, the mutilated homicide victim, the precise plans of the youngster who committed suicide in the garage. This enthusiasm is as tasteless as prurient sexual interest, for it uses the tabooed subject as the means to shock readers, to call attention to the reporting rather than to the subject. Death can be terrible and horrifying. But its terror and horror are best made known through understatement. In sensitive areas, the whisper speaks louder than the shout.

Mencher counsels students that "a sensitivity to personal feelings is essential to the journalist, not because invasions of privacy are illegal, but because compassion is a compelling moral demand."

That moral imperative is basic to good journalism. It should guide reporters, photographers and editors daily—especially in their handling of traumatic death. Unfortunately, many factors can cloud journalists' judgment: the demands of rapidly approaching deadlines, competition with other newsgathering organizations, pressure from peers and the desire for fame and fortune, to name just a few.

Journalists should bear in mind that the traditional standards for deciding what is newsworthy—timeliness, conflict, novelty, prominence, proximity, impact and so forth—have no ethical foundation. At their core they are amoral; that is, no moral judgment is involved in their application.

And the law is not much help, either. Libel and invasion of privacy precedents provide journalists with a better blueprint for what they can *get away with* than what they *should* do. That is not the best criterion on which to base responsible reporting. That's why most reputable newspapers, radio stations and television networks now have formal codes of ethics that set standards for what they consider to be appropriate professional behavior. They emphasize responsibility, accuracy and, especially, fairness.

In its code of ethics, for example, the Society of Professional Journalists notes that members must "at all times show respect for the dignity, privacy rights and well-being of people encountered in the course of gathering and presenting the news." It stresses that "the news media must guard against invading a person's right to privacy" and that "the media should not pander to morbid curiosity about the details of vice and crime."

Nevertheless, as I wrote in my book, *The Murder of a Shopping Bag Lady*, the biography of a homeless woman whose brutal slaying I covered for the *New York Daily News*:

> The making of a cynic begins early in a newspaperman's career....I had written hundreds of such stories over the years until they had all begun to blend together. Who could remember them all? ...Children

burned in fires, plane crashes, murders. Just change the names and dates; they're all the same. Bang them out—and keep your eye out for the twist, the new angle, the irony that will make this story different from the one last week.

Avoiding that seen-it-all, been-everywhere, know-it-all attitude is sometimes difficult for a seasoned veteran. And, sadly, up-and-coming beginners are often quick to emulate it as a kind of badge of professional honor. That's a big mistake. If not held in check, it can infect an entire career and do much unintended harm to innocent people.

Guarding against such cynicism is the moral duty of every responsible journalist. The good ones know they must constantly question their motives. When confronted with how to handle potentially harmful information, they ask themselves:

1. Is the questionable material significant beyond mere sensationalism or titillation? What makes it so? Does the public have a need to know? Why?

2. Who are the people who might be hurt by the questionable material? And how might they be hurt?

3. Am I being compassionate to those affected—treating them as human beings deserving of respect or merely as a means to my journalistic end?

4. If I feel the good that will come of using questionable material will outweigh the harm, have I examined all possible alternatives?

5. If the roles were reversed and I was a stakeholder, how would I feel?

6. What are the possible consequences of my actions? Short term? Long term?

7. How will my readers or listeners react? Can I justify my decision to them?

8. How can I include others with different perspectives into my decisionmaking process?

9. Are there others—funeral directors, hospital officials, police or fire officials, family spokespersons, etc.—I

might deal with to avoid invading the privacy of mourning family members?

10. Am I willing to take full responsibility for my decision?

When journalists meet the challenge of covering traumatic death responsibly, with fairness and compassion, the results can be not only dramatic, but also helpful to those involved. Nowhere in recent memory is that shown more clearly than in the immediate aftermath of the bombing of Oklahoma City's Alfred P. Murrah Federal Building, where 169 persons were killed and more than 500 injured in April 1995.

J.E. McReynolds, an editorial writer for the *Daily Oklahoman* wrote these words only days after the bombing:

> I have seen reporters in our newsroom struggling to maintain control. They have covered mass murders and drive-by shootings. They have been to five-car smashups and seen kids burned by a member of their own family. They have seen all kinds of evil, but they have not seen this kind.

> One of them started crying...thinking herself a "monster" because she was reporting the story and others were pulling people out of the federal building. Another wrote through tears when she learned a friend and father of five was among the missing .

> We are a hard bunch, we journalists, too hard for our own good. But no one is too hard to cry along with the mother of the child in the photograph that will forever symbolize this tragedy. In her reunion with the police officer and firefighter who tried in vain to save the child, the woman helped us all let go of whatever emotion we'd been saving.

In their coverage of the bombing and its aftermath, *Daily Oklahoman* staffers constantly reminded themselves that "We were Oklahomans covering Oklahomans," said assistant city editor Don Mecoy. "We didn't have to restrain our reporters from being overly gruesome; they are experienced people and they knew where the boundaries were." The paper had no choice but to write about blood and bodies and decapitated children. But it wisely refused to dwell morbidly on those details.

In its first day of coverage, the most prominently displayed pictures concentrated not on bodies—though some, of course, were shown—but on the devastation of the federal building, a local landmark. On the second day, the Page One picture showed a *survivor* in bed and smiling. "That was a very conscious decision," said Mecoy. "We felt that was the direction in which the story should be moving. We didn't make it with the specific intent of providing therapy for our readers." But for many it had that effect.

Day after day, the paper put out special sections on the disaster, broadening its coverage with each issue. The logo for the section was "Terror in the Heartland." But, said Mecoy, "After the President and Billy Graham came, we changed the focus. We called the section "Together in the Heartland."

Without shortchanging readers one iota, the *Daily Oklahoman* — with its thorough, thoughtful and sensitive coverage—helped heal the wounds of this enormous tragedy and aided thousands of people, not just in Oklahoma but across the nation, deal with their grief.

In that, there is a lesson for journalists everywhere.

16. The Response of Schools and Teachers

ROBERT G. STEVENSON. PH..D.

> To speak of an enemy gives it strength.
>
> —African Proverb

In the fall of each year the public schools in New Jersey are closed for two days so that educators can attend a statewide convention. The annual conference offers lectures and work-shops aimed at improving teaching/counseling skills and helping educators develop programs to better serve the needs of their students. On another weekend, there is a conference for school board members and public school administrators. In 1990 a teacher and an administrator offered a workshop at one of these fall conventions to help educators develop a program to prepare schools to face crises, especially those involving student and staff grief following a death. Only one educator, an administrator, attended. He was there because of the recent suicide of a student. In light of the impact that grief has on students, on memory and on the learning process, the presenters were baffled at the apparent lack of response to a workshop whose value to educators seemed self evident.

In the spring of that same year, the administrator was presenting the same topic at another conference and the size of the crowd necessitated a second session since over 400 administrators wished to attend and the room held only 200. A poll of those attending showed that each of these administrators came from a school that had experienced a student or staff death that year. At both conferences there had been a variety of topics that could have been selected by the participants. The topic of coping with student loss and speakers were the same at each conference. The drastic shift in numbers was hard to understand. It seemed as though some educators saw a need for knowledge of how best to cope with trauma only in the *aftermath* of some traumatic event. Even then, this was a need that might soon be forgotten, if not addressed quickly. If that was the case, this type of thinking is certainly not new. In fact, it may well be many centuries old.

The quote that begins this chapter comes from Africa. When tracking an animal they have wounded, Namibian hunters will not speak about the object of their quest. They believe that to speak of it will cause it to grow stronger, while they will grow weaker. This traditional practice has been passed on for countless generations. It can be found in similar customs in Asia, Europe and among the native peoples of North America. There is some basis for this belief. Speaking of the greater speed, strength or cunning of the prey can be discouraging. To allow talk that causes people to focus on the difficulty of their task can be disheartening and may create failure as a type of self-fulfilling prophesy. However, it must be remembered that these hunters already know what to do from past experience, including planning and practice, and have developed the skills with which to accomplish their task.

A modern form of this proverb can be heard from concerned groups who say that crisis preparation is not effective, nor is it a task for schools. Further, there is no need for young people to learn about death, since it will not be part of their lives for many years and, it is assumed, they will not think of it unless we draw it to their attention. In extreme cases, these groups argue, such lessons may even cause traumatic events (such as youth suicide or violence) rather than prevent them or help young people cope with them when they do occur. The difference in maintaining silence in this case, is that schools may do so without first creating the plans for dealing with traumatic events or helping staff and students to develop the skills necessary to carry out such plans.

A traumatic event is one that involves a wound or emotional shock that can cause lasting physical or emotional damage. We believe that schools must be prepared to cope with physical injury or illness. For this reason we hire school nurses to be present in order to care for the health of students and to be present in event of an accident, serious injury or sudden illness. Most schools do not wait for such events to occur to decide where to turn for medical help. Medical programs are developed to track student health, monitor immunization compliance and provide regular health screening. The danger of exposure to blood-borne pathogens (Hepatitis-B, HIV, etc.) is addressed by instructing staff members on the use of universal precautions in dealing with student injury or illness.

We prepare to some extent for physical trauma to occur. Why are we reluctant to take the same precautions in relation to the possible emotional or psychological aftermath of a traumatic event? One possible explanation is that we do not fully under-stand the impact that traumatic events have on the functioning of a school.

EFFECTS ON STUDENTS

Traumatic events produce losses directly and have associated losses as well, whether actual or threatened. These include: loss of friends or loved ones, relationships, security, hope, health, feelings of trust or even the loss of childhood innocence. When dealing with these losses, children may react in any of a variety of ways. Both children and their schools must learn to cope with behaviors that may include emotional numbing, guilt, anger, fear of the future.

Emotional numbing can vary from a brief period of shock, to a reaction where children believe, in effect, that if feelings hurt this much, they will "refuse" to feel anything at all. Guilt and anger are often linked and may result in apathy (a withdrawing from life) or in acting out. This acting out from guilt and/or anger may be directed at others through verbal abuse or even physical vio-lence. Such violence may start as playful pushing or wrestling but can quickly turn serious. This violence may also be directed back at the child him/herself in a pattern of accidents, deliberate self-injury or punishment-seeking behavior. Fear of the future comes from a child's concern that the future is unknown and he/she may be unable to cope with crises that could arise in this un-known future. Examples of this fear may be seen in students who resist any further change in their lives or their environment. This can be taken to a point where a student may deliberately fail one or more required courses to avoid the changes, and possible losses, that would accompany graduation.

If they are not addressed, these fears may even develop into a type of free-floating anxiety. In such cases, every change requiring action on the part of the individual becomes an immediate crisis. The effects of anxiety on schoolwork have been demonstrated by a number of researchers. Students experience a shorter attention span and difficulty in concentrating, which is often accompanied by a drop in grades. In varying degrees many of these students perceive themselves to be helpless in coping with life and have shown signs of depression, increased episodes of daydreaming and withdrawal from socialization with peers. These students also complain of physical aches and pains more often than their peers.

Preparing Schools

It is now widely held that the most effective way of assisting people to cope more effectively with traumatic crises is to do so in advance of the actual event or situation. After the onset of a crisis there can be a period of "psychic annulment." This concept was first used by Caprio in 1950 to describe the difficulty people have assimilating information in times of crisis. He applied the concept to grief following a death, but it has wide applicability to any individual who has suffered a traumatic loss. Any attempt to develop and implement effective support systems for students or protocols for dealing with a crisis in the midst of that crisis or after they have experienced some traumatic event will probably not be effective. Such attempts, when they fail, may even make a difficult situation worse. In times of crisis, there is not the luxury of time: time for reflection, time for evaluation, time for education of staff and parents or time for intervention in a calm and thoughtful manner.

Programs now exist to help students, educators and parents to cope with traumatic events that many of them may one day face. These programs address grief and loss, youth suicide, health issues including both life threatening illness and sexually transmitted diseases), violence in our society (including assault, rape and violent death), and war (with its special impact on the military family).

Can school programs prevent or lessen the pain of loss, or prevent trauma in times of crisis? Quite probably, the answer is no. No program can prevent the pain of loss. No one program can address all possible effects of traumatic losses. However, if students and staff are prepared for possible traumatic losses, such preparation may keep the traumatic effects from being worse than they may otherwise be. In times of traumatic loss and its aftermath, people feel a loss of control over their lives. This is especially true in the case of children and adolescents who may already be dealing with feelings of helplessness from prior losses. It is also true of children who may feel powerless in a world run by adults. There are a number of programs that have been shown to help young people cope with a traumatic loss. These students have some points in common. These programs help students by increasing feelings of self-worth, show students how they can draw on support systems (such as family, friends, educators or religious advisors), help students to develop a belief that they can have some control over events in their lives, allow students to feel more secure in a hostile world, assist students to identify and cope with the feeling of guilt that may accompany a traumatic loss, explain the process of grief, explain that even when everything is done in the "right way" bad things can still happen and that these things (whether they include a death, a change in family structure, or an illness) are not necessarily anyone's fault.

The following recommendations may prove helpful to parents and educators who want to see their schools implement programs that can help young people to deal with traumatic loss.

Recommendation #1. Establish a committee of parents, educators and community resource personnel to develop a crisis response plan. When this task is assigned to one person or group, some community resources may not be identified, some responses may not be considered, some individuals or groups may be underutilized while others are burdened with unrealistic demands. Interested persons who do not have an opportunity to participate may react with anger, becoming a negative factor when crisis response plans are implemented.

It is important for every school to have a crisis response plan because key people in the school and the community are identified as part of such a plan. A clear chain of command is established, roles are assigned to staff members and all members of the school community are informed of available support and the fastest way to draw on that support.

Recommendation #2. Staff members should be trained to assist students in the wake of a traumatic loss. One of the most important roles assigned to staff members is to assist students to cope with the effects of traumatic loss. This task cannot be left to one or two people. There are often situations, such as the death of a student or staff member, where even the most capable individual would be quickly overwhelmed by the number of students wanting or needing help. Not every faculty member will be able to provide assistance to affected students. Not all educators have come to terms with their personal issues related to death and loss. Some staff members may not be able to speak with students about emotional issues, such as AIDS or other STDs. Assistance to students coping with traumatic loss may be too much for staff members who have had recent losses of their own.

Recommendation #3. Professional development programs must be provided for interested staff members and should be available to representatives from parent organizations and community groups. Such staff development programs should enable participants to:

- understand the components of the grief process;
- identify the signs of destructive or complicated grief;
- possess effective communication skills (active listening, discrete questioning, emotional support, appropriate advice and, when necessary, referral);
- utilize school and community resources effectively; and
- develop a knowledge of themselves, their students' needs, the established priorities of the school and community, and the *limits* of their ability to help.

Recommendation #4. Knowledge of the grief process should include the tasks of grieving: understanding, grieving, commemorating and moving on. The grief process is a starting point for recovery. Such recovery may be more difficult after a traumatic loss.

These four tasks were described by Sandra Fox and served as the basis for her "Good Grief Program" in Boston, Massachusetts. She believed that to successfully complete the grief process, a child needs to:

Understand: The child must understand that *death is universal.* All things that live will, one day, die. It is no one's fault that things are this way. This is simply part of life. The child must understand that the deceased person no longer feels anything because a dead body no longer functions as it once did. Finally, the child, apart from the religious beliefs of his/her family, must understand that the physical aspects of death are irreversible. *Death is permanent.*

Grieve: There are many feelings connected with bereavement, especially sadness, anger and guilt. The child must be able to both *experience* and to *express* the feelings that are part of the grief process. Following a traumatic loss, children may be unwilling to experience their feelings and, even if they do, may still be unable to express the feelings connected to the loss.

Commemorate: The child needs to remember the life of the person who died, both good things and bad, to *mourn the real person* who is gone. Where possible, the child should also play some role in helping to decide how the deceased will be remembered. There are some cases where this can be extremely difficult, as in the case of students who wanted to have a school-based memorial for a deceased classmate when the family was firm in stating that they wanted no memorial or ritual of any kind in the school.

Here is one case in which the need for both a chain of command and clear definition of staff roles is clear. It has been said that the essence of tragedy is the conflict of "right versus right." This sort of situation fits that definition exactly. Although many people may have input, the decision in a case such as this must be made at the highest levels in the chain of command. If anyone sets plans in motion prematurely, the results can hurt many people. The rights and needs of all parties must be considered to decide on an appropriate response and that decision must carry the full weight of the school administration.

Move on: When the child has moved through the grief process, he/she will need to take the final step of getting on with life. It is necessary to return to the business of being a child with all of the living, loving and learning that childhood entails.

An individual death or an injury to a friend or family member may, at first, present a crisis to a single child. However, this crisis extends to other members of the school community when this child returns to interact with teachers and classmates or when, as often happens, it is someone in the school community who was first asked to inform the child.

Recommendation #5. There must be clear guidelines available for any staff member who attempts to assist a student coping with a traumatic loss. The adults who offer support to students after a traumatic loss will ideally follow a set of basic guidelines. The following items form a starting point for such guidelines .

GUIDELINES FOR ASSISTING STUDENTS

- *Allow time for students to meet with teachers.* Following a traumatic loss, the needs of the student(s) must take priority over inflexible schedules.
- *Listen.* Pay attention to what the student is saying. Do not think of possible answers until he/she is finished.
- *Encourage the student to identify and list all of the issues to be discussed.* This may include both the recent loss and past losses still being dealt with by a student. Do not try to limit the student's list because the length of this list is not a problem. A long list may at first appear frightening or overwhelming, but it can also be used to show a young person how much strength they have shown in being able to cope with so many past losses.
- *Allow the student to establish priorities.* Ask the student, "What do you want to deal with first?" With this starting point, the student can identify the meaning he/she has given to each event.
- *Understand how the young person views the traumatic event.* If the student believes this loss has created a void, how will this void be filled? If it seen as an enemy, what resources will the student use to combat it? It may even offer some gain, such as a more stable environment after the protracted illness and

death of a family member. If so, how will the student cope with possible feelings of guilt?

- *Help the student distinguish between actual and anticipated losses.* Is the student more concerned with the effects of past and present losses, or with the possibility of losses in the future?

- *Stress the student's right to let others know his/her feelings.* If a student needs to talk about the loss, he/she has a right to do so. If the student wants others to be able to help or to understand his/her behavior, he/she has a responsibility to speak of his/her loss. A traumatic loss can make a person different. Others can be of help, but the student must be willing to let them.

- *Focus on one issue at a time.* This will avoid the overwhelming situation of trying to deal with several issues at once. It can also reduce the confusion of moving too quickly from one issue to another.

- *Remember that the schools's function is to educate the whole person.* Each student carries baggage in the form of a history containing personal events that can have a major effect on learning. A traumatic loss interacts with these events and cannot be dealt with in isolation. In the wake of traumatic loss, life can seem like a puzzle where no two pieces match and some are missing. Teachers and parents together can provide many of the pieces that the young person may need to make sense of this puzzle and to complete the picture of his/her future.

- *Remember that young people may see some losses as traumatic that would not be judged as that by serious adults.* With less experience of significant life events (deaths, divorce, violence), children and young adults may experience a loss as traumatic partly because such an experience is new to them. They have been thrust into a completely strange situation, and they can't be sure what will happen, or what they will feel, next.

- *Maintain regular lines of communication between school and home.* Home-school efforts to assist children following a traumatic loss must be marked by *cooperation,* not by competition. Children see clearly how well the important adults in their lives are coping with a traumatic loss. If educators and parents send contradictory messages, it will only complicate the recovery of the child. By keeping home–school communication open, such apparent contradictions may be minimized.

- *Support efforts must be appropriate to the age and developmental level of the child and to a school setting.* Young children may seek more physical contact at home in the form of hugs and kisses. In a school setting, such physical contact could present problems. A close substitute would be to allow the child to sit near an adult during some activities, or to assign him/her a role in helping the teacher. The child can then feel special or close by working with the teacher in a special way. Adolescents may not wish to be singled out in any class setting. Their communications and contact related to their loss will often be kept private. They may want class to go on as usual to reinforce the feeling that there are still things in life that are not touched by the loss, that are as they were before the loss occurred.

Recommendation #6. Schools must build into their response plans the understanding that a cause of death can magnify the traumatic effects of that loss. Some causes of death can produce a grief reaction that is different from that which follows a death caused by illness or accident. Suicide is such a cause. Those who are alive after someone they loved, knew or identified with dies as the result of a completed suicide are called *survivors of suicide.* The grief of these survivors is different for one or more of the following reasons: The death is sudden and seldom anticipated, is often violent, takes place in the presence of other stressors, accentuates feelings of regret and/or guilt, causes survivors to feel a loss of control over their lives. This loss of control is made worse by a flood of emotions, and survivors feel they are being avoided by others. A death from AIDS can also complicate the grief reaction and create a situation in which young people may have special needs. AIDS-related grief can produce:

- *isolation*—friends of family members of the deceased being avoided through fear or misunderstanding.
- *lack of social support*—memorials or other rituals that typically follow a death are sometimes not available after an AIDS-related death.

- *feelings of guilt*—social sanctions may cause special feelings of guilt for those students who were friends of the deceased, or who believe they have engaged in high-risk behavior.
- *anger/violence*—Strong emotions may be released within the school community and if there is no outlet provided, these feelings can produce incidents of violence.

Recommendation #7. School response plans must accommodate the broadest possible use since death is not the only traumatic loss that today's young people may face. Violence in our schools is growing at a rapid rate. It might comfort some to think that this is a phenomenon linked only to inner-city schools, but violence is reaching into every area of the country with greater frequency. It may be the random violence of a drive-by "gang-banging" or the more selective violence of an act of self-destruction. When a violent attack takes place or a death has occurred as the result of violence, the pain and confusion left in its wake can touch every student in a school, or in many schools. However, the possibility of violence is a crisis that is faced by students and by schools across the country on a daily basis. Such a loss of feelings of security is, in itself, a traumatic loss for some. Some schools have reacted to an episode of violence by starting programs to address students' feelings of a lack of security and their need to address issues involving personal safety. Now is the time for all schools to become proactive by addressing these needs among their students, and a possible side-effect may well be the prevention of the violence itself.

A similar conclusion can be drawn about health issues connected to HIV and AIDS. A school can deny the real risk confronting students who may be sexually active or be engaged in other behaviors, such as drug abuse. They can say that no deaths have occurred or that no students are yet known to be HIV positive. However, television, radio, movies, and newspapers are filled with stories on a daily basis that show the immunity students feel, and schools seemingly reinforce with silence, is only an illusion. Although it may not be as openly acknowledged as the concern over violence, the possibility of contracting an HIV infection is one that exists in every school in this country. We can again try to distance ourselves with myths. Just as we might want to believe that violence only takes place in urban schools, we may try to draw comfort from the belief in the myth that

AIDS is a gay disease. By focusing on, and isolating, one element of the school community, this illusion can reduce anxiety for many in the short term, but in the long run it may prove fatal for some and can be harmful for everyone. If parents and educators work together now to help our children, it can avoid the finger-pointing and accusations later, when it may too late for some young people and the crises faced by the survivors will have multiplied.

Recommendation #8. Continue to support communication among all concerned parties after a traumatic loss. Silence, even with the best of intent, serves only to isolate people and may cause them to be further traumatized. Some people remain silent to avoid causing further pain. The pain comes from the loss and its effects, not from speaking about it. Communication after a loss may be painful, but it also helps with healing by allowing the externalization of emotions and fears in a supportive atmosphere.

CONCLUSION

The emotional health and physical safety of our children are clearly issues that are both serious and decisive. When a traumatic event affects a school community, it can be almost impossible to ignore. When one or more its members must cope with traumatic loss, a school community must act in ways that will aid recovery if we are to avoid the death of academic learning, of emotional growth, of personal potential, of optimism and dreams.

The trial-and-error methods of coping with traumatic loss employed by many young people have been less than effective because these young people often fail to utilize the support systems available to them. A common technique with which young people attempt to deal with crises is denial. This offers some short term relief from stress, but does not provide a method facing issues any more effectively in the future. School systems that do not acknowledge the losses of their students are also practicing denial.

Prior planning is the most effective way for schools to prepare students and staff to deal with the losses we may encounter in life. It takes courage to step forward and offer help when some-one has suffered a traumatic loss since this act involves people in situations they might have chosen to avoid. It can take even greater courage for a school community to plan in advance for ways to respond to possible losses. There will be those who will not understand, who will quote the old proverbs.

To speak of *this* enemy will give strength. However, it will not be to the death or other loss, it will be to those who must cope with it. If we are willing to speak about possible losses, about the pain of traumatic loss, and about our planned response, such talk will give strength to us and our ability to help those in our care. If we design and carry out a comprehensive plan, we may even begin a new proverb:

To speak of an enemy gives us strength.

17. Government's Role in Disaster Response

LAURA BOYD, PH. D.

I am a member of the House of Representatives of the State of Oklahoma and additionally practice as a marriage and family therapist, a career I have enjoyed for over 20 years. I also have experience as a Registered Traumatologist, having worked numerous instate disasters and several national disasters beginning with the Oakland earthquake of 1989. All of my training, all of my experience as a clinician (including much work with oncology patients and their families) and all of the study for my Ph.D. in counseling psychology could not have predicted the skills necessary to respond as an elected lawmaker nor as the leader for one of the crisis debriefing teams following the April 19, 1995, bombing in Oklahoma City.

I have the luxury of hindsight and self-analysis, supported by personal written notes over the 45 days immediately following the April tragedy. Yet I am fully aware of being only midstream in our recovery process as a community, a state and a nation. There is no escaping my continued responsibility as healer and facilitator required particularly by the profile of public office.

I continue to be personally touched, to be poignantly reminded of my public responsibility, and to be individually thrust into my own healing needs as a result of the unique opportunity of traveling this nation attending various professional meetings within the realm of my normal duties and being sought out by Americans from all walks of life who have not yet had the opportunity to express their pain, grief or impotence over this tragedy and who desperately need to do so.

All loss is traumatic. Whether we are enduring the loss of a job, a relationship, a loved one, a pet or a wallet, each of these are losses; and the singularly defining difference is simply one of degree.

Indeed, mass trauma is unique in terms of the numbers of victims versus the number of unscathed helping professionals or leaders who are available for response. In mass trauma events the necessary amount of resources required for responding can be overwhelming: physical resources such as ground crews, security, medical teams; emotional crews such as debriefing teams, therapists, friends and family; spiritual teams such as chaplains and clergy; and financial needs for such basics as housing, eyeglasses and transportation. Broad scale group trauma or mass trauma demands exorbitant amounts of these resources. It demands timeliness and accessibility to resources. It demands coordination of numerous individuals, agencies, and functions; and it demands accountability to victims, their families and the public at large.

Traumatologists are aware that underlying all of these notable and predictable demands in times of crisis exists the basic principle that only early and comprehensive response to each level of need will prevent future secondary tragedies from occurring.

There are numerous similarities in mass trauma and individual trauma or family disaster. Trauma is often defined as any in-stance over which we have no control and yet suffer subsequent loss. The importance of the issue of control and lack of control cannot be overestimated. *Our* recovery deserves *our* direction and definition of need and respect for *our* timing. Whether as individuals or as a larger collective body of citizens, five ques-tions must be answered before the circle of healing can reach conclusion: 1) what happened? 2) why did it happen? 3) why did I do what I did when it happened? 4) will it happen? 5) what will I do if it happens again?

Another similarity of individual or family trauma and mass trauma is that victims experience a shattering of belief systems and an altering of function and expectation at multiple levels: physical, emotional, psychological, spiritual and perhaps finan-cial. As part of the healing process, each of us needs to tell our own story. We need to tell it in our own way and as many times as is individually necessary in order to experience some mastery of the incident.

As for my own experience of the April 19th bombing, I was aware within two minutes of the tragedy a mile from the Capitol. Stories circulated immediately of a daycare center being involved.

My initial response was to encourage individuals to carefully seek accurate data as soon as possible, an awkward attempt yet an important one to keep hysteria minimized.

Fearing additional security vulnerabilities, the State Capitol was formally evacuated within approximately two hours of the original blast. Heading to my home district, 30 miles south of Oklahoma City on the Interstate, I felt the surreal nature of a science fiction movie. Exits from the Interstate to downtown were blocked off and secured by law officers. Radios and televisions blasted facts and rumors continually in an attempt to keep the public informed. Cellular phones were restricted for emergency channels only. I was passed by more than a dozen speeding patrol cars headed to the disaster site in response to a statewide call for help. *Everyone* was focused particularly on the plight of the children!

Unique to mass trauma and its recovery process are two elements: the cultural perspective in which the trauma occurs and those stories needed by individuals and groups in order to endure.

Whether technically accurate or not, Oklahoma has a statewide and national image of being in the middle of the Bible Belt, and of being conservative both religiously and politically. Politics, government and professionals in general are often popular targets of skepticism. Therapy and mental health are still very slowly being accepted as health options. For much of the population the need for counseling or mental health services is perceived as an embarrassment and/or weakness. Simultaneously Oklahomans are known for and are proud of their independence and self-sufficiency.

As with any tragedy, the bombing of April 19th provided a brief window of opportunity for Oklahomans and for the nation to examine our belief systems and to reevaluate archaic, constraining ideologies. Oklahoma certainly met this challenge. Today across this nation reference is made to the "Oklahoma standard", i.e., a tough, thorough, persevering and caring banner of citizen response. Suddenly, leadership became trustworthy. Needing help was not a sign of weakness; it became an opportunity to demonstrate care for one another.

Our next challenge and the challenge of America is to maintain those newly evidenced aspects of our belief systems and abilities. We must incorporate these behaviors as permanent resources of both our reality and our mythology.

Cultural stories provide the strength necessary to face our losses and to demand a recovery. "God gives us no more than we can handle" is a underlying principal of Oklahoma existence. From the time of the land rush and the dust bowl, to the heartbreak of the Bombing, this premise has provided the strength and fortitude that we need as individuals and as community.

The first 18 days after the bombing saw extremes the typical fluctuating climate of Oklahoma. Torrential rains, painful windchills, periods of sauna-like temperatures and the dramatically fluctuating force with which these changes occurred are not strange patterns to Oklahomans. At the same time their abruptness required one more set of accommodations on behalf of a grieving populace. "God's tears" was the description bestowed on the elements of rain and cold. Explanations of "God's grieving" on days when it seemed the rain made no sense and of "gifts from God" for days when the cold seemed unbearable were heralded. Indeed, all were aware that the potential of finding victims alive and bodies in a condition to be identified would be supported by cold weather.

The role demonstrated by government in mass trauma defines the complexity and efficiency of the recovery process. It is my belief that the purpose of government in general, in good times and bad, is to make recovery possible and to give individuals the opportunity to take care of themselves. Some elected officials believe it is important for "government to get out of the way" so that individuals can do it themselves. There is a slight and important difference in these two philosophies. Self-responsibility is the goal in both. However, responsibility without opportunity is useless to a single parent with needy children, to an unemployed family or to a young adult who sees no hope of improving the plight of the next generation.

I believe that government must respond to its constituents in both symbolic and substantive ways.

As is the case with any professional responding to individual trauma, government in response to mass trauma must a) listen and b) demonstrate accountability. We have already discussed the importance to the individual of "telling their story" in as many ways and as many times as necessary. In mass trauma this requirement also exists. Victims and their families must have access to accurate information throughout the traumatic and post-traumatic periods. They demand a government that demonstrates not only listening, but a willingness to hear and therefore respond.

In the case of the Oklahoma City bombing, state workers were also victims either directly from the bombing or from the displacement of their work sites or from their individual heroic responses to the rescue of other bombing victims. Through our willingness to listen and to demonstrate a responsiveness to all those affected, government sends the reassuring message that it cares and is competent to respond.

Government must be accountable for the actions of itself as an entity in those decisions made on behalf of the populace whether good or bad, graceful or awkward, right or wrong in retrospect. Government must also be accountable to the group of victims as a whole. Families, individuals, rescue workers, state employees, etc. will all have needs that must be validated and attended. Simultaneously, government cannot package a response and hand it out as though a one-size fits-all approach will work. As elected officials we must all be cognizant of the different feelings and behaviors and levels of impact on numerous individuals affected by the trauma.

In mass trauma if government will be accessible and swift in its response, then citizens receive the message of competence and power in its leaders. If government behaves decisively, the people are reassured. If government is sincere and flexible in tailoring its interactions with various groups and individuals, the people experience their leaders as responsive and respectful. If government gives itself the latitude for innovation and creativity in times of crisis, it will be known to the citizens as personal and protective. Like any good parent the role of Big Brother Government in times of mass crisis is to repeatedly demonstrate its caring and its competence.

Finally and equally important government can offer avenues for all those desiring to be involved in the response effort to have an important and valued role. There are many tasks from soliciting donations to carrying out specifically defined needs and actions. Through its organizational capacity, government can offer avenues for citizen action. It must be willing to recognize not only the suffering but also the most minor contributions of all involved in the recovery effort.

Our experience in Oklahoma has led to some specific clarifications and redefinitions by our state government as direct result of this bombing experience. With a little help, we have come to recognize and define victims as those who were either physically and/or emotionally and mentally impacted by this bombing. We have recognized the parity of biomedical and mental health professionals in responding to the treatment of victims. We likewise remain acutely respectful of the power and potential from local units of control whether those be governmental bodies and entities, or families, or health care organizations.

For most, it is clear that in time of mass trauma there is no appropriate venue for a moments indulgence of political sparring or partnership. Our tasks presently are to continue our healing and to maintain our awareness of these gifts of learning.

The world hopes along with us that these acts of terrorism are never repeated. At the same time, there is a backdrop of basic considerations which each unit of government whether local or state can provide to facilitate the recovery effort of a mass trauma. The first major area includes that of health care reform. States can facilitate their response effort by providing the opportunity for citizens to predetermine advance directives for their own health care in terminal situations. Accessibility for citizens to treatment, inclusion of home care medical services, parity of biomedical and mental health needs, and freedom to choose a variety of desired professionals allow for a health care system most responsive to large numbers of affected citizens.

The second major area providing a backdrop for response is that of insurance reform. States can address this arena of debate prior to tragedy. Whether each state prefers some mechanism for universal coverage, small group insurance reform, the development of risk pools, the availability of medical IRAs, etc., insurance reform must be a political topic of this decade.

Thirdly, states must have an efficient and comprehensive disaster plan in place. This plan must not only be on paper, but must be supported with adequate and frequent training and exercise.

Perhaps the most important cultural arena in which all states and all citizens can participate and impact our future is that of violence prevention. Until we as a human race recognize that violence and crime are not synonymous and therefore that reducing crime does not equate with preventing violence, we will be forced to restrict our dwindling resources to the arenas of building prisons and responding incrementally where tragedy strikes. We must recognize the cultural violence that permeates our media, especially in film. We must reallocate our resources to support families at whatever juncture they experience turmoil in the crossroads of life. That support could be teaching young parents how to work with infant and preschool children, or it could be supporting families through the teenage years. Wherever we invest preventive and supportive resources, we are also investing in a future that can become violence-free. Violence is not a fact of life anymore than the bubonic plague, which was once considered a fact of life. With the skills, knowledge, experience and resources we have available, we can create a culture of nonviolence.

The Oklahoma Legislature passed numerous pieces of both substantive and symbolic legislation as a result of the April bombing. The following is a list of those bills and resolutions passed between April 24 and May 26, 1995, by this legislature in response to the bombing of the Alfred P. Murrah Federal Building, Oklahoma City, in which 169 innocent victims died. Our current responsibilities as a government are to see that these measures are fully and expeditiously enacted and to remain accessible to as yet-to-be identified requirements for the healing of a state population of three and a quarter million citizens.

LEGISLATION RELATED TO THE BOMBING OF THE ALFRED P. MURRAH FEDERAL BUILDING

The legislative session was deeply affected by the tragic bombing of the federal building in Oklahoma City on April 19, 1995. In response to the tragedy and the weeks of rescue, search, and recovery efforts, the Legislature passed numerous bills and resolutions.

Substantive

SCR 25 creates a 20-member Joint Legislative Commission on the Alfred P. Murrah Federal Building Disaster Response for coordinating the state response to the disaster. The Commission were required to report by October 1, 1995, the state's share for funding needs arising from the bombing.

HB 1706 creates the Murrah Crime Victims Compensation Act, administered by the Administrator of the Oklahoma Crime Victims Compensation Board. Monies received for the program can be used to compensate victims and families of victims involved in the bombing tragedy.

HJR 1047 authorizes paid administrative leave for April 19 through May 19, 1995, for state employees who had immediate family members killed or missing as a result of the bombing.

HB 1462, among other provisions, excludes those benefit wages paid to an employee who was separated from employment as a direct result of a natural disaster, fire, flood or explosion on and after April 19, 1995, from benefit wages charged against an employer for persons claiming unemployment compensation.

SCR 24 urges members of Oklahoma's congressional delegation to seek federal assistance to pay for repair costs incurred by the City of Oklahoma City and Oklahoma State Government.

HB 1722 appropriates $100,000 for district attorneys to prosecute persons involved in the bombing.

Symbolic

HB 1249 creates the "Heart of the Heartland License Plates" to honor victims of the bombing. The fee for the special plates will be $25 above other vehicle registration fees, $20 of which is to be deposited to the Heart of the Heartland Scholarship Fund created by the bill. The fund is created as a trust fund with the members of the State Board of Higher Regents as trustees. Funds are to be used to educate students in state supported higher education institutions who were injured in the bombing or children of bombing victims who attend state supported higher education institutions who were injured in the bombing or children of bombing victims who attend state-supported colleges or universities.

SB 412 authorizes the awarding of the Oklahoma Alfred P. Murrah Service Medal to members of the Oklahoma National Guard, nonuniformed employees of the Oklahoma Military Department and other persons deemed appropriate by the Adjutant General for service in the disaster relief operations.

SR 16 urges broadcasters and sponsors of the "G. Gordon Liddy Show" and other talk shows that encourage hate and violence to withdraw their financial support.

HCR 1030, HCR 1044, HCR 1056, SR 14, SR 1, and *SR 20* express the state's deep gratitude for the efforts of federal, state, local, private and volunteer workers who responded to the tragedy.

HR 1027 praises the efforts of New York Task Force One, a coalition from the police and fire departments and the emergency service unit of New York City. The Legislature praised the Oklahoma media for their extensive broadcasting during the tragedy, the ethical conduct of journalists and the media's role in collecting supplies.

HCR 1057 commended State Trooper Charles Hanger for his arrest of bombing suspect Timothy J. McVeigh near the Billings exit on I-35.

Conclusion

KENNETH J. DOKA, PH.D.

There are five critical points that thread through the concluding chapters.

1. Grief is a highly individual reaction.

No one experiences or copes with a loss, whether sudden or similar, in the same way. Each person responds very individually to loss. As the chapters in the book indicate, this can be the result of many factors including:

- The nature and quality of the relationship with the deceased
- The circumstances and type of loss
- Psychological aspects of the bereaved including their grieving styles and coping strengths
- The availability of social support
- Cultural and spiritual factors
- The presence of concurrent crises and stressors

When dealing with bereaved, it is essential to explore that unique experience of loss and develop suitable interventions based on the needs and style of the individual.

2. Different types of sudden loss create unique issues for survivors.

While grief is a highly individual experience, we also recognize that each situation of loss creates special issues for survivors. It is helpful for counselors to recognize the distinct stressors of each particular type of loss. For example, the involvement of media and the criminal justice system may complicate grief for survivors of suicide, homicide and disasters. In accidents, the perceptions of preventability may generate intense guilt and pain. Caregivers working with such survivors need to educate themselves on the particular problems of different losses. This knowledge can help as they advocate for their clients and validate and explore client responses. We do not minimize the individuality of loss. Each survivor will react and cope in his or her own way.

3. Survivors of sudden loss are often coping simultaneously with both grief and the loss of their normal world.

Survivors of sudden loss face two difficulties. First, they are coping with significant losses. These may include not only the death of someone they have loved, but in the case of accident or disaster, may involve multiple losses. In addition, there may be many secondary losses as well. These refer to other losses that are related to the primary loss. For example, in an automobile accident, one may lose a car and injure oneself, even be party to a lawsuit or criminal case.

In addition to these losses, there may be a loss to one's sense of normalcy. We may assume that the world is generally a safe and predictable place. One gets in a car, goes to work and then returns home. A sudden loss may make one feel that the world is a very dangerous place so that even simple acts now cause anxiety. In short, sudden loss assaults a sense of safety and predictability. Often that sense of safety has to be addressed early in the interventive process.

4. Survivors of sudden loss need both short and long term intervention.

Many of the chapters have emphasized the need for survivors to receive counseling. Yet these chapters have also stressed that this interventive process needs to be phased over the short and long term. One of the great strengths of Critical Incident Stress De-briefing (CISD) is that it provides a mode of approach that includes both short- and long-term interventions. Whatever process is used, the role of ritual can be a critical tool.

5. Caregivers at all levels may be affected by traumatic loss so self-care is critical.

Many of the chapters have emphasized the extensive effects of sudden and traumatic loss. In many cases, all the caregivers, on all levels may be affected. For example, in a horrible fire two adolescents were killed. Their deaths troubled not only surviving family and friends but a host of others such as firefighters, emergency personnel, police, funeral director and the mother's counselor.

In such situations self-care is critical. Some of this is the responsibility of caregivers themselves. Caregivers need to acknowledge and validate their own needs, practice effective lifestyle management, find respite and tap into their own spirituality. But part of this is an organizational responsibility as well. Organizations should provide opportunities for ongoing support such as debriefings, support groups, rituals, opportunities for individual counseling and in-service education. Even in the midst of crisis taking care of caregivers remains a critical priority.

6. Communities need to be proactive.

It would be nice to think we can eliminate sudden loss. That would, of course, be impossible. Yet this does not mean we can ignore the root causes. Many times, sudden losses are in fact preventable. In addition, we can develop effective ways to intervene. While each situation is idiosyncratic, there are policies and procedures that can be in place. For example, police and emergency room personnel can be trained in humane ways to break bad news. Organizations such as schools or governments should have policies, procedures and crisis teams in place. These plans should be periodically reviewed.

Any book, especially one produced for a teleconference, has a certain incompleteness. Surely there are far more areas of sudden loss to explore, from natural disasters and accidents and sudden infant death syndrome to the reactions of involved caregivers such as nurses. Unfortunately every work has limits to comprehensiveness.

We hope that both this book and the teleconference itself will help educate a wide range of caregivers on the distinct issues raised after sudden loss. For in few other types of loss is the need for care so profound.

18. An Annotated Resource List on Traumatic Loss

MARY BETH WILLIAMS
WITH THE ASSISTANCE OF MICHELLE LEDBETTER

Books on Trauma for Professionals

Baures, M. (1994). *Undaunted spirits: Portraits of recovery from trauma.* Philadelphia, PA: The Charles Press. This book includes 16 face-to-face interviews with resilient, well-known individuals who have had positive transformations after traumatic events. Creativity is one major means to go beyond trauma.

Figley, C. R. (Ed.) (1985). *Trauma and its wake: The study and treatment of post-traumatic stress disorder.* New York: Brunner/Mazel. This classic work examines the effects of stressful events on a variety of populations including survivors of crime, rape and catastrophe. Chapters on treatment of children, incest survivors and others offer helpful models of clinical intervention that are applicable today.

Figley, C. R. (Ed.) (1986). *Trauma and its wake, Vol. II: Traumatic stress theory, research and intervention.* New York: Brunner/Mazel. This book presents theory, research data and intervention programs and methods for the treatment of PTSD. Of particular interest to those in the field of loss and bereavement are chapters dealing with the mobilization of support networks, family counseling and post-traumatic adaptation of homicide survivor victims.

Figley, C. R. (Ed.) (1995). *Compassion fatigue: Coping with secondary traumatic stress disorder in those who treat the traumatized.* New York: Brunner/Mazel. This book focuses on crisis and trauma counselors who become victim to secondary traumatic stress disorder or "compassion fatigue" as a result of helping or wanting to help a traumatized person. The 11 chapters address characteristics of traumatized caregivers and effective prevention programs and provide varied case examples as well as theoretical models.

Foy, D. W. (Ed.) (1992). *Treating PTSD: Cognitive-behavioral strategies.* New York: The Guilford Press. The volume provides behavioral strategies to assess and treat survivors of combat, battering and sexual assault. It includes basic treatment principles to apply across different types of trauma that fall under the rubric of cognitive-behavioral interventions.

Gibson, M. (1991). *Order from chaos: Responding to traumatic events.* Birmingham, England: Venture Press. This book outlines the plans, training, techniques and self-care skills that can be used by professional and volunteer helpers in crisis situations, particularly disasters. An entire chapter deals with the emotional needs of the bereaved during and after crises.

Harway, M. (Ed.) (1995). *Treating the changing family: Handling normative and unusual events.* New York: John Wiley & Sons, Inc. This new book provides an overview of issues and problems faced by today's families and how to survive them. Among the issues covered in terms of how they impact family functioning are trauma, illness and AIDS.

Hudnall-Stamm, B. (Ed.) (1995). *Secondary traumatic stress: Self-care issues for clinicians, researchers and educators.* Lutherville, MD: Sidran Press. This book is a compilation of writings to help professionals deal with ongoing exposure to traumatic material. It addresses clinical and ethical issues.

Herman, J. (1992). *Trauma and recovery.* Glenview, IL: Basic Books. This comprehensive text looks at the diagnosis and treatment of traumatic disorders. It includes an examination of the concept of complex PTSD. The stages of recovery that are discussed in detail are safety, remembrance and mourning, and reconnection. Mourning involves the resolution of traumatic loss.

James, B. (1989). *Treating traumatized children: New insights and creative interventions.* Lexington, MA: Lexington Books. This comprehensive book provides specific guidance and tools for treating children who have been traumatized in a variety of situations. It includes assessment instruments and exercises.

Janoff-Bulman, R. (1992). *Shattered assumptions: Towards a new psychology of trauma.* New York: The Free Press. Traumatic events shatter victims' fundamental assumptions that the world is safe, kind and meaningful and that the self is worthy. This book examines the impact of traumatic events, including sudden losses leading to complicated bereavement and provides strategies to help survivors integrate those events into their lives.

Journal of Traumatic Stress. Published four times a year by Plenum Press. 233 Spring Street. New York, NY 10013.

Matsakis, A. (1994). *Post-traumatic stress disorder: A complete treatment guide.* Oakland, CA: New Harbinger Publications. This book is designed to serve as an introduction to PTSD and its treatment for clinicians who want to learn how to work with survivors of trauma. Numerous exercises and client handouts are included. It is a preliminary overview of the field.

Meichenbaum, D. (1994). *A clinical handbook/practical therapist manual for assessing and treating adults with post-traumatic stress disorder.* Waterloo, Ontario, Canada: Institute Press. This book is the result of a two-year project designed to summarize relevant literature and provide a practical clinical guidebook that looks at skills. It also includes a critical analysis of current PTSD intervention practice.

Ochberg, F. M. (Ed.) (1988). *Post-traumatic therapy and victims of violence.* New York: Brunner/Mazel. This volume examines treatment of a variety of traumatic, violent events. Relevant to persons working with traumatic loss and bereavement are chapters dealing with the homicide of a child and the crime victims' movement, as well as general chapters on treatment issues.

Pearlman, L. A., & Saakvitne, K. W. (1995) *Trauma and the therapist: Countertransference and vicarious traumatization in psychotherapy with incest survivors.* New York: W. W. Norton. This book addresses the needs of therapists who work with traumatized individuals and explores the role and experience of the therapist in that therapeutic relationship. The authors offer many suggestions to avoid countertransference/vicarious traumatization.

Peterson, K. C., Prout, M., & Schwarz, R. A. (1991). *Post-traumatic stress disorder: A clinician's guide.* New York: Plenum Press. Part I of this book deals with the diagnosis and assessment of PTSD; Part II presents an excellent overview of a variety of models of PTSD and theoretical explanations. Part III outlines therapeutic interventions in the areas of psychotherapy, behavioral treatment, hypnotherapy, group treatment, work with children and families and pharmacology.

Saigh, P. A. (Ed.) (1992). *Posttraumatic stress disorder: A behavioral approach to assessment and treatment.* Boston, MA: Allyn & Bacon. This book presents an integrated approach to the assessment and treatment of PTSD in victims of rape, abduction, combat, physical abuse and natural disasters.

Scott, M. J., & Stradling, S. G. (1992). *Counseling for post-traumatic stress disorder.* London, England: Sage Publications. This book provides clear, detailed guidelines to counsel clients with PTSD from single, dramatic events as well as enduring circumstances. The authors present a variety of techniques and illustrative cases to treat PTSD and concurrent anxiety, depression and irritability.

Sorensen, E. S. (1993). *Children's stress and coping: A family perspective.* New York: The Guilford Press. This book examines how stress is perceived by children in the family setting. It includes appraisal strategies and suggests needed research projects.

Tedeschi, R. G., & Calhoun, L. G. (1995). *Trauma and transformation: Growth in the aftermath of suffering.* Thousand Oaks, CA: Sage. This book is designed to help readers focus on positive outcomes of trauma and traumatic loss, using a cognitive framework that incorporates elements of self-constructivist development theory of McCann and Pearlman. It looks at ways to help survivors of trauma and traumatic loss examine and change their belief systems to cultivate compassion and understanding and includes a model of personal coping.

Ursano, R. J., McGaughey, B. G., & Fullerton, C. S. (Eds.) (1994). *Individual and community responses to trauma and disaster: The structure of human chaos.* New York: Cambridge University Press. The authors show that a sense of order and predictability of human responses exists after the chaos of disaster and trauma. The reality of the world as global village makes disaster planning a necessity. Psychological effects of trauma, including traumatic loss, are illustrated in a variety of settings.

Watts, R., & de L. Horne, D. J. (Eds.) (1994). *Coping with trauma: The victim and the helper.* Brisbane, Australia: Australian Academic Press. This readable, practical book examines the nature of trauma and the impact of traumatic experiences on both victim and helper. Of interest to readers are chapters on traumatic accidents and large-scale road accidents that often result in sudden, traumatic death and complicated bereavement reactions.

Williams, M. B., & Sommer, J. F., Jr. (Eds.) (1994). *Handbook of post-traumatic therapy.* Westport, CT: Greenwood Press. This extensive, edited work is designed as a practical resource for the treatment of a variety of traumatic events that involve loss, grief and bereavement reactions. Treatment protocols for survivors of homicide, disaster, abuse, school crises, torture and other populations are included, as are chapters describing the importance of providing safety in the therapy setting and ethical issues of treatment designed as a practical resource for the treatment of a variety of traumatic events, which involve loss, grief and bereavement reactions.

Wilson, **J. P.** (1989). *Trauma, transformation and healing: An integrative approach to theory, research and post-traumatic therapy.* New York: Brunner/ Mazel. Wilson's interactive model of PTSD has been extremely helpful in conceptualizing the interaction of stressor, person and environmental aspects in healing. Wilson is particularly interested in the role of modulating factors between stressor and outcome. This book also lists general intervention strategies and principles for treatment of trauma.

Wilson, **J. P.**, **& Raphael**, **B.** (Eds.) (1993). *International handbook of traumatic stress syndromes.* New York: Plenum Press. This multi-authored, 84-chapter text covers major areas of trauma research, intervention and theory relating to war, disaster, children, torture, social policy, Critical Incident Stress Debriefing (CISD) and work. The book is heavily weighted toward quantitative studies.

Young, **M. A.** (1993). *Victim assistance: Frontiers and fundamentals.* Washington, DC: NOVA & Dubuque, IO: Kendall/Hunt Publishing Co. This comprehensive manual for professionals deals with victims of crime and presents training in outline form. It also includes guidelines for the administration of victim service programs.

Young, **M. A.** (1994). *Responding to communities in crisis: The training manual of the Crisis Response Team.* Washington, D.C.: NOVA and Dubuque, IA: Kendall/ Hunt Publishing Co. This manual, presented in outline format, is a textbook for crisis team training. It includes lessons on dealing with emotional aftermath of catastrophes.

Books for Child Survivors of Trauma

Alexander, **D. W.** (1992). *Books for Children: It happened to me: A story for child victims of crime or trauma. I can't remember. Something bad happened: A story for children who have felt the impact of crime or trauma. All my feelings: A story for children who have felt the impact of crime or trauma.* Huntington, NY: Bureau for At-risk Youth. These coloring/workbooks are designed for early elementary school students. They identify the various components of PTSD and help with healing.

Alexander, **D. W.** (1993). *Books for Teens: The way I feel: A story for teens coping with crime or trauma. It happened in Autumn: A story for teens coping with a loved one's homicide.* Huntington, NY: Bureau for At-risk Youth. These two books are part of a 6-volume series designed for teens who have been exposed to crime and trauma. They are short and include space for completing exercises.

Davis, N. (1988). *Once upon a time: Therapeutic stories to heal abused children.* Oxon Hill, MD: Author. This compilation of short stories is designed to help children (and adults) deal with a variety of issues that are a result of trauma and abuse. Stories are metaphorical and can stimulate discussion and treatment.

Davis, N. (1995). *Audio tape: Stories for traumatized children.* Oxon Hill, MD; Author.

Books for School Professionals and Others Who Develop Programs for Children

Beckmann, R. (1990). *Children who grieve: A manual for conducting support groups.* Holmes Beach, FL: Learning Publications, Inc. This workbook provides guidelines for support groups and handouts for exercises.

Capuzzi, D. (1994). *Suicide prevention in the schools: Guidelines for middle and high school settings.* Alexandria, VA: American Counseling Association. This book includes lessons designed to develop and prepare a crisis team, inservice guidelines, group counseling options, classroom presentations and parent education workshops. A variety of handouts are available.

Cull, J. G. & Giel, W. S. (1992). *Suicide probability scale.* Los Angeles, CA: Western Psychological Services. This 36-item scale uses a four-point Likert Scale to identify four subscales of suicidality, including hopelessness, suicidal ideation, negative self-evaluation and hostility. It is a quickly scored screening device designed for adolescents and adults (Ages 13 +). It can be used as a way to monitor and document changes in ideation.

Dunne, E., McIntosh, J., & Dunne-Maxim, K. (1987). *Suicide and its aftermath: Understanding and counseling the survivors.* New York: W. W. Norton & Co. This book offers essays addressing many perspectives of suicide. Special chapters deal with sibling survival and adolescent suicide.

Haasl, B., & Marnocha, J. (1990). *Bereavement support group program for children: Manual and workbook.* Muncie, IL: Accelerated Development, Inc. This leader's manual and participant's workbook for five-session programs for grieving children ages 5–15 includes basic outlines and supplemental activities. It deals with internal processing of grief as well as external, public expression of mourning. A reading list for each session is included.

Hannaford, M. J., & Popkin, M. (1992). *Windows: Healing and helping through loss.* Atlanta, GA: Active Parenting, Inc. This full-video based program with a leader's guide is designed for loss education for teens and adults. It focuses on the needs of individuals who have experienced loss as well as those who want to be helpers. It can be used as a crisis-intervention program.

Johnson, S. W., & Maile, L. J. (1987). *Suicide and the schools.* Springfield, IL: Charles C. Thomas. This book discusses issues of prevention, intervention and postvention as well as characteristics of at-risk students and responsibilities of school staff. It also includes suggestions for conducting suicide prevention workshops.

Lagoro, J. (1993). *Life cycle: Classroom activities for helping children live with daily change and loss.* Tucson, AZ: Zephyr Press. Elementary-level activities for children who have experienced major losses are included in this book.

Landy, L., (1988). *Child support through small group counseling.* Mt. Dora, FL: Kidsrights. A death counseling group program is included in this selection of small group counseling protocols for children ages 6–12.

Machin, L. (1993). *Working with young people in loss situations.* Harlow Essex, England: Longman Group. This collection of worksheets and trigger pictures in reproducible drawings and explanatory narratives are designed to illustrate a variety of loss situations. Grief as a response to loss is featured in many of the pictures.

McEvoy, M. L. & McEvoy, A. W. (1994). *Preventing youth suicide: A handbook for educators and human service professionals.* Holmes Beach, FL: Learning Publications. This book provides strategies for crisis response and intervention, postvention protocols and peer counseling programs. It emphasizes the need to reduce suicide contagion.

Morrow, G. (1987). *The compassionate school: A practical guide to educating abused and traumatized children.* Englewood Cliffs, NJ: Prentice-Hall, Inc. This book is designed to help school administrators, counselors, teachers and support-service personnel identify and work with children of trauma, including those who have lost a significant attachment figure through death or abandonment, and are grieving that traumatic loss. It includes suggestions for developing a staff support system to help these children, which includes a teacher-assistance team.

National Association of School Psychologists (1991). *Resources in crisis intervention: School, family and community applications.* Silver Spring, MD: NASP. This collection of articles, papers and lessons overviews crisis intervention principles, children's reactions to crises, responses to specific crises by professionals and parents and case examples. It was designed to provide resources to children and families of Operation Desert Storm.

Oates, M. D. (1993). *Death in the school community: A handbook for counselors, teachers and administrators.* Alexandria, VA: American Counseling Association. This book encourages schools to plan responses to a death. It includes step-by-step action plans and ways to cope with resulting PTSD as well as techniques for leading loss and grief groups.

Petersen, S. & Straub, R. L. (1992). *School crisis survival guide.* West Nyack, NY: The Center for Applied Research in Education. This volume provides practical ideas to respond to crisis in the schools such as deaths and natural disasters. Ways to counsel grieving students are included, as well as disaster plans. It provides lesson plans for grades K–12 to help students deal with crisis and tragedy and includes reproducible sheets and step-by-step guidelines.

Pitcher, G. D., & Poland, S. (1992). *Crisis intervention in the schools.* New York: The Guilford Press. This book examines school responses to a variety of child-centered crises, including divorce, family violence and suicide, serious bus accidents, school violence and natural disasters. It includes case studies, sample to-do lists for crisis team members, crisis plan drills, materials and checklists.

Richgarn, R. . V. (1995). *Perspectives on college student suicide.* Amityville, NY: Baywood Publishing Co., Inc. This book uses the perspective of the college student to examine the experience of suicide and illustrates how to react to suicidal situations on campus. Because suicide is the second leading cause of death in college-age individuals, this book calls for an activist attitude toward the problem.

Schmidt, J. J. (1991). *A survival guide for the elementary/middle school counselor.* West Nyack, NY: The Center for Applied Research in Education. This book contains a chapter entitled "Crisis Intervention: Being Prepared," which describes how to set up a crisis plan, conduct an inservice, do crisis counseling and work with critical cases of potential suicide and child abuse.

Steele, W. (1992). *Preventing self-destruction: A manual for school crisis response teams.* Holmes Beach, FL: Learning Publications, Inc. This book describes the need for crisis teams, suggests how to develop them and describes the losses that accompany traumatic experiences. It includes interview techniques with students and families and describes ways to deal with traumatic loss, including loss from suicide.

Stevenson, R. G. (Ed.) (1995). *What will we do? Preparing a school community to cope with crises.* Amityville, NY: Baywood Publishing Co., Inc. This book is a guide for educators and parents who wish to prepare for, understand and deal with school crises. It presents specific steps for coping with future crises and examines the benefits and potential risks of dealing with issues of death, loss, violence and war.

Webb, N. B. (Ed.) (1991). *Play therapy with children in crisis.* New York: The Guilford Press. This book is designed as a casebook and illustrates a variety of play therapy techniques including storytelling, games, puppets, art and dolls. Techniques are presented by type of crisis situation.

Webb, N. B. (1993). *Helping bereaved children: A handbook for practitioners.* New York: The Guilford Press. This volume examines the area of childhood bereavement and includes an extensive chapter on assessment and a variety of case studies ranging from death of a parent to death of a teacher and school counselor.

Welch, I. D., Zawistoski, R. M., & Smart, D. W. (1988). *Encountering death: Structured activities for death awareness.* Muncie, IN: Accelerated Development, Inc. This book of experiential activities provides information on topics of death and dying. It can be used with teens and adults in individual and group settings. A chapter on traumatic death is included.

Books for Adult Survivors of Trauma and their Families

Allen, J. G. (1992). *Coping with trauma: A guide to self-understanding.* Washington, DC: American Psychiatric Press. This book is designed to help laypersons understand the impact of traumatic experiences. The book is also de-

signed to help partners and families of traumatized individuals. It includes
sections on memory, attachment and dissociative disorders.

Catherall, D. R. (1992). *Back from the brink: A family's guide to overcoming traumatic stress.* New York: Bantam. This guide for trauma survivors and their families shows how to deal with a survivor of trauma as well as how to be a survivor. Confronting loss is a major feature of the book. It is designed for laymen as a beginning guide.

Cohen, B. M., Barnes, M., & Rankin, A. B. (1995). *Managing traumatic stress through art: Drawing from the center.* Lutherville, MD: The Sidran Press. This book provides step-by-step art experiences designed to help those who do them understand, manage and transform the aftereffects of trauma. It is practical, useful and shows the ways in which art making and writing can assist healing from severe trauma.

Cole, D. (1992). *After great pain: A new life emerges.* New York: Summit Books. The author uses her experiences to illustrate how one individual grows after traumas of deaths of those close to her and being held hostage. It lists many theoretical resources as well as gives a model for others to use for healing.

Flannery, R. B., Jr. (1992). *Post-traumatic stress disorder: The victim's guide to healing and recovery.* New York: The Crossroad Publishing Company. This book is written for the victim of PTSD and the victim's family. It is designed to show those individuals how to recover from trauma's debilitating effects and looks at both the psychology and biology of PTSD. Project SMART (Stress Management And Relaxation Training) skills are also presented.

Fried, H. (1990). *Fragments of a life: The road to Auschwitz.* London: Robert Hale. Fried, a Swedish psychologist who works with Holocaust survivors, as a Romanian, Transylvanian teen, was assaulted and traumatized through her capture and eventual trip to Auschwitz. This is an excellent story of one remarkable woman's resilience and recovery.

Gayton, R. (1995). *The forgiving place: Choosing peace after violent trauma.* Waco, TX: WRS Publishing. This book is the story of loss of the author's wife to a brutal murder and his story of healing. He uses his personal experience to show other show to come to terms with suffering and how to find a new commitment to life. The author is a clinical psychologist in private practice.

Matsakis, A. (1992). *I can't get over it: A handbook for trauma survivors.* Oakland, CA: New Harbinger Publications, Inc. This book explains how post-traumatic stress disorder affects survivors of a variety of traumas including disasters, rape, crime and violence. It addresses survivors directly and helps survivors self-diagnose and then get appropriate treatment. It includes a variety of techniques and self-help suggestions for safe recovery.

Muss, D. (1991). *The trauma trap: A self-help programme for overcoming post-traumatic stress disorder.* London, England: Doubleday. This innovative program uses a specific technique called the "rewind technique" to help survivors of natural and man-made traumas and disasters. It is written in understandable language for the lay reader but includes suggestions for counselors, as well.

Books for Survivors of Loss

Akner, L. F. (1993). *How to survive the loss of a parent: A guide for adults.* New York: William Morrow & Co. The book explains how the traumatic loss, though inevitable, is different from other losses. It gives ways to work through the grief.

Bozarth-Campbell, A. R. (1986). *Life is good-bye, life is hello: Grieving well through all kinds of loss,* second edition. Center City, MN: Hazelden Foundation. The author, as an episcopal priest and therapist, looks at grief and the accompanying losses as well as styles of grieving, the changes that occur with grief and the essentials needed to grieve.

Caplan, S., & Lang, G. (1995). *Grief's courageous journey: A workbook.* Oakland, CA: New Harbinger Publications. This book presents a compassionate program of steps to help survivors cope with their losses and the accompanying changes. This book contains journal exercises and suggestions for the creation of rituals. It also includes a facilitator's guide for a 10-session support group.

Cornils, S. P. (1992). *The mourning after: How to manage grief wisely.* Saratoga, CA: R & E Publishers. This book for survivors offers hope and help for resolving grief. It examines manifestations of grief and the work of mourning. The steps are presented within a religious perspective.

Davies, P. (1988). *Grief: Climb toward understanding. Self-help when you are struggling.* New York: Carol Communications. This collection of poetry was begun by the author when her 13-year-old son was killed in a plane crash. It includes space for readers to add their own notes or poetry. The book shows the author's struggle and includes helpful references, a very helpful checklist detailing what to do when someone dies, questions to ask and how to create a memorial card.

Deits, B. (1992, rev. ed). *Life after loss: A personal guide dealing with death, divorce, job change and relocation.* Tuscon, AZ: Fisher Books. This book provides skills for healthy recovery, including how to cry, how to write a good-bye letter, how to deal with emotions and how to cope.

Edelman, H. (1994). *Motherless daughters: The legacy of loss.* Reading, MA: Addison-Wesley Publishing Co. Stories of women whose mothers have died early in their lives and how absence of a mother shapes identity are the focii of this book.

Feinstein, D., & Mayo, P. E. (1990). *Rituals for living and dying: How we can turn loss and the fear of death into an affirmation of life.* New York: Harper Collins Publishers, Inc. This work describes the journey of a family as members face the impending death of the father. It illustrates the ways in which ritual can help a family come to terms with loss.

Graves, S. (1994). *Expressions of healing: Embracing the process of grief.* North Hollywood, CA: Newcastle Publishing. This book is designed to combine expression, grief and recovery in a workbook format and includes over 20 journaling and art exercises. Exercises help the reader to "name" emotions, nurture the self and deal with physical aftereffects of trauma.

Grollman, E. A. (1990). *Talking about death: A dialogue between parent and child.* Boston, MA: Beacon Press. This compassionate guide is designed for children and adults to read together and answers the questions children ask about death. It also includes extensive resource lists.

James, J. W., & Cherry, F. (1989). *The grief recovery handbook: A clearly defined program for moving beyond loss.* New York: Harper Collins Publishers, Inc. This book presents a five-step program designed to help those who are experiencing emotional loss including loss of a child, spouse, parent, sibling, or job.

Lightner, C., & Hathaway, N. (1990). *Giving sorrow words: How to cope with grief and get on with your life.* Minneapolis, MN: CompCare Publishers. This work describes how individuals cope with grief and loss. It describes the cycle of grief, good grief, bad grief, sudden death, anticipated death and ways to cope with grief.

Marshall, F. (1993). *Losing a parent: A personal guide to coping with that special grief that comes with losing a parent.* Tuscon, AZ: Fisher Books. This book looks at the impact of the sudden death of a parent as well as terminal illness. It includes suggestions how to locate help, how to support a surviving parent and inheritance issues.

Metrick, S. B. (1994). *Crossing the bridge: Creating ceremonies for grieving and healing from life's losses.* Berkeley, CA: Celestial Arts. This book discusses rituals to find wholeness in the face of loss. It discusses and defines loss, whether sudden or anticipated and the impact of loss. Rituals using creative expression and ceremony are included.

Peck, R., & Stefanics, C. (1987). *Learning to say good-bye: Dealing with death and dying.* Muncie, IN: Accelerated Development, Inc. This book was written by a healthcare professional and a layman to normalize the occurrence of death. It presents ways to help dying persons and their families in a humanistic approach to working with the terminally ill. It also describes thanatology programs for healthcare.

Rando, T. A. (1988). *How to go on living when someone you love dies.* New York: Lexington Books. This book is written for the general public and includes suggestions for ways to deal with sudden and anticipated death. It gives self-help techniques to take care of business, work on unfinished business, take care of self and when to get help from others.

Shaw, E. (1994). *What to do when a loved one dies: A practical and compassionate guide to dealing with death on life's terms.* Irvine, CA: Dickens Press. This book presents excellent guidelines describing what to do when a death occurs and is a sourcebook for decisionmaking. It has an extensive listing of support groups, resources and other sources of help. Its approach is extremely detailed and includes sections on dealing with catastrophic deaths and the death of pets.

Sissom, R. (1994). *Moving beyond grief: Lessons from those who have lived through sorrow.* Grand Rapids, MI: Discovery House. This religiously-oriented book offers stories of persons who have learned to cope with grief and trauma.

Soder-Alderfer, K. (1994). *With those who grieve: 20 grief survivors share their stories of loss, pain and hope.* Elgin, IL: Lion Publishing. This book describes the healing process of grief and looks at its effects as well as how to find and offer help. Grief stories cross the lifespan.

Staudacher, C. (1987). *Beyond grief: A guide for recovering from the death of a loved one.* Oakland, CA: New Harbinger Publications. This guide for survivors, whether lay persons or professionals, gives general information about grieving and ways to survive specific types of death. It also presents guidelines to create support groups as well as guidelines for offering support to others.

Tagliaferre, L, & Harbaugh, G. L. (1990). *Recovery from loss: A personalized guide to the grieving process.* Deerfield Beach, FL: Heath Communications, Inc. This book grew out of the untimely death of the first author's wife and looks at tasks of grief acknowledgement, feeling, substitution, detachment and recon-struction across physical, intellectual, emotional and spiritual domains. This book contains an interesting analysis of personality types (Myers-Briggs) in relation to loss and grief.

Tatelbaum, J. (1984). *The courage to grieve: Creative living, recovery and growth through grief.* New York: HarperCollins Publishers, Inc. This book offers ways to understand and recover from the intense emotional process that is part of the grieving process.

Wolfelt, A. D. (1992). *Understanding grief: Helping yourself heal.* Muncie, IN: Accelerated Development, Inc. This book is based on the philosophy that we do not "get over" grief but learn to "live with" it. It is designed to help the reader become an expert on his/her own experiences and explore how he/she thinks and feels. It looks at the healing needs of survivors and gives outlines for running survivor support groups.

Woodson, M. (1994). *Making it through the toughest days of grief.* Grand Rapids, Mi: Zondervan Publishing House. This book offers practical advice to get through lonely days, angry days and special holidays. It offers many personal stories as well.

Zagranski, D. (1994). *Stuck for words: What to say when someone is grieving.* Melbourne, Australia: Hill of Content Publishing Co. This book provides suggestions for the ordinary person as to what to do and say to someone who is grieving. It also suggests ways for those who are grieving to say what they need and when to get help.

Books for Child Survivors of Loss

Alderman, L. (1989). *Why did daddy die: Helping children cope with the loss of a parent.* New York: Pocket Books. The author tells how she guided her own children through grief. She describes phases of grief and children's views of death.

Heegaard, M. (1991). *Coping with death and grief.* Minneapolis, MN: Wood-land Press. This book includes stories about young people, grades 3-6, who deal with grief. It provides facts about death that are developmentally based.

Heegaard, M. (1991). *When something terrible happens: Children can learn to cope with grief* (ages 6-12) and *When someone very special dies: Children can learn to cope with grief.* Minneapolis, MN: Woodland Press. These two books teach basic concepts of death and help children, through their workbook format, express feelings and increase coping skills. Children use their own personal stories to complete the pages as they draw the events and their accompanying feelings.

Palmer, P. (1995). *I wish I could hold your hand: A child's guide to grief and loss*. San Obispo, CA: Impact Publishers. This book helps the growing child identify feelings and learn to accept and deal with those feelings surrounding death and traumatic loss.

For a comprehensive bibliography of books about death for children presented in a developmental fashion, see Charles A. Corr's chapter in:

Doka, K. J. (Ed.) (1995). *Children mourning; mourning children*. Washington, D.C.: Hospice Foundation of America.

Books on Loss and Grief Written for Professionals and Volunteers

Adams, D. W., & Deveau, E. J. (Eds.) (1995). *Beyond the innocence of childhood*, Vols. 1–3. Amityvile, NY: Baywood Publishing Co. This three-volume set brings together a variety of educators, researchers and practitioners who share knowledge and expertise concerning ways to help children and adolescents deal with life threats, dying, death and bereavement.

Allen, N. H. (1991). *Survivor-victims of homicide: Murder is only the beginning*. New York: Hemisphere. This book looks at the differences between dealing with murder and other deaths. It notes that the horrendous memories of murder live forever and stresses the value of impact statements.

Ashton, J. & Ashton, D. (1994). *Loss and grief recovery: Help caring for children with disabilities, chronic or terminal illness*. Amityville, NY: Baywood Publishing Company, Inc. This book helps the reader recognize and control ways to resolve grief and focuses primarily on caring for children with disabilities or illness. The authors use personal experience of the chronic illness of their own son to illustrate the grief process and tools for recovery.

Bertman, S. L. (1991). *Facing death: Images, insights and interventions*. New York: Taylor & Francis Publishing Co. This book draws upon the arts and humanities as well as literary works and pop culture images of death, loss and suffering to discuss how we feel and think about death. The author uses these resources to lead workshops about death. The book provides suggestions for death education.

Cool, A.S. & Dworkin, D. S. (1992). *Helping the bereaved: Therapeutic interventions for children, adolescents and adults*. New York: Basic Books. This book focuses on therapeutic interventions with bereaved individuals and groups. It gives therapists specific therapeutic techniques including development of ethical wills and rituals. It also addresses the development of groups for children and adults.

Hansen, J.C. (Ed.) . (1984). *Death and grief in the family*. Rockville, MD: Aspen Publications. This edited book includes chapters to help professionals deal with survivors of specific traumas of suicide, cancer, youth illness, sibling death and others.

Jacobs, S. (1993). *Pathologic grief: Maladaptation to loss.* Washington, DC: American Psychiatric Press, Inc. This book presents a scholarly and systematic evaluation of pathologic grief and bereavement. It provides definitions of pathologic grief and suggestions for treatment and looks at PTSD after loss as a disorder of adaptation. The book also looks at the role of trauma in shaping emotional responses to traumatic loss.

Kastenbaum, R. (1992). *The psychology of death,* 2nd Ed. New York: Springer Publishing Company. This book examines deathbed scenes, explores facts and meanings of mortality and looks at changing conceptions of death and death anxiety. It includes a discussion of the developmental perspective of these issues.

Klass, D. (1988). *Parental grief: Solace and resolution.* New York: Springer Publishing Company. This book explores parental bereavement and its resolution; it looks at the role of peer groups, self-help groups, support groups for parents of murdered children and groups for children with long-term illnesses.

Larson, D. G. (1993). *Helper's Journey: Working with people facing grief, loss and life-threatening illness.* Champaign, IL: Research Press. This book is designed for volunteers, counselors and clergy who work in direct caregiving roles with survivors and those facing death. It gives practical suggestions as well as exercises and activities designed to develop coping skills.

Lee, C. (1994). *Good grief: Experiencing loss.* London, England: Fourth Estate Limited. This book examines family prejudices, family grieving experiences and difficulties of mourning.

Leick, N., & Davidsen-Nielsen, M. (1991). *Healing pain: Attachment, loss and grief therapy.* London, England: Tavistock/Routledge. This Scandinavian work, translated into English, describes treatment methods for grief work and provides direction as to how to work with both normal and pathological grief. It examines crisis intervention after severely traumatic events, delayed grief and avoided grief.

Lundin, T. (Ed). (1995). *Grief and bereavement: Proceedings from the Fourth International Conference on Grief and Bereavement in Contemporary Society.* Stockholm, Sweden: Swedish National Association for Mental Health. This work includes key note addresses and a selection of papers from the conference. One interesting paper describes the impact of the research process on researchers.

Mogenson, G. (1995). *Greeting the angels: An imaginal view of the mourning process.* Amityville, NY: Baywood Publishing Company. This book examines the imaginal dimension of the mourning process. It describes how the bereaved relate to images of the dead, which return to heal and be healed, and the spiritual process that accompanies this aspect of mourning. The author believes that the dead teach the bereaved how to mourn them and uses dream theory, poetry, Jungian psychology to elucidate the themes.

Morgan, E. (1984). *Dealing creatively with death: A manual of death education and simple burial* (10th ed.). Burnsville, NC: Celo Press. The premise of this book is that death education is for all. It looks at bereavement from the personal view of the author as well as issues of burial, cremation, death ceremonies and organ donation. It includes a variety of sample forms.

Papadatou, D., & Papadatou, C. (Eds.) (1991). *Children and death.* New York: Hemisphere Publishing Co. This book looks at death from a developmental perspective. It describes group and family interventions with dying children and programs for their care as well as parental grief reactions to the loss of a child. It also examines stress in professionals who work with death.

Parkes, C. M., & Weirs, R. S. (1983). *Recovery from bereavement.* Northvale, NJ: Jason Aronson, Inc. This classic book describes the results of a research study with widows and widowers. It looks at why some people recover and lets the bereaved speak.

Raphael, B. (1983). The anatomy of bereavement. Northvale, NJ: Jason Aronson, Inc. This thorough, comprehensive work looks at the impact of death at various stages and ages. It describes the experience of loss and coping with death and disaster and is a classic in the field.

Rando, T. A. (1993). *Treatment of complicated mourning.* Champaign, IL: Research Press. This book focuses on individual assessment and treatment of adult bereavement. It presents a therapeutic approach to the treatment of traumatic death.

Redmond, L. M. (1989). *Surviving when someone you love was murdered: A professional's guide to group grief therapy for families and friends of murdered victims.* Clearwater, FL: Psychological Consultation and Education Services, Inc. This book examines issues of complicated mourning for friends and families of murder victims.

Rosen, H. (1986). *Unspoken grief: Coping with childhood sibling loss.* Lexington, MA: Lexington Books. This book provides suggestions how to cope with and survive from the death of a sibling. It includes an interview questionnaire to be used with the family, projective tests for use with surviving children and a death anxiety questionnaire.

Rosof, B. D. (1994). *The worst loss: How families heal from the death of a child.* New York: Henry Holt & Co., Inc. The death of a child overwhelms many people. This book describes the losses that the death of a child brings to parents and siblings as well as potential PTSD reactions and the work of grief. It gives practical advice from a therapist's point of view.

Shapiro, E. R. (1994). *Grief as a family process: A developmental approach to clinical practice.* New York: Guilford. This book integrates a variety of theories into a systematic developmental model that describes how grief can enhance the growth of the family system. The sociocultural context of grief is empha-sized throughout the book.

Simas, B. (1979). *A time to grieve: Loss as a universal human experience.* Milwaukee, WI: Families International Incorporated. This book is designed for professionals who will counsel clients on issues relating to loss and grief. It examines emotional reactions to grief including fear of loss and ways to cope with that loss.

Sprang, G., & McNeil, J. (1995). *The many faces of bereavement: The nature and treatment of natural, traumatic and stigmatized grief.* New York: Brunner/

Mazel. This book provides an overview of traumatic grief and the specific situations leading to traumatic grief (e.g. murder, critical incidents). It includes assessment protocols, debriefing strategies and treatment interventions.

Stroebe, M. S., Stroebe, W., & Hanssom, R. O. (1993). *Handbook of bereavement: Theory, research and intervention.* New York: Cambridge University Press. This excellent resource for professionals looks at theory and research of bereavement from a variety of perspectives. It examines the impact of conjugal bereavement, counseling theories and the role of self-help groups. It also includes an extensive reference list. The book is technical and based on scientific knowledge.

Swedish National Association for Mental Health (1994). *Book of abstracts: Fourth International Conference on Grief and Bereavement in Contemporary Society.* Stockholm, Sweden: Author. This monograph includes 227 abstracts that address issues of traumatic loss, pathological grief and bereavement. Research and training issues are also included.

Walsh, F., & McGoldrick, M. (Eds.) (1991). *Living beyond loss: Death in the family.* New York: W. W. Norton. This edited work looks at how the field of family therapy treats death and discusses the family impact of death and loss. It uses both systems and developmental perspectives.

Williams, M. B., & Nurmi, L. A. (1994). *Death of a co-worker: Personal and institutional responses.* Helsinki, Finland: Poliisin Oppikirjasarja. This monograph uses a series of cases to illustrate the impact that the death of a co-worker has on an institution and its members. It examines diagnosis of PTSR and PTSD and describes debriefing strategies and treatment planning.

Wolfelt, A. (1983, 1991). *Helping children cope with grief.* Muncie, IL: Accelerated Development, Inc. The seventh printing of this book provides a good description of children's reactions to death and the caregiving skills needed for those children. It is written for parents, teachers and counselors and advocates death education for adults and includes material for death education workshops.

Worden, W. (1991). *Grief counseling and grief therapy, 2nd ed.: A handbook for the mental health practitioner.* New York: Springer Publishing Company. This book details ways to help clients accomplish tasks of mourning to avoid unresolved grief and its complications. A chapter on grieving traumatic losses is included, as are sketches for role plays in training.

Zisook, S. (Ed.) (1987). *Biopsychosocial aspects of bereavement.* Washington, DC: American Psychiatric Press. This edited work includes chapters on psychological adjustment to unnatural dying, outcome predictors of bereavement, vulnerability factors and a chapter on the Texas Revised Inventory of Grief.

Tapes and Videos

David's Story: A Teen Suicide. Covington, TN: Sunburst Communications. This 28-minute video discusses why friends of a suicide victim did or did not see the suicide coming. The film examines the warning signs of suicide.

Davis, N. (1995). Audio Tapes. *Healing the Heart; Letting Go; Therapeutic Stores for Trauma and Stress; Stories to Heal the Grieving Heart.* 6178 Oxon Hill Rd. Suite 306, Oxon Hill, MD 2074 (301-567-9297). These audio tapes contain collections of therapeutic stories designed to ease the process of grieving, explain stages of grief, address the intuitive side of the mind and help the listener find what he/she needs within the self. They are designed for the intuitive, right side of the brain. Visual imagery and relaxation exercises are also included.

Organizations, Journals, Conferences

American Association of Suicidology
Denver, CO
303-692-0985
Promotes public awareness, research and education.

Association for Death Education and Counseling
638 Prospect Ave., Hartford, CT 06105
203-232-4825
Promotes effective death education and counseling. The organization does research and will co-sponsor.

Bereavement: A Magazine of Hope and Healing
8133 Telegraph Drive, Colorado Springs, CO 80920
719-282-1948

Candlelighter's Foundation
2025 Eye St. NW, Suite 1011, Washington, DC 20006
Helps parents of children with cancer.

Compassionate Friends
P. O. Box 3696, Oak Brook, IL 60522
703-990-0010, 312-323-5010
Offers support, friendship and understanding to parents and siblings grieving the death of a child.

Concerns of Police Survivors, Inc. (COPS)
9423 A Marlboro Pike, Upper Marlboro, MD 20772
301-599-0445

Death Studies
Hannelore Wass, Ed., Hemisphere Publishing Corporation
1010 Vermont Avenue, Washington, DC 20005

Heartbeat
2015 Devon St., Colorado Springs, CO 80909
719-596-2575
Mutual support group for those who have lost someone through suicide.

In Loving Memory
1416 Green Run Lane, Reston, VA
703-435-0608
Mutual support, friendship and help for parents who have lost their only child or all of their children.

MADD (Mothers Against Drunk Driving)
669 Airport Freeway, Suite 310, Hurst, TX 76053
800–Get–MADD

Mothers of AIDS Patients (MAP)
P. O. Box 1763, Lomia, CA 09717

National Association of Military Widows
4023 25th Rd N., Arlington, VA 22207
703–527–4565

National Sudden Infant Death Syndrome Alliance
10500 Little Patuxent Parkway #420, Columbia, MD 21044–3505
410–964–8000 or 800–221–7437
Provides emotional support for families of SIDS victims; the organization has local chapters.

National Sudden Infant Death Syndrome Resource Center
8201 Greensboro Drive Suite 600, McLean, VA 22102
703–821–8955

OMEGA: Journal of Death and Dying
R. J. Kastenbaum and K. J. Doka, Eds.
Amityville, NY: Baywood Publishing Company, Inc.
Association for Death Education Counseling Affiliated Journal

POMC (Parents of Murdered Children)
100 East Eighth Street, Room B–41, Cincinnati, OH 45202
513–721–5683
Provides self help groups to support persons who survive the death of children through murder.

Ray of Hope For Suicide Survivors
319–337–9880

Survivors
993 "C" Santa Fe Ave, Vista, CA 92083
Mutual help and 12–step step program to recover from grief due to the death of a loved one.

Survivors of Suicide
P.O. Box 82262, Lincoln, NE 68423
414–442–4638
Helps families and friends of suicide victims cope with grief and refers to other survivor groups; has manuals and materials to start groups.

Tender Hearts/Triplet Connection
PO Box 99571, Stockton, CA 95209
209–474–0885
Network of parents who have lost one or more children in multiple births.

Theos (They Help Each Other Spiritually)
Theos Foundation
410 Penn Hills Mall, Pittsburgh, PA 15235
412-243-4299
Helps persons whose spouses have died.

Unite, Inc.
Jeanes Hospital
7600 Central Ave, Philadelphia, PA 19111
215-728-3777
Support for parents grieving miscarriage, stillbirth and infant death.

Victims of Pam Am 103 "The Truth Must Be Known"
135 Algonquin Parkway, Whippany, NJ 07981
Mutual support group for families and friends who lost a loved one on the flight.

Professional Organizations

Association for Death Education and Counseling (ADEC)
638 Prospect Avenue, Hartford, CT 06105
203-232-4825

International Association for Trauma Counselors
1033 La Posada Drive, Suite 220, Austin, TX 78752-3880
512-454-8626
This multidisciplinary professional organization offers certification for persons counseling victims of trauma, debriefers and other trauma-related professionals. It sponsors an annual national conference and various trainings.

International Society for Traumatic Stress Studies
60 Revere Drive Suite 500 Northbrook, IL 60062
708-480-9028
This multi-disciplinary organization is the pioneer organization in the field of trauma. It sponsors an annual meeting and publishes *The Journal of Traumatic Stress*. Members are in the forefront of trauma research, education, professional scholarship and training.

National Organization of Victim's Assistance
717 D. St. NW Washington, DC 20004
This private, nonprofit organization of victim and witness assistance programs and practitioners provides national advocacy, direct services, training in critical incident stress debriefing, technical assistance and other training. It has numerous curricula available.

References

Commentary   by Kenneth Doka

Doka, Kenneth J. (1989). *Disenfranchised Grief: Recognizing Hidden Sorrow.* Lexington, MA: Lexington Press.

Leviton, Daniel (1991) *Horrendous Death, Health, and Well-Being.* Washington, D.C.: Hemisphere Publishing Company.

Chapter 2   by Stephen P. Hersh

National Stroke Association (1996).

Center for Disease Control, U.S. Public Health Service.

National Heart, Lung & Blood Institute, National Institutes of Health.

National Center for Health Statistics.

Nuland, Sherwin B. (1994). *How We Die.* New York: Alfred P. Knopf.

Chapter 3   by Janice Harris Lord

Amick-McMullen, A., Kilpatrick, D., Veronen, L., & Smith, S. (1989). "Family survivors of homicide victims: Theoretical perspectives and an exploratory study." *Journal of Traumatic Stress,* 2(1), 21–35.

Awooner-Renner, S. (1993). "I desperately needed to see my son." *British Medical Journal (BMJ),* 32, 356.

Ditchick, F. (1990). "The reactions of husbands and wives to the death of their child and its effect on the marital relationship." Adelphi University: Unpublished dissertation.

Lehman, D. & Wortman, C. (1987). "Long-term effects of losing a spouse or child in a motor vehicle crash." *Journal of Personality and Social Psychology,* 52(1), 218, 231.

Mercer, D. (1991). "The role of religious affiliation and activity in recovery from drunk driving bereavement and injury." Unpublished manuscript.

Mercer, D. (1993, October). "Drunk driving victimization or non-victimization effects on volunteer victim advocates." Paper presented at the annual conference of the International Society for Traumatic Stress Studies, San Antonio, TX.

Mercer, D. (1994). Victim impact panels' effects on victim participants. Preliminary report on first-year findings of a three-year project, drunk driving victim impact panels: Victim outcomes. Research funded by the Department of Health and Human Services, National Institute for Mental Health, grant no. 1-RO1-MH 48987.

Miller, T.R. & Blincoe, L.D. (1994). "Incidence and cost of alcohol-involved crashes." *Accident Analysis & Prevention,* 26(5), 583–591.

NHTSA (National Highway Traffic Safety Administration) (August 1995). *Fatal accident reporting system.* Washington, DC.

Osmont, K. (1993). "The value of viewing in grief work reconciliation: A psychologist's perspective." *The Forum Newsletter* of the Association for Death Education and Counseling, November–December.

Rinear, E. (1988). "Psychosoclal aspects of parental response patterns to the death of a child by homicide." *Journal of Traumatic Stress*, *1*(3), 305-322.

Rynearson, E.K & McCreery, J.M. (1993). "Bereavement after homicide: A synergism of trauma and loss." *American Journal of Psychiatry*, 150(2), 258-261.

Schanfield, S., Swain, B., & Benjamin, G. (1987). "Parents' responses to the death of adult children from accidents and concur: A comparison." *Omega*, 289-297.

Wolfelt, A. (1992). *Understanding Grief: Helping yourself heal.* Muncie, Indiana: Accelerated Development Publishers.

Wortman, C. (1985). "Reactions to victims of life crisis: support attempts that fail." In I.G. Sarason and B.R. Sarason (Eds.) *Social Support Theory. Research and Application.* Dordreeht, The Netherlands: Marinus Nijhoff.

Weinberg, N. (1985). "The health care social worker's role in facilitating grief work: An empirical study." *Social Work in Health Care*, 10(3), 107-117.

Weiss, R. (1988). "Loss and Recovery." Paper presented at The Society for the Psychological Study of Social Issues.

Recommended Reading

Books

Grollman, Earl A. (1993*) Straight talk about death for teenagers: How to cope with losing someone you love.* Boston, MA: Beacon Press.

Lord, J. (1986) *No time for good-byes: coping with sorrow anger and injustice after a tragic death.* Ventura, CA: Pathfinder Publishing.

Mercer, D. (1994) *Injury: Learning to live again.* Ventura, CA: Pathfinder Publishing.

Saperstein, Robert, J.D. and Saperstein, Dana, Ph.D. (1994) *Surviving An Auto Accident: A guide to your physical economic and emotional recovery.* Ventura, CA: Pathfinder Publishing.

Brochures

(All of the following are available by calling Mothers Against Drunk Driving at 1-800 GET-MADD, ext. 231. One copy is free. If you wish additional copies, you will receive ordering information.)

Victim Information Pamphlet–A guide through the criminal justice system.
How You Can Help–For Emergency Room support.
Financial Recovery After a Drunk Driving Crash–For all crash victims.
Someone You Know Drinks and Drives–For those who want to prevent drunk driving.
Helping Children Cope With Death–For caregivers of grieving children.
Straight Talk About Death For Teenagers–For grieving teenagers.
We Hurt Too–For adult siblings of someone killed.
Your Grief: You're Not Going Crazy–For all grieving persons.
Don't Call Me Lucky–For the injured and their families.
Closed Head Injury: A Common Complication of Vehicular Crashes–For all occupants of a vehicle involved in a crash, whether or not they believe they were injured.
Men and Mourning–A man's journey through grief.
Drunk Driving: An Unacknowledged Form of Child Endangerment in America–For those concerned about a person who drives drunk with children in the vehicle.

Will It Always Feel This Way?—For the parent whose child has been killed.
Monday Mourning—For businesses when an employee becomes a crash victim.
A Screening Instrument for the Selection of Victim Impact Panelists.

Chapter 4   by Judith M. Stillion

Alexander, V. (1991). "Grief after suicide: Giving voice to the loss." *Journal of Geriatric Psychiatry*. 24(21, 277-291).

Allen, B.G., Calhoun, L.D., Cann, A., & Tedeschi, R.G. (1993-94). "The effect of cause of death on responses to the bereaved: Suicide compared to accident and natural causes." *Omega*. 28(1), 39-48.

Barrett, T.W., & Scott, T.B. (1990). "Suicide bereavement and recovery patterns compared with non-suicide bereavement patterns." *Suicide and Life-Threatening Behavior*. 20. 1-15.

Brent, D., Pepper, J., Moritz, G., Allman, C., Friend, A., Schweers, J., Roth, C., Balach, L., & Harrington, K. (1992). "Psychiatric effects of exposure to suicide among the friends and acquaintances of adolescent suicide victims." *Journal of the American Academy of Child and Adolescent Psychiatry*. 31, 629-640.

Calhoun, L.G. (1982). "The aftermath of childhood suicide: Influences on the perception of the parent." *Journal of Community Psychology*, 10, 250-254.

Calhoun, L.G., & Allen, B.G. (1991). "Social reactions to the survivor of a suicide in the family: A review of the literature." *Omega*. 23(2). 95-97.

Calhoun, L.G., Selby, J. W., & Abernathy, (1984). "Suicidal death: Social reactions to bereaved survivors," *The Journal of Psychology*, 116, 261-266.

Calhoun, L.G., Selby, J.W., & Faulsdch (1980). "Reactions to the parents of the child suicide: A study of social impressions." *Journal of Consulting and Clinical Psychology*. 48(4), 535-536.

Calhoun, L.G., Selby, J.W., & Faulstich (1982). "The aftermath of childhood suicides: Influences on the perception of the parent." *Journal of Community Psychology*. 10, 250-254.

Calhoun, L.G., Selby, J.W., & Selby, L.E. (1982). "The psychological aftermath of suicide: An analysis of current evidence." *Clinical Psychology Review*. 1, 409-420.

Calhoun, L.G., Selby, J.W., & Steelman, J.K. (1988-89). "A collation of funeral directors' impressions of suicidal deaths." *Omega*. 19(4), 365-373.

Calhoun, L.G., Selby, J.W., & Walton, P.B. (1985-86). "Suicidal death of a spouse: The social perception of the survivor." *Omega*. 16(4), 283-288.

Carter, B.F., & Brooks, A. (1990, May). "Suicide postvention: Crisis or opportunity?" *The School Counselor*. 37, 378-389.

Demi, A.S. (1984). "Social adjustment of widows after a sudden death: Suicide and non-suicide survivors compared." *Death Education*. 8 (Suppl.), 91-III.

Farberow, N.L, Gallagher, D., Gilewski, M., & Thompson, L. (1987). "An examination of the early impact of bereavement on psychological distress in survivors of suicide." *Gerontologist*. 27, 592-598.

Farberow, N.L, Gallagher-Thompson, D., Gilewski, M., & Thompson, L. (1992a). "The role of social supports in the bereavement process of surviving spouses of suicide and natural deaths." *Suicide and life-threatening behavior*. 22(1), Spring, 107-124.

Farberow, N.L., Gallagher-Thompson, D., Gilewski, M., & Thompson, L. (1992b). "Changes in grief and mental health of bereaved spouses of older suicides." *Journal of Gerontology: Psychological Sciences.* 47, 357–366.

Gibson, J.A., Range, L.M., & Anderson, H.N. (1987). "Adolescents' attitudes toward suicide: Does knowledge that the parents are divorced make a difference?." *Journal of Divorce,* 163–167.

Gilewski, M. J., Farberow, N.L., Gallagher, D.E., & Thompson, L.W. (1991). "Interaction of depression and bereavement on mental health in the elderly," *Psychology and Aging.* 6(1), 67–75.

Gordon, R.S., Range, L.M., & Edwards, R.P. (1987). "Generational differences in reactions to adolescent suicide." *Journal of Community Psychology.* 15, 268–274.

Hazell, P., & Lewin, T. (1993, Summer). "An evaluation of postvention following adolescent suicide." *Suicide and Life-threatening Behavior.* 23(2).

Kovarksy, R.S. (1989). "Loneliness and disturbed grief: A comparison of parents who lost a child to suicide or accidental death." *Archives of Psychiatric Nursing.* 3, 86–96.

McIntosh, J.L. (1993, Summer). "Control group studies of suicide survivors: A review and critique." *Suicide and Life-threatening Behavior.* 23(2).

McIntosh, J.L., & Kelly, L.D.(1992). "Survivors' reactions: Suicide vs. other causes." *Crisis.* 13, 82–93.

Miles, M.S., & Demi, A.S. (1991). "A comparison of guilt in bereaved parents whose children died by suicide, accident, or chronic disease." *Omega.* 24, 203–215.

Pennebaker, J.W., & O'Heeron, R.C. (1984). "Confiding in others and illness rate among spouses of suicide and accidental death victims." *Journal of Abnormal Psychology.* 93, 473–476.

Range, L.M., & Thompson, K.E. (1984). "Community responses following suicide, homicide, and other deaths: The perspective of potential comforters." *The Journal of Psychology.* 121(2), 193–198.

Range, L.M., & Calhoun, L.G. (1990). "Responses following suicide and other types of death: The perspective of the bereaved." *Omega.* 21(4). 311–320.

Range, L.M., & Niss, N.M. (1990). "Long-term bereavement from suicide, homicide, accidents, and natural deaths." *Death Studies.* 14. 423–433.

Reed, M.D., & Greenwald, J.Y. (1991). "Survivor-victim status, attachment, and sudden death bereavement." *Suicide and life threatening Behavior.* 21(4), 385–401.

Rudestam, K.E., & Imbroll, D. (1983). "Societal reactions to a child's death by suicide." *Journal of Consulting and Clinical Psychology.* 51(3). 461–462.

Saunders, J.M. (1981). "A process of bereavement resolution: Uncoupled identity." *Western Journal of Nursing Research.* 3, 319–332.

Shneidman, E.S. (1971). "Prevention, intervention, and postvention of suicide." *Annals of Internal Medicine.* 75, 453–458.

Shneidman, E.S. (1981). "Postvention: The care of the bereaved." *Suicide and Life-threatening Behavior.* 11(4), 349–359.

Shneidman, E.S. (1975). "Postvention: The care of the bereaved." In R. O. Pasnau (Ed.), *Consultation-liaison psychiatry* (pp. 245–256). New York: Grune & Stratton.

Smith, J. (1991). "Suicide intervention in schools: General considerations." In A.A.

Leenaars & S. Wenckstern (Eds.), *Suicide prevention in schools.* New York: Hemisphere Publishing Co.

Stillion, J.M., & McDowell, E.E. (1996). *Suicide across the life span: Premature Exits* (2nd edition). Washington: Hemisphere Publishing Co.

Trolley, B.C. (1993). "Kaleidoscope of aid for patents whose child died by suicidal and sudden, non-suicidal means." *Omega.* 27(3), 239-250.

Van Der Wal, J. (1989-90). "The aftermath of suicide: A review of empirical evidence." *Omega.* 20(2), 149-171.

Wenckstern, S., & Leenaars, A.A. (1991). "Suicide postvention: A case illustration in a secondary school." In A.A. Leenaars & S. Wenckstern (Eds.), *Suicide prevention in schools* (pp. 181-195). New York: Hemisphere.

Chapter 5   by Lula M. Redmond

This material was excerpted from: *Surviving When Someone You Love Was Murdered; Professional's Guide To Group Grief Therapy For Families and Friends Of Murder Victims.* (1989). ISBN 0-9624592-0-8 Lula M. Redmond, author and publisher.

The book and accompanying video are available from Psychological Consultation and Education Services, Inc. P.O. Box 6111, Clearwater, FL. 34618-6111
For orders: Book:. 26.95; Video: 134.95; Book and Video Pack:. 144.95
All prices include shipping and handling. No C.O.D. Orders accepted. Foreign orders must be in U.S. Currency plus $10.00 additional postage cost.

Commentary   by Kenneth J. Doka

Doka, Kenneth J. (1984). "Expectation of Death, Participation in Funeral Arrangements and Grief Adjustment." *Omega,* 15, 19-30.

Doka, Kenneth J. and Morgan, John (1993). *Death and Spirituality.* Farmingdale, NY: Baywood Press.

Chapter 7   by Charles R. Figley

American Psychiatric Association. (1980). *Diagnostic and Statistical Manual of Mental Disorders* (3rd Edition). Washington, DC: Author.

American Psychiatric Association. (1987). *Diagnostic and Statistical Manual of Mental Disorders.* (3rd Edition—Revision.) Washington, DC: Author.

Agger, I. (1994). *The blue room (Det Blla Varelse,* originally published in Danish by Forlag of Copenhagen in 1992). Trauma and testimony among refugee women, a psycho-social exploration. Translated into English by Mary Bille. London: Zed Books.

Baker, J. E. (in press). "Treating Parental Grief: Minimizing the Impact of the Death of a Child." In C. R. Figley, B. Bride, and N. Mazza (Eds.). *Death and Trauma.* London: Taylor & Francis.

Callahan, R. and Callahan, J. (in press). "Thought Field Therapy: An Algorithm for Eliminating the Suffering of Grief Trauma." In C. R. Figley, B. Bride, and N. Mazza (Eds.). *Death and Trauma.* London: Taylor & Francis.

Cummock, V. (1995). "Surviving an airplane disaster—my personal story." Invited keynote address at the Annual Meeting of the Association for Death Education and Counselors, Miami, April.

Denny, N. (1995). "The orienting reflex as a partial explanation for the effectiveness of EMDR and TFT." *Traumatology*, Volume 1, Issue 1, Article 1.

Donovan, D. (1991). Traumatology: "A field whose time has come." *Journal of Traumatic Stress*, 4(3), 433–436.

Einspruch, E. L. and Forman, B. D. (1988). "Neuro-linguistic programming in the treatment of phobias." *Psychotherapy in Private Practice*, 6(1), 91–100.

Eth, S. and Pynoos, R. (1985). *Post-Traumatic Stress Disorder in Children*. Washington, DC: American Psychiatric Press.

Figley, C. R. (Ed.) (1978). *Stress disorders among Vietnam veterans: Theory, research, and treatment*. New York: Brunner/Mazel.

Figley, C. R. (1982). "Traumatization and comfort: Close relationship may be hazardous to your health." Invited lecture, Texas Tech University, Lubbock, Texas.

Figley, C. R. (1983). "Catastrophes: An overview of family reactions." In C. R. Figley & H. I. McCubbin (Eds.), *Stress and the Family, Volume 2: Coping with Catastrophe*, pp. 3–20, New York: Brunner/Mazel.

Figley, C. R. (1984). "Treating post-traumatic stress disorder: The algorithmic approach." *American Academy of Psychiatry and the Law Newsletter*, 9(3), 7–9.

Figley, C. R. (1985). "Role of the family: Both haven and headache." In Lystad, M. (Ed.), *Role Stressors and Supports for Emergency Workers*. Washington, DC. DHHS Publication No. (ADM) 85-1408.

Figley, C. R. (1986). "Post-traumatic stress: The role of the family." *Journal of Crisis Intervention*, 3, 58–70.

Figley, C. R. (1988). "Toward a field of traumatic stress studies." *Journal of Traumatic Stress*, 1(1), 3–11.

Figley, C. R. (1989a). *Helping traumatized families*. San Francisco: Jossey-Bass.

Figley, C. R. (Ed.) (1989b). *Treating stress in families*. New York: Brunner/Mazel.

Figley, C. R. (Ed.) *Compassion Fatigue: Coping with secondary traumatic stress disorder*. New York: Brunner/Mazel.

Figley, C. R. and Carbonell, J. (1995). "Treating PTSD: What Works and What Does Not." Invited symposium, Family Therapy Networker's Symposium, Washington, DC, March.

Figley, C. R. and Southerly, W. T. (1980). "Psychosocial adjustment of recently returned veterans." In C. R. Figley and S. Leventman (Ed.), *Strangers at Home: Vietnam Veterans Since the War*. New York: Praeger.

Gerbode, F. (1992). *Beyond Psychology: An Introduction to Metapsychology*. Palo Alto: IRM Press.

Glick, I. O., Weis, R. S. and Parkes, C. M. (1974). *The first year of bereavement*. New York: Wiley.

Hogancamp, V. E. and Figley, C. R. (1983). "War: Bringing the Battle Home." In C. R. Figley and H. I. McCubbin (Eds.). *Stress and the Family, Volume II: Coping with Catastrophe*. New York: Brunner/Mazel, 148–165.

Horowitz, S. H. (in press). "Treating Families with Traumatic Loss: The Rochester Model." In C. R. Figley, B. Bride, and N. Mazza (Eds.). *Death and Trauma*. London: Taylor & Francis.

Kubler-Ross, E. (1969). *On death and dying: What the dying have to teach doctors, nurses, clergy, and their own families*. New York: Macmillan.

Lehrman, S. (1956). "Reactions to untimely death." *Psychiatric Quarterly*, 30, 564–578.

Lifton, R. J. (1969). *Death in Life*. New York: Vintage Books.

Lindemann, E. (1944). "Symptomatology and management of acute grief." *American Journal of Psychiatry*, 101, 141–148.

Koziey, P. W. and McLeod, G. L. (1987). "Visual-kinesthetic dissociation in treatment of victims of rape." *Professional Psychology: Research and Practice*, 18(3), 276–282.

MacLean, M. (1986). "The neurolinguistic programming model." In F. J. Turner (Ed.). *Social Work Treatment: Interlocking theoretical approaches*, 3rd Ed., pp 341–373.

Parkes, C. M. (1972). *Bereavement: Studies of grief in adult life*. New York: International Universities Press.

Parkes, C. M. and Brown, R. J. (1972). "Health after bereavement: A controlled study of young Boston widows and widowers." *Psychosomatic Medicine*, 34, 449–461.

Parkes, C. M. and Weiss, R. S. (1983). *Recovery from bereavement*. New York: Basic Books.

Rando, T. A. (1983). "An investigation of grief and adaptation in parents whose children have died from cancer." *Journal of Pediatric Psychology*, 8(1), 3–20.

Rando, T. A. (1984). *Grief, dying, and death: Clinical interventions for caregivers*. Champaign, Ill: Research Press.

Rando, T. A. (1986). *Loss and anticipatory grief*. Boston: Lexington Books.

Rando, T. A. (1993). *Treatment of Complicated Mourning*. Champaign, Illinois: Research Press

Raphael, B. (1983). *The Anatomy of Bereavement*. New York: Basic Books.

Raphael, B. (1986). *When disaster strikes: How individuals and communities cope with catastrophe*. New York: Basic.

Redmond (1989). *Surviving: When someone you love was murdered*. Clearwater, Florida: Psychological Consultation and Education Services.

Rogers, C. (1951). *Client-Centered Therapy*. New York: Norton.

Shapiro, F. (1995). *Eye Movement Desensitization and Reprocessing: Basic Principles, Protocols and Procedures*. New York: Guilford.

Solomon, R. and Shapiro, F. (in press). "Eye Movement Desensitization, and Reprocessing: A Therapeutic Tool for Trauma and Grief." In C. R. Figley, B. Bride, and N. Mazza (Eds.). *Death and Trauma*. London: Taylor & Francis.

Simpson, M. A. (1977). "Death and modern poetry." In H. Feifel (Ed.) *New Meanings of Death*, pp 313–333. New York: McGraw-Hill.

Simpson, M. A. (1979). *The Facts of Death*. Englewood Cliffs NJ: Prentice-Hall.

Simpson, M. A. (1980). "Research in Thanatology; problems of methodology." *Death Education*, 108, 4, 139–150.

Simpson, M. A. (1993). "Bitter waters: The effects on children of the stresses of unrest and oppression." IN J. Wilson and B. Raphael (Eds). *The International Handbook of Traumatic Stress Syndromes*. New York: Plenum.

Spilka, B., Friedman, L., and Rosenberg, D. (1978). "Death and Vietnam: Some combat veteran experiences and perspectives." In C. R. Figley (Ed.), *Stress disorders among Vietnam veterans: Theory, research, and treatment.* New York: Brunner/Mazel.

Chapter 8 — by Vanderlyn R. Pine

1. For a full discussion see Vanderlyn R. Pine (Ed.), et. al., *Acute Grief and the Funeral* (1976). Springfield, Illinois: Charles C. Thomas, Publisher.

2. For a full discussion see Vanderlyn R. Pine, "Dying, Death and Social Behavior," in Ivan K. Goldberg, Arthur C. Carr, Bernard B. Schoenberg, and Austin H. Kutscher (Eds.), *Psychosocial Aspects of Anticipatory Grief (1974).* New York, New York: Columbia University Press, Chapter 6, pp. 31-47.

3. For a full discussion of this see Colin Murray Parkes, *Bereavement: Studies of Grief in Adult Life* (I972). New York, New York: International Universities Press, Inc.

4. For a full discussion of this see Erich Lindemann, "Symptomatology and Management of Acute Grief," in Robert Fulton (Ed.), *Death and Identity,* revised edition (1976). Bowie, Maryland: The Charles Press Publishers, Inc.., pp. 210-221.

5. For a full discussion of this see Goldberg, Carr, Schoenberg, and Kutscher (Eds.), *Psychosocial Aspects of Anticipatory Grief, op. cit.*

6. For a full discussion of this see Pine, "Dying, Death and Social Behavior," *op. cit.*

7. For a full discussion of this see Vanderlyn R. Pine, "Grief, Bereavement, and Mourning: The Realities of Loss" in Pine, *et. al., Acute Grief and the Funeral, op. cit.,* pp. 105-114.

8. For a full discussion see Avery D. Weisman, *On Dying and Denying: A Psychiatric Study of Terminality* 1972). New York, New York: Behavioral Publications, Inc.

9. For a full discussion see Robert Kastenbaum and Ruth Aisenberg, *The Psychology of Death* (1972). New York, New York: Springer Publishing Company, Inc., Chapter 14, pp. 354-392.

10. For a full discussion see Vanderlyn R. Pine, "The Social Context of Disaster," in Vanderlyn R. Pine (Ed.), *Responding to Disaster* (1974). Milwaukee, Wisconsin: Bulfin Printers, pp. 1-10.

11. For a full discussion see Vanderlyn R. Pine, "Comparative Funeral Practices," in *Practical Anthropology* 16 (March-April, 1969), pp. 49-62.

12. The term "death overload" may be compared and contrasted to Robert Kastenbaum's "bereavement overload" in *Death, Society and Human Experience,* second edition (1981). St. Louis, Missouri: the C.V. Mosby Company.

Chapter 9 — by Dana G. Cable

Caplan, G. (1969). "Opportunities for school psychologists in the primary prevention of mental disorders in children." In A. Bindman & A. Spiegel (Eds.), *Perspectives in community mental health.* Chicago: Aldine.

Mitchell, J. T. (1983). "When disaster strikes: The critical incident stress debriefing process." *Journal of Emergency Medical Services*, 8, 36-39.

Mitchell, J. T. (1988). "Development and function of a critical incident stress debriefing team." *Journal of Emergency Services*, 13(1), 42-46.

Mitchell, J. T. & Berg, G. (1990). *Emergency services stress.* Englewood Cliffs, NJ.: Prentice Hall.

Mitchell, J. T. & Everly, G. S. (1995). *Critical incident stress debriefing: An operations manual for the prevention of trauma among emergency service and disaster workers.* (2nd ed.). Baltimore, MD: Chevron.

Rando, T. A. (1993). *Treatment of Complicated Mourning.* Champaign, IL. Research Press.

Sanders, C. M. (1989). *Grief: The mourning after.* New York John Wiley & Sons.

Scurfield, R. (1985). Post-trauma stress assessment and treatment: Overview and formulations. In C. Figley (Ed.), *Trauma and its wake: The study and Treatment of post-traumatic stress disorder.* New York: Brunner Mazel.

Worden, J. W. (1991). *Grief counseling and grief therapy.* (2nd ed.). New York. Springer.

Chapter 10   **by O. Duane Weeks**

Boatright, Connie J. (1985). "Children as victims of disaster," pp. 131-49 in Appleton-Century-Crofts.

Bradach, K. and Jordan, J. 1995 "Long-term effects of a family history of traumatic death on adolescent individuation," *Death Studies 1994*) July-August: 315-36.

Carter, B. F. and Brooks, A. (1991). "Child and adolescent survivors of suicide, Pp. 231-58 in A. Leenaars (Ed.) *Life Span Perspectives of Suicide: Time-Lines in the Suicide Process.* New York, NY: Plenum Press.

DeSpelder, L. A. and Strickland, A. (1992). *The Last Dance: Encountering Death and Dying.* Mayfield Publishing Company.

Eth, S. and Pynoos, R. (1985). "Interaction of trauma and grief in childhood," Pp. 169-86 in S. Eth and R. Pynoos (Eds.) *Post-Traumatic Stress Disorder in Children.* Washington, DC: American Psychiatric Press.

Fulton, R. (1994). "The funeral in contemporary society," Pp. 288-312 in R. Fulton and R. Bendiksen (Eds.), *Death and ?.* The Charles Press.

Howarth, G. (1993). "Investigating deathwork: a personal account," pp. 221-37 in D. Clark (Ed.) *The Sociology of Death.* Oxford, U.K.: Blackwell Publishers.

Kearl, Michael C. (1989). *Endings: A Sociology of Death and Dying.* New York, NY: Oxford University Press.

McCown D. E. and Davies, B. (1995). "Patterns of grief in young children following the death of a sibling." *Death Studies.* 19(1) January-February:41-53.

Nader, K., Pynoos, R., Fairbanks, L., and C. Frederick 1990 "Children's PTSD reactions one year after a sniper attack at their school." *American Journal of Psychiatry*, 147(11) November:1526-30.

Pynoos R. and Eth S. (1985). "Children traumatized by witnessing acts of personal violence: Homicide, rape, or suicide behavior," Washington, DC: American Psychiatric Press, Inc.

Pynoos, R., Frederick, C., Nader, K., Arroyo, W., Steinberg. A., Eth, S., Nunes, F., and L. Fairbanks (1987). "Life threat and posttraumatic stress in school-age children." *Archives of General Psychiatry*. 44 December:1057-63.

Pynoos, R. and Nader, K. (1990). "Children's exposure to violence and traumatic death." *Psychiatric Annals*. 20(6) June:334-44.

 Schwarz, E. and Kowalski, J. (1991). "Posttraumatic stress disorder after a school shooting: Effects of symptom threshold selection and diagnosis by DSM-III, DSM-III-R, or proposed DSM-IV," *American Journal of Psychiatry*, 148(5) May: 592-7.

Rando, T. (1993). *Treatment of Complicated Mourning*. Champaign, IL:. Research Press.

Raphael, B. (1983). *The Anatomy of Bereavement*. New York, NY: Basic Books.

Redmond, L. M. (1989). *Surviving When Someone You Love Was Murdered*. Education Services, Inc.

Wenckstern S. and Leenaars, A. (1993). "Trauma and suicide in our schools." *Death Studies*, 17 March-April:151-71.

Wolfelt, A. 1992 *Understanding Grief: Helping Yourself Heal*. Muncie, IN: Accelerated Development Publishers, Inc.

1994 *Creating Meaningful Funeral Ceremonies: A Guide for Caregivers*. Fort Collins, CO: Companion Press

Chapter 11   by Therese A. Rando

American Psychiatric Association. (1987). *Diagnostic and statistical manual of mental disorders*, third edition, revised. Washington, DC: Author.

Amick-McMullan, A., Kilpatrick, D, Veronen, L., & Smith, S. (1989) Family survivors of homicide victims: Theoretical perspectives and an exploratory study. *Journal of Traumatic Stress*, 2, 21-35.

Bugen, L. (1979). Human grief: A model for prediction and intervention. In L. Bugen (Ed.), *Death and dying: Theory, research, practice*. Dubuque, IA: William C. Brown.

Figley, C. (1985) Introduction. In C. Figley (Ed.), *Trauma and its wake: The study and treatment of post-traumatic stress disorder*. New York: Brunner/Mazel.

Horowitz, M. (1985) Disasters and psychological responses to stress. *Psychiatric Annals*, 15, 161-167.

Horowitz, M. (1986). *Stress response syndromes* (2nd ed.). Northvale, NJ: Jason Aronson.

Kastenbaum, R. (1969). Death and bereavement in later life. In A.H. Kutscher (Ed.), *Death and bereavement*. Springfield, IL. Charles C. Thomas.

Linday, J., Gree, B., Grace, M., & Titchener, J. (1983). Psychotherapy with survivors of the Beverly Hills Supper Club fire. *American Journal of Psychotherapy*, 37, 593-610.

Merriam–Webster Inc. (1987), *Webster's ninth new collegiate dictionary.* Springfield, MA: Author.

Ochberg, F (1988). *Post-traumatic therapy and victims of violence.* In F. Ochberg (Ed.), Post-traumatic therapy and victims of violence. New York: Brunner/Mazel.

Platt, L. (1991, April 25). Workshop on "Interventions for complicated Grief: Helping the Survivors of Sudden and Violent Death." Presented at the 13th annual conference of the Association for Death Education and Counseling, Duluth, MN.

Rando, T (1984). *Grief, dying and death: Clinical interventions for caregivers.* Champaign, IL: Research Press.

Rando, T. (1993) *Treatment of complicated mourning.* Champaign, IL: Research Press.

Raphael, B. (1983). *The anatomy of bereavement.* New York: Basic Books.

Raphael, B. (1986). *When disaster strikes: How individuals and communities cope with catastrophe.* New York: Basic Books.

Redmond, L. (1989) *Surviving: When someone you love was murdered.* Clearwater, FL: Psychological Consultation and Education Services.

Rynearson, E. (1987) Psychological adjustment to unnatural dying. In S. Zisook (Ed.), *Biopsychosocial aspects of bereavement.* Washington, DC: American Psychiatric Press.

Rynearson, E. (1988). The homicide of a child. In F. Ochberg (Ed.), *Post-traumatic therapy and victims of violence.* New York: Brunner/Mazel.

Chapter 12   by Terry Martin and Kenneth J. Doka

Friedman, M. & Rosenman, R.H. (1974). *Type A behavior and your heart.* New York: Knopf.

Gray, John (1992). *Men are from Mars, women are from Venus: A practical guide for improving communication and getting what you want in your relationship.* New York: Harper Collins.

Matthews, K.A. (1989). Coronary heart disease and Type A behaviors: Update on and alternative to the Booth-Kewley and Friedman (1987) quantitative review. *Psychological Bulletin,* 104, 373-380.

Mitchell, J. T. (1983). When disaster strikes: The critical incident stress debriefing process. *Journal of Emergency Medical Services,* 8, 36-39.

Mitchell, J. T. &Bray, G. (1990). *Emergency services stress.* Englewood Cliffs, NJ: Prentice-Hall.

Nelan, B. W. (1993, May 10). Armed forces: Annie get your gun. *Time,* 141, 38-43.

Rando, T. A. (1993). *Treatment of complicated mourning.* Champaign, IL. Research Press.

Ryan, D. R. (1989). Underestimated grief, in K. Doka (Ed.), *Disenfranchised grief: Handling hidden sorrow* (pp. 127-133). Lexington, MA.: Lexington Books.

Shoenman, E. (1995). Arrivederci! Binford (A. Cadiff, Director). In C. Finestra (Producer), *Home Improvement.* New York: American Broadcasting Company.

United States Bureau of the Census. (1994). *Statistical abstracts of the United States.* Washington, DC: Bureau of the Census: Author.

Staudacher, C. (1991). *Men and grief.* Oakland, Ca.: New Harbinger Publishers.

Stolley, Richard, B. (1964). Work, memories, old friends, *Life Magazine,* 56, pp. 34-36.

Worden, J. William (1991). *Grief counseling and grief therapy: A handbook for the mental health practitioner* (2nd ed.). New York: Springer.

World almanac and book of facts (1995). Mahwah, N.J: Funk and Wagnals Corp.

Chapter 13   by Lois Chapman Dick

Burge, J.H. (1984), *Occupational Stress in Policing,* Fresno, CA: Pioneer Publishing.

Emergency Medical Update, Vol. 7, No.. 12, October 1994, Lockert-Jackson & Associates, Inc., P.O. Box 11380, Bainbridge Island, WA 98110.

Everly, G. Jr. (1980), *A Clinical Guide to the Treatment of the Human Stress Response,* New York: Plenum Press.

Figley, C.R. (1986) *Trauma and Its Wake - The Study and Treatment of Post-traumatic Stress Disorder,* New York: Brunner/Mazel, Publishers.

Smith, D. (1988), *Firefighters,* New York: Doubleday.

Tubesing, N.L. & D.A. (Eds.). *Structured Exercises in Stress Management - A Whole Person Handbook for Trainers, Educators and Group Leaders.* Duluth, MN: Whole Person Press.

Chapter 16   by Robert G. Stevenson

Dunne, E.J., J.L. McIntosh, and K. Dunne-Maxim (Eds.), *Suicide and Its Aftermath: Understanding and Counseling the Survivors,* W.W. Norton and Company, New York, 1987.

Fox, S.S., "Good Grief: Positive Interventions for Children and Adolescents," Preventive Psychiatry: Early Intervention and Situational Crisis Management, S.C. Klagsbrun, et al, Eds., Charles Press, Philadelphia, 1989, pp. 83-92.

Grollman, E.A. *Bereaved Children and Teens: A Supportive Guide for Parents and Professionals,* Beacon Press, Boston, 1995.

Grollman, E.A., *Talking About Death: A Dialogue Between Parent and Child,* Beacon Press, Boston, Massachusetts, 1990.

Stevenson, R.G., "AIDS Related Grief: Helping Young People to Understand the Impact of Societal Values on the Grief Process," *Illness. Crises and Loss,* 1:2, pp. 56-59.

Stevenson, R.G., "Teen Suicide: Sources, Signals and Prevention," *The Dying and Bereaved Teenager,* J.D. Morgan, Ed., Charles Press, Philadelphia, 1990, pp. 135-139.

Stevenson, R.G. (Ed.) *What Will We Do? Preparing A School Community To Cope With Crises,* Baywood Press, Amityville, NY, 1994.

Biographical Information

Laura W. Boyd, Ph.D., is a member of the Oklahoma House of Representatives, a licensed marriage and family therapist and a family and divorce mediator with 20 years in clinical practice augmented by 15 years of university teaching on both graduate and undergraduate levels.

Dana G. Cable, Ph.D., is a professor of psychology at Hood College in Frederick, Maryland and maintains a private practice as a licensed psychologist and certified death educator and grief counselor, specializing in grief and death related issues. He is on the editorial board of the *American Journal of Hospice and Palliative Care.*

Bonnie Carroll is the founder and president of Tragedy Assistance Program for Survivors (TAPS), a national nonprofit network of peer support and assistance for military families who have lost loved ones in the line of duty. She is an officer of the Alaska National Guard.

Victoria Cummock is an activist working primarily in the areas of disaster crisis management, aviation security, and counter-terrorism. She works to raise awareness among mental health providers, educators, counselors, and disaster professionals regarding the special needs of families of homicide victims.

Lois Chapman Dick, M.S.W., has a private practice in the state of Washington, including emphasis on matters of trauma, stress and grief, but frequently travels around the country to provide training sessions and counseling in these fields. She is the editor of the ADEC newsletter.

Kenneth J. Doka, Ph.D., is professor of gerontology at the College of New Rochelle in New York. He is also an ordained Lutheran minister and a sociologist, associate editor of *Omega,* and the editor of *Journeys,* a newsletter for the bereaved published by the Hospice Foundation of America.

Charles R. Figley, Ph.D., is a professor of social work at Florida State University (FSU). He directs the FSU Marriage and Family Therapy Center and heads their traumatic stress intervention and training program. He was the founding editor of the *Journal of Traumatic Stress.*

Earl A. Grollman, D.D., is a rabbi, a pioneer in the fields of death education and crisis intervention and the author of 24 books about death and dying. He speaks frequently at conferences and symposia, and is often called to scenes of traumatic injury and death as a counselor to both victims' families and to caregivers.

Stephen P. Hersh, M.D. F.A.P.A., is a psychiatrist and director of the Medical Illness Counseling Center, a nonprofit clinic dealing with the chronically and terminally ill and their families. He is Clinical Professor of Psychiatry, Behavioral Sciences and Pediatrics at George Washington University School of Medicine.

Lisa Hudson, M.S., has a master's degree in psychiatric nursing from the Medical College of Georgia and specializes in loss and grief counseling as a psychotherapist in private practice.

Brian Kates is Deputy Editorial Page Editor of the New York Daily News. He has taught writing, reporting, and ethics courses at New York University and at Columbia University Graduate School of Journalism. He is also an officer in a family-owned corporation that publishes *The American Funeral Director.*

Janice Harris Lord, A.C.S.W., M.S.S.W., is Director of Victim Programs for Mothers Against Drunk Driving (MADD). Her professional focus has been on families of victims of drunk drivers and crime. In 1993, she received the U.S. Department of Justice Award for Outstanding Work with Victims of Crime.

Terry L. Martin, Ph.D., is an Assistant Professor of Psychology at Hood College in Frederick, Maryland, and has written frequently on death, dying and bereavement. He has served on the Board of Directors of ADEC and maintains a private counseling practice, specializing in grief counseling.

Vanderlyn R. Pine, Ph.D., is a professor of sociology at the State University of New York, New Paltz. He has served as Director of Graduate Studies for the M.S./M.S.W. program and as chair of the Sociology department. He serves on advisory boards at New

York Medical College, Columbia University, and the University of Minnesota.

Therese A. Rando, Ph.D., is a clinical psychologist in private practice in Rhode Island and is clinical director of Rando Associates, Ltd. which provides psychotherapy, training, and consultation, specializing in loss and grief, traumatic stress and the psychosocial care of the chronically and terminally ill.

Lula M. Redmond, R.N., M.S., is a licensed marriage and family therapist as well as having a degree in nursing. She began one of the first group therapy treatment programs for homicide survivors and before that set up educational programs for hospices throughout the United States.

Dianne Ruby survived the homicide of her best friend and her unborn daughter's father, a soldier in the U.S. Army, in December 1993. Since then she has trained and practices in the support and assistance to survivors of homicide and military death.

Robert G. Stevenson, Ph.D., is a secondary school teacher and counselor in New Jersey where he has taught a course on death and dying since 1972. He is director of the ADEC Education Institute and for 10 years was chairman of the Columbia University seminar on death.

Judith M. Stillion, Ph.D., is a professor of psychology at Western Carolina University and serves there as Associate Vice Chancellor for Academic Affairs. She was a charter member of ADEC and its president from 1987 to 1989. She is an associate editor of *Death Studies* and has edited the News and Notes section for six years.

O. Duane Weeks, Ph.D., has been a licensed funeral director and embalmer for over 30 years and owns four funeral homes in the State of Washington. His interest in death education and grief-related issues led him to a doctorate in sociology from the University of Minnesota.

Mary Beth Williams, Ph.D., L.C.S.W., has written extensively in the field of traumatic stress and is a board member of the International Society for Traumatic Stress Studies. She has a private practice in Warrenton, Virginia.

ORDER FORM

LIVING WITH GRIEF: AFTER SUDDEN LOSS

Edited by Kenneth J. Doka, Ph.D. $16.95

ISBN: 1-56032-578-X

For bulk quantity orders, call Hospice Foundation of America
1-800-854-3402
or write Hospice Foundation of America
      Suite 300, 2001 S Street, NW
      Washington, DC 20009

For single copies, write Taylor & Francis (see address below).

PAYMENT OPTIONS

____ Enclosed is my check or money order, payable to Taylor & Francis
in U.S. funds only.

Please charge my ____ Visa ____ MC ____ Amex

Card # _____ Exp. _____

Signature _____

Telephone *(required for credit card purchase)*

P.O.# _____ Date _____

BILL/SHIP TO

Name _____

Institution _____

Address _____

_____

City _____ State ____ Zip _____

____ Subtotal   ____ Shipping & Handling[*]

____ Sales Tax (PA only)   ____ Total

[*] Add $2.50 for book orders $50 and under.

Send Order Form To:
    Taylor & Francis
    1900 Frost Road, Suite 101
    Bristol, PA 19007-1598

    TO ORDER BY PHONE, CALL TOLL FREE 1-800-821-8312
      Or send orders on our 24-hour telefax, 215-785-5515
Orders can also be placed via the Internet at bkorders@tandfpa.com